Dickens characters illustrated by the Victorian artist Kyd (Joseph Clayton Clarke), clockwise from top left: Uriah Heep (David Copperfield), *Mr Micawber* (David Copperfield), *'The Marchioness'* (The Old Curiosity Shop), *Dick Swiveller* (The Old Curiosity Shop), *Mrs Bardell* (Pickwick Papers) *and Mr Stiggins* (Pickwick Papers).

Charles Dickens

A celebration of his life and work

Charles Mosley

Charles Dickens at 18, painted 1830 by his aunt Janet Barrow; an unsigned miniature exists which is allegedly the earliest likeness of Dickens, but this portrait is of unimpeachable provenance.

WORTH PRESS

Gad's Hill Place, near Rochester, Kent – Dickens's home from 1857 to his death.

Charles Dickens

A celebration of his life and work

Charles Mosley

Dickens in 1839, an oil portrait by his friend Daniel Maclise (above).

Dickens in the late 1850s (right).

Contents

Reader's Guide 6
The Making of Charles Dickens 8
A Charles Dickens Timeline 20
Charles Dickens's World 26
Collectable Dickens 34
Pickwick Papers (1837) 38
Oliver Twist (1838) 50
Nicholas Nickleby (1839) 62
The Old Curiosity Shop (1841) 76
Barnaby Rudge (1841) 88
A Christmas Carol (1843) 98
Martin Chuzzlewit (1844) 110
Dombey and Son (1848) 120
David Copperfield (1850) 132
Bleak House (1853) 146

'Covent Garden' by Phoebus Levin, painted in 1864.

Hard Times (1854)	160
Little Dorrit (1857)	166
A Tale of Two Cities (1859)	176
Great Expectations (1861)	182
Our Mutual Friend (1865)	190
The Mystery of Edwin Drood (1870)	196
Dickens's Stories	202
Dickens's Plays	204
Dickens's Poetry	206
Dickens's Illustrators	208
Dickens Abroad	212
How Dickens Changed the World	228
Selected Bibliography	232
Index	234

Reader's Guide

The section on Dickens's major works (pages 38–201) deals with all the novels and *A Christmas Carol*. (The latter, due to its huge popularity, is here treated as an honorary novel.) They are arranged in chronological order of publication. Each novel's character who has any speaking role is listed at the start of each 'chapter' covering a given novel alphabetically by surname or main part of sobriquet, e.g. 'Dodger, The Artful' rather than 'Artful Dodger, The'. There usually follows a brief sketch of how he or she fits into the story.

The list is not confined to humans. Animals are included provided they forward the plot, the speaking role qualification being waived. Bill Sikes's dog fails to make the grade, being a mere ornamental appendage to Bill and even in his tragic and undeserved death getting upstaged by his master's clumsy but spectacular one. Barnaby Rudge's raven Grip and the two important dogs, Dora Copperfield's Jip and Henry Gowan's Lion, do feature. Similarly, as in the case of *A Christmas Carol*, with supernatural beings. Again, the alphabetisation focuses on the main substantive, e.g. 'Christmas Past, Ghost of' rather than 'Past, Ghost of Christmas'.

Major characters are shown with larger headings, and sometimes have quite long entries. This category includes Grip, Jip and Lion. Brief details of the actors/actresses who have played the character (other than in the case of Grip, Jip and Lion), and the sort of vehicle they have appeared in (such as film or televisation) feature at the end of each character paragraph.

Considerations of space mean only the best-known actors/actresses can be included. Some of the more obscure stage performances of Dickens's works, especially where benefit nights or charity matinées, and still more so where just a sketch was mounted, or even a single scene, have proved impossible to track down. Before the television age dramatisations of Dickens were so frequent as to constitute an industry in its own right, not just an offshoot of the entertainment sector.

After each list of characters a 'Story Commentary' follows. This, while aiming to encompass the essential elements of the plot, cannot be a substitute for reading the entire novel. How could it, when at most it is 1,500 words long against a novel's 300,000 or even 400,000? What it does try to do is highlight any contradictions, puzzles, character conundrums or especially tricky twists in the novel under discussion, offering solutions. This is a 'celebration' of Dickens, so lacks classroom ornaments such as footnotes. And the word 'offering' is stressed. Dogmatic pronouncements (often equally unsupported by hard evidence, however) can be left to the likes of F R Leavis.

A cartoon of Charles Dickens by André Gill, from a coloured engraving in L'Eclipse *(Paris), 14 June 1868.*

Similarly, 'A Charles Dickens Timeline' tags the salient germane events throughout not just Dickens's life but either side of it where helpful. 'Charles Dickens's World', at any rate as regards Britain, pinpoints chiefly the principal places where events in the novels take place, secondly places which Dickens visited or where he lived. Abroad it is more the other way round. Where mentioned at all, only buildings that survive are shown. It was sad to discover how many of the hotels and inns and taverns Dickens used during his lifetime have since been demolished, even relatively recently, usually by his fellow countrymen property developers rather than enemy action in either World War.

The bibliography in this book is but a starting point for the study of Dickens. The Slater and Ackroyd biographies mentioned in it between them provide in their turn bibliographies, Ackroyd's constituting a near-lifetime's task list of further reading. Dickens's novels by themselves, a magnificent and nutritious feast, take about five months steady pegging away to devour. On the other hand they are invariably better written than books about Dickens by other people (Angus Wilson's being an exception). So tackle them first. This may sound daunting, so do not be afraid to skip Dickens's longer passages. You can always return to them later. He is to be sampled like a department store gift picnic hamper. If that means wolfing the caviare and smoked salmon first, leaving the scotch eggs and individual pork pies till another day, so be it.

The Making of Charles Dickens

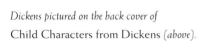

The best-known novelist of all time and across all countries. Creator of household-name characters. Coiner of immortal catch-phrases. Chief promoter, if not co-inventor (with Prince Albert in support), of the Victorian Christmas, whose rich food, plentiful liquor and overindulgence in both beguile us still, as do its round games, flirtation, songs and facetious banter – all carried out against pagan foliage of fir tree, holly and mistletoe. These, while not neglecting the festival's Christian element, were to Dickens what made Christmas 'merry'. And 'merry', with 'jolly', was his highest word of praise.

What else was he? A leading journalist. One who had progressed to that higher calling after apprenticeship as a first-rate public speech reporter, itself root of his gift for dialogue. Indeed in the 19th century's equivalent of what is now the media/entertainment industry he was very much an all-rounder. Magazine editor. Newspaper ditto. Book and even copy-editor (of the clown Joey Grimaldi's memoirs). Pioneer book-packager (usually thought a modern publishing development). Gifted amateur actor and play director, stage manager and dramatist. Even public reciter of his own works, and a very well remunerated one too.

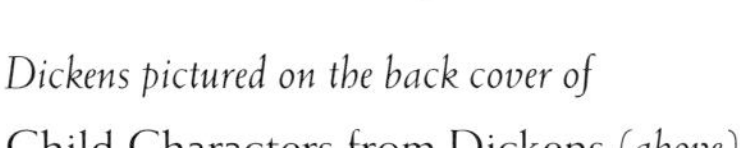

Dickens pictured on the back cover of Child Characters from Dickens *(above).*

Catherine Hogarth (below).

He was a campaigner, also thought a modern calling. Example? Against such outrages as the Sunday ban on any public activity resembling pleasure, when it was the one day of the week a sweated work-force got substantial free time.

The above accomplishments make him sound a paragon. He wasn't. In his books he extolled family togetherness. But he eventually lost patience with, then contrived a separation from, his wife Catherine. Her offence? To be a passive creature unequal to his high-velocity existence.

He paid insufficient attention to his 10 children, the bearing of whom had enfeebled Catherine. With so many, and given his other activities, this was inevitable. But here we have his daughter Katey's take on the matter, a bitter one: 'My father was like a madman when my mother left home,' she said. ' … He did not care a damn what happened to any of us.'

Dickens had carried 'family togetherness' to bizarre lengths from the moment he married Catherine Hogarth, finding more congenial female companionship in first one

Dickens with his daughters Mamie and Katey at Gad's Hill Place (right).

Angela Burdett-Coutts (middle).

Urania Cottage, Shepherd's Bush (below).

of her sisters then a second, both of whom he installed under his roof. He seems not to have had affairs with either, though he may have been in love with Mary, the elder. But his obvious delight in their company, plus his increasing exasperation when in Catherine's, helped kill his marriage.

Charles John Huffam Dickens was nonetheless among the very greatest of the eminent Victorians. He shared the energy that is so typical of them. He was a great walker, regularly clocking up as many as 20 miles a day. Like Gladstone, he tried weaning prostitutes from their sordid trade. This involved two stages. First, their rehabilitation at a Shepherd's Bush refuge by the (to us) unfortunate name of Urania Cottage, funded by Dickens's millionaire patroness Angela Burdett-Coutts. Second, their chaste employment, as maidservants or seamstresses, say, in the Colonies. The chastity dream could turn sour. The first shipment of ex-Urania girls foundered, as it were, when the girls slipped back into prostitution while still at sea.

So Dickens well merits his self-description as 'The Inimitable'. His disciple Evelyn Waugh (of whom more later) implied he was one of the two 'most daemonic of the masters', the other being Balzac. Fourteen full-length novels justify 'daemonic', not simply in bulk, but variety of characters, colourfulness of dialogue and intricacy of plot. The last element especially. Dickens produced them as serials, mostly monthly ones, stretching a year and more. There could be no going back to revise a scene, plant an early hint of a story's later development or tie up loose ends.

Moreover, he wrote each instalment in great meaty chunks of up to 16,000 words. It was a productivity rate the very contemplation of which would have laid low most authors. Eventually its execution did exactly that to Dickens. He died at 58.

He could write two novels simultaneously, the current one overlapped by the next, and often while he undertook editor's duties concerning a third publication altogether. He left but a single novel unfinished, one he titled a mystery.

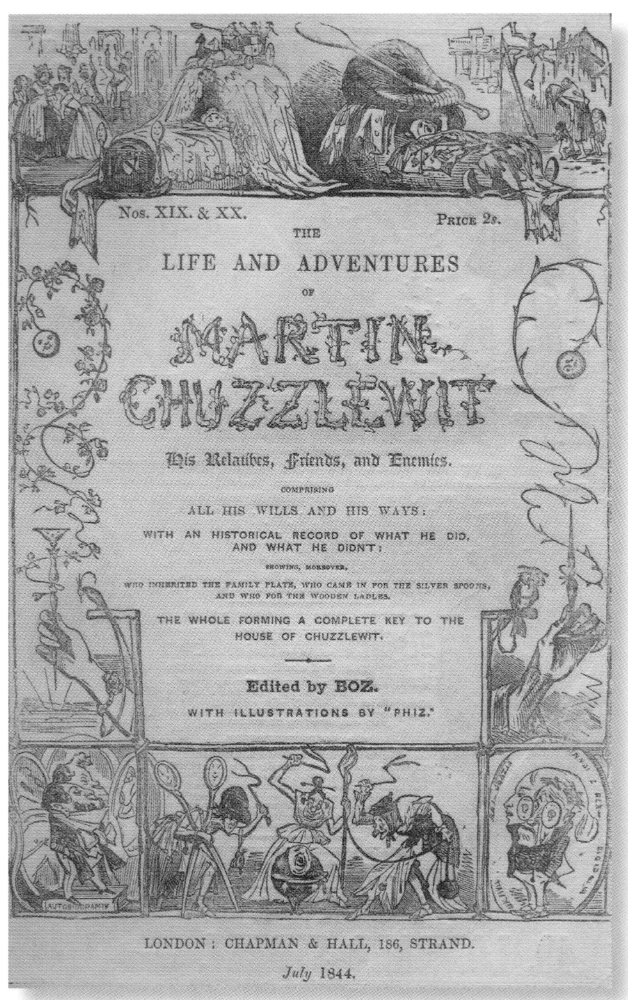

Nos. XIX. & XX. PRICE 2s.

THE LIFE AND ADVENTURES OF MARTIN CHUZZLEWIT

His Relatives, Friends, and Enemies.

COMPRISING ALL HIS WILLS AND HIS WAYS: WITH AN HISTORICAL RECORD OF WHAT HE DID, AND WHAT HE DIDN'T: SHOWING, MOREOVER, WHO INHERITED THE FAMILY PLATE, WHO CAME IN FOR THE SILVER SPOONS, AND WHO FOR THE WOODEN LADLES.

THE WHOLE FORMING A COMPLETE KEY TO THE HOUSE OF CHUZZLEWIT.

Edited by BOZ.

WITH ILLUSTRATIONS BY "PHIZ."

LONDON: CHAPMAN & HALL, 186, STRAND.

July 1844.

He was arguably the inventor of the mystery tale, grandsire of both the whodunnit and its less domesticated sibling the thriller, plus the character type on which both hinge, the private investigator — Nadgett in *Martin Chuzzlewit*. Then there is the comedy of predominantly lower-class manners, forerunner of today's sitcom. Also melodrama, the Victorian literary-cum-dramatic art form *par excellence* and forerunner of today's soaps. Though no revolutionary in politics, Dickens truly overthrew the existing order in fiction.

As a periodicals editor, ultimately of four magazine titles, he commissioned, scrutinised, made changes to and saw through the press up to 80 contributions a month. Of two of the titles he was also a leading shareholder. And of the last of them he was also co-publisher. He briefly took the helm of the *Daily News*, a national newspaper. As well as novels he wrote stories, plays, essays and verse.

Stories? The term is accurate but does him scant justice. The chief five, his *Christmas Books*, each runs to around 30,000 words. Hefty novellas even by Victorian standards. And virtually novels proper by terser modern ones.

They were tailor-made for the Victorian public's Christmas spending spree. In flavour they resemble lexical sweetmeats, fashioned by a master chef spinner of tales to complement a real confectioner's Yuletide bon-bons.

Martin Chuzzlewit, *July 1844 number (above).*

Best wishes for the New Year, illustration from The Chimes *as reproduced in* Through the Year with Dickens, *compiled by Dickens's eldest daughter (right). Artist not credited.*

They are little known now, bar *A Christmas Carol*. The essence of Dickens, this contains dollops of treacle more sugary than the richest Carême dessert, yet also hard nuggets of Grand Guignol. The result, dark yet seductive, and concentrated enough to be consumable in a single evening's steady devouring, like a luxury-brand box of chocolates, is among the best-loved of all his works.

Mixing sugar with Grand Guignol was a Dickens literary trick. He had a savage streak, as we have seen over his wife. Linked to it was his fascination with violent crimes, especially murder. Lastly, there was the sentimentality already alluded to. The two contrasting dispositions – now dark, now saccharine – often fuse in a single person, particularly among Americans, who have always revered him.

Dickens is also one of the great travel writers. And not just, as with *American*

Notes and *Pictures from Italy*, in describing foreign parts. He revelled in the nuts and bolts of how you got there. Transport inspired him as much as did destination.

His very first novel, *Pickwick Papers*, positively creaks with coaches. They formed the long-distance articulated lorry-cum-charabanc-cum-fibre optic cable system of their time. They conveyed luggage, passengers and major communications but were unwieldy and top-heavy, hauled across variable terrain by teams of horses which for sheer trickiness resembled an insubordinate cavalry squadron. Coachmen needed the skills of a modern super-tanker pilot and a crowd-control policeman after a disputed goal at a Celtic *v* Rangers football match. Yet Dickens's propagandist powers have had the effect of converting this vital tool of transport and keeping-in-touch to a 'Merry England' greetings card motif.

But unintentionally. Which needs stressing. Dickens has Mr Pickwick refer to their dangers. Pickwick even gets personally overturned in a carriage accident. In *Nicholas Nickleby*, Dickens capsizes a full-blown mail coach, and in snow. For him the coach-and-horses world was more dramatic than romantic, the exception being a lyrical description of Tom Pinch's ride to London in *Martin Chuzzlewit*.

Railways, the chief 19th-century transport innovation, inspired Dickens quite as much. He kills the villain in *Dombey and Son* with a train, having in an earlier chapter devoted several paragraphs of purplish prose to a fanciful similarity between the swiftly moving London–Birmingham express and the March of Death. Mr Dombey he based partly on George Hudson, the 'Railway King', whose boom-and-bust projects his readers would have known all about. Dickens's writings were so absorbing that Mrs Gaskell in *Cranford* has Captain Brown run over by a train while deep in the current episode of *Pickwick Papers*.

Italian peasants illustration in Pictures from Italy *(top).*

A 1905 Christmas card featuring Mr and Mrs Peerybingle from The Cricket on the Hearth *– one of the* Christmas Books *(above).*

The 1865 Staplehurst railway accident (below).

Nor did Dickens merely write about railway dramas. In 1865, five years before his death, he was involved as passenger in a train crash on the Folkstone–London line in Kent. Characteristically, he ignored his own injuries to help others. For he practised as well as preached benevolence (unlike his humbugging evangelical characters). This included raising funds for indigent colleagues in the literary world. And he was a notoriously soft touch for begging-letter-writers.

Dickens's house in Broadstairs, which became a museum in the 1970s (above).

Dickens's birthplace in Portsea, Portsmouth (below).

Dickens agitated for all sorts of betterment of the general human condition. He urged sympathy with children rather than dismissing them as 'limbs of Satan'. He thought any public appointment should go to whoever merited it, however lowborn. He pushed for imaginative rather than arid schooling and a rational, humane legal system, not the reactionary restrictive practice of his day.

Dickens was a restless man. He often took his family to live abroad. But never for more than a year, and usually much less. Semi-flits, perhaps. They were nonetheless proper relocations, not extended holidays.

He twice toured America. He spent whole summers away from whatever was his main residence, mostly by the sea at Broadstairs, in Kent, but over three years during the 1850s at Boulogne, across that sea.

Not even in his Kentish or Continental retreats did he vegetate. He would dash up to London on publishing business from Broadstairs. And in the winter of 1844–45 he made the then arduous Genoa–London–Genoa round trip – via Venice too – all to give a reading to some friends in London of his latest work.

He attended and got up public dinners throughout the United Kingdom. He explored its more far-flung reaches for background colour to tint his novels with. When he embarked on his public readings, he performed up and down the provinces, as well as in London.

Dickens was not a true Cockney, being born on the edge of Portsmouth rather than within sound of Bow Bells. Indeed he claimed to be country-bred. But he is the nearest thing to an honorary one. Stylistically, he has the Cockney wit's love of ponderous sarcasm: ' … there was considerable difficulty in inducing Oliver [Twist] to take upon himself the office of respiration – a troublesome practice, but one which custom has rendered necessary to our easy existence … '

His Cockney characters, not least the nicest and wittiest of them, Sam Weller, are his best creations. This operated professionally, not just artistically. Sam's arrival in *Pickwick Papers* boosted the serial's readership and made Dickens's reputation. It explains why he never ditched 'low' comic scenes from his other novels, even when they sat uneasily with ever more sophisticated ones involving major characters and plot developments.

Dickens's family was from the petty bourgeoisie. His mother's father Charles Barrow was a dishonest senior functionary in the Royal Navy pay office who eventually absconded to the Isle of Man, then as now largely outside UK jurisdiction. Dickens's father John was an improvident but apparently honest clerk in the same department, who retired in his late thirties on ill health grounds, taking a pension and trying his hand at other activities, including journalism. So demanding a secondary career rather calls in question his ill health – perhaps therefore his honesty in pleading it to his employers before pocketing their pension.

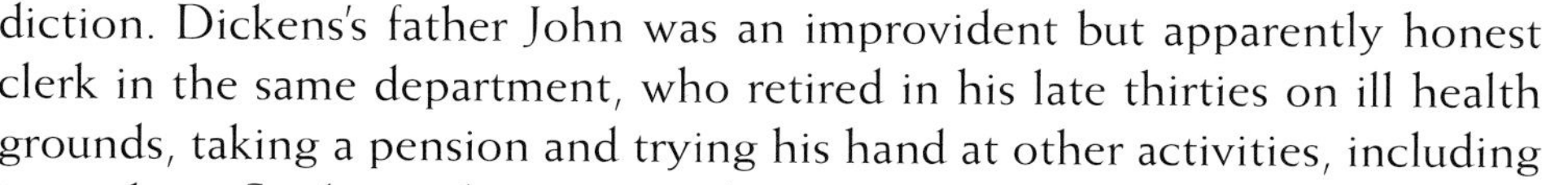

Dickens's parents, Elizabeth and John (above).

An illustration by Kyd from Dombey and Son *showing Toots, head boy at Dr Blimber's academy (below).*

Dickens's paternal grandparents were butler and housekeeper to Lord Crewe. Dickens shows an acute sense of the gradations of status between servant, also the pecking order among small business-owners, junior-rank functionaries and shopkeepers. He excels at subtle variations in their views of the world and each other.

He is less convincing when handling labourers or factory workers. He tends in his early books to make them, if a 'good' character, sturdy-limbed and noble in outlook. Later, such beings are excessively homely, with a tendency to forelock-tugging to their 'betters', though not without that slightly bemused, almost ironic detachment which, among the English lower classes at any rate, avoids pure obsequiousness.

Cardboard cut-out characterisation was Dickens's vice in youth. His Early Period love-interest juveniles are good-looking (reasonably enough; plain ones would have displeased readers), but with boring feelings, boringly expressed. Madeline Bray in *Nicholas Nickleby* is distilled nullity, her counterpart Kate Nickleby very little more.

The two-dimensionality of his Early Period 'baddies' is worse still, near silhouettes in their lack of depth. It includes speech. Dickens had a problem here. He dared

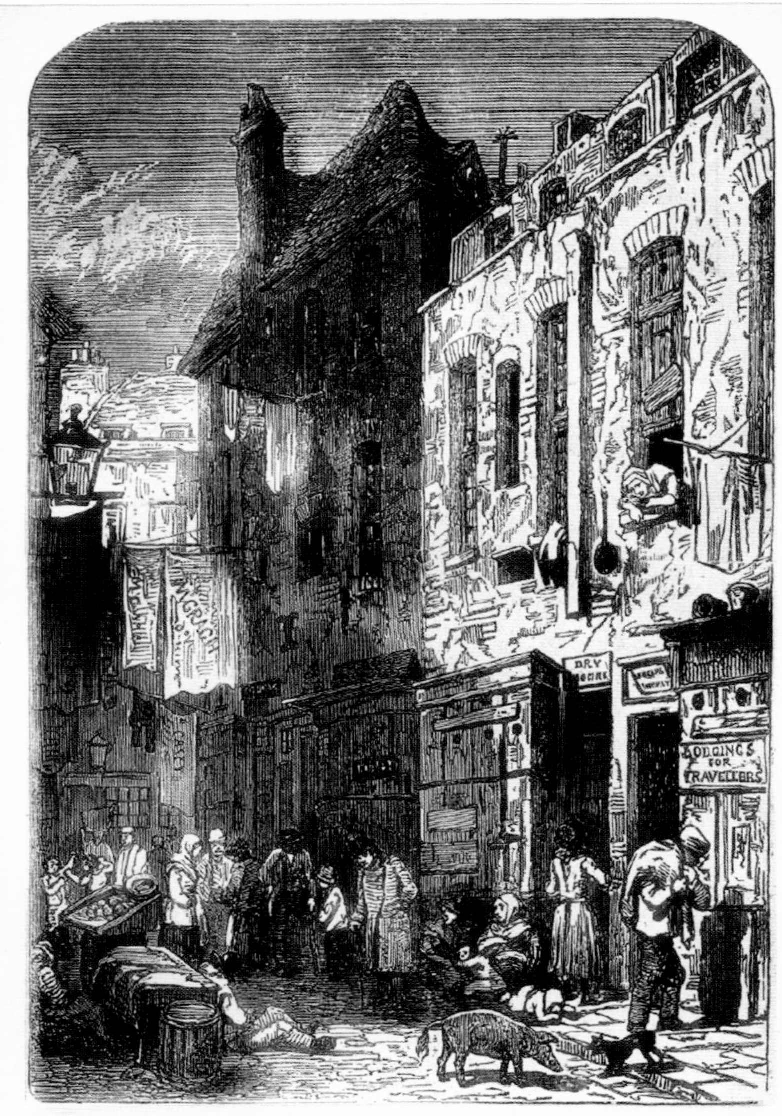

An exceptionally squalid part of London. Note the pig.

not make curses too obscene or blasphemous. His public would have deserted him. So to illustrate a character's wickedness he fell back on such tired props as shifty glances, evil leers and the biting of one's lip.

And in his dialogue he used archaic terms such as 'drab', meaning 'whore', addressed to the prostitute Nancy by Fagin; or 'she devil', addressed to her by Bill Sikes. Bill's bogusly Miltonic-Shakespearean imprecations when on the run ('Wolves tear your throats', 'you white-livered hound') might *just* sound plausible in a spoilt priest turned Mafia don after a very old-fashioned English language school tuition. They hardly fit an 1830s thug bred among the London 'rookeries', or slum tenements. One is reminded of Jimmie Waterford in Muriel Spark's *Robinson*, whose weird speech mixes period colloquialisms from P G Wodehouse with the stately idiom of the King James Bible.

And for Dickens it is as if there had been no progress in literary portraiture since the medieval allegories: warped souls are betrayed by a repulsive physiognomy. Or in plain words, his nasty characters have correspondingly nasty faces.

Aristocrats largely elude Dickens too, though 'Cousin' (Lord) Feenix in *Dombey and Son*, and Sir Leicester Dedlock in *Bleak House*, come over as something better than caricatures. But his chief defect of vision, as the novelist and critic Anthony Powell observed, was his inability to understand how almost anyone, but particularly upper middle-class professionals or businessmen, earn their livings.

This will have come from Dickens's achieving independence as a writer while very young. It deprived him of artistically valuable experience in prosaic commercial occupations along the way. And his project-managing may have been little sharper than that of his famously scatty father, the original of Mr Micawber. As a book-packager Dickens tended to splash out on elaborate production, to the detriment of profits. Similarly with his charity theatre shows. But in negotiating he was pretty 'cute', as Victorians put it. He argued his own corner effectively enough against publishers. Just as well. Literary agents barely existed then.

Dickens owed more to his family than literary models. A kinsman rented with Dickens the box in Doctors' Commons (see *David Copperfield* 'Characters' against Mrs Crupp for explanation) that the teenage Dickens and other freelance reporters occupied when reporting speeches. His maternal uncle John Barrow was owner-editor of the newspaper where the slightly older teenage Charles got his first experience of parliamentary speech-reporting.

So although Dickens became a superb novelist beholden to nobody but his readers, at the start of his career he owed as much to family string-pulling as do the Barnacle upper-class sprigs in the Circumlocution Office who he goes for in *Little Dorrit*.

He suffered from the typically petty bourgeois anxiety to be thought a 'gentleman', even though, or perhaps because, he wasn't one, or not quite. It is a preoccupation he passes on to several characters, notably David Copperfield and Pip in *Great Expectations*.

Even when Dickens had become the most successful author of the century he dressed a little too loudly, much as his disciple Evelyn Waugh would get himself up to look like a bookie. It ran wholly counter to the age, for by the 1840s and 1850s, Dickens's prime, the tight-fitting, gaudy plumage of Regency bucks and their successors, the dandies of the 1820s and 1830s, was retreating before looser-cut outfits in drabber hues.

It doesn't matter that Dickens embodied contradictions: sentimental satirist, sharp dresser in an ever more subfusc age, would-be gentleman brute to his wife, above all provincial-origin urbanite. No native topographer, whether Cockney rough diamond, jaded Fleet Street hack, earnest Hampstead humanitarian or drawling West End exquisite, has painted London better than does the Pompey-born Dickens. Nobody can have known it better. And even in the 19th century there was a lot to know. Dickens lived, worked, loved and suffered there as both child and man. He sets episodes in nearly all his novels there. And those episodes are among the most dramatic in, and vital to, their encasing stories.

A fashion plate dated 1850 from Petit Courier des Dames *(above). An inspiration to London ladies and gentlemen of the period.*

Dickens characters have imposed their names on London streets. Brownlow, the benevolent father-substitute in *Oliver Twist*, is now also a mews behind Dickens's house at the time, which was in Doughty Street, on Bloomsbury's eastern fringe. Dombey is commemorated in a thoroughfare two blocks west. Just south of the Thames, near the old Marshalsea debtors' prison, sheaves of streets (Clennam, Copperfield, Doyce, Little Dorrit, Quilp and Weller) are christened after Dickens characters.

The courtyard of the White Hart Inn in Southwark (right) where Mr Pickwick first meets Sam Weller. Dickens describes the inns in this area, 'Great, rambling, queer old places they are, with galleries, and passages, and staircases, wide enough and antiquated enough to furnish material for a hundred ghost stories.'

And most of us know individuals who have barely read Dickens, or only did so back in childhood, yet who spout Dickens catch-phrases and behave, especially when elderly ladies and in a contrary mood, exactly in that exasperating, warped-logic, monomanic, tunnel-vision fashion that he alone of all novelists is wholly fluent in echoing.

Greater London is Dickens's oyster. He sets scenes in the Kentish fringes; the East End slums; the City and its western buffer zone (Clerkenwell, Holborn and Law Court land); the blue-chip districts of Mayfair and Belgravia; the shabby genteel Borough and Southwark; the then wholly rural Petersham, Richmond and Twickenham.

Ellen Ternan.

Dickens ranges in his novel scenes, as he did personally during his marathon walks, from the Surrey side of the Thames to the Hampstead heights and beyond, up to Barnet and the gateway to the North. He is not absolutely ubiquitous. London's southern outskirts he largely ignores. Conceivably, as regards his later novels, because during his last dozen years he clandestinely kept a young actress he was besotted with, Ellen Ternan, in a house in Peckham, in southeast London. Whether she was actually Dickens's mistress remains uncertain. Most of his recent biographers think she was.

Nearby Norwood also exudes sexual whiffs. It is where the feline Mr Carker in *Dombey and Son* has his villa, adorned inside, not with manly landscapes or wholesome genre paintings, but with 'prints and pictures ... of one voluptuous cast'. Carker's books, Dickens hints, are mostly rather voluptuous too – at the very least erotic, conceivably downright smut. In his next novel Dickens makes Norwood the setting for David Copperfield's wooing of his first wife Dora. This time the sexuality is straightforward enough – on the surface. But it is calamitous in the longer run, for Dora's child-wife inadequacy cannot support David's burgeoning literary career, any more than Dickens's real-life Catherine could his.

As to London's northwest, Dickens on another occasion installed Ellen Ternan there too. And that is an area he ignores in his novels, but probably due to the area's lack of melodramatic colour rather than any senescent sexual guilt. Back in the 1830s he had sent Bill Sikes to Hendon as part of the latter's frenzied getaway after murdering Nancy but instantly lugged him back to face the music in a spot more congenial to Dickens's strong sense of box office: a tumbledown riparian warehouse on Jacob's Island at Rotherhithe.

The Thames was in Dickens's day not just the capital's main through-way, but its chief sewer. Its grimier reaches, from, say, Hungerford Bridge downstream to the Pool of London, fascinate him. He keeps us off its upper waters till *Great Expectations* (Hammersmith). But the unlovely lower ones intrude into his narrative time and again. He wallows, as it were, in the Thames's then smelly contents, as deadly to human immersion in his day as they were life-giving to trade.

'The Pool of the Thames' by W Miller, from an original painting by Sir A W Callcott RA, c.1840

The adjective 'Dickensian' carries instant recognition, much as 'Victorian' does. The two terms even complement each other. 'Dickensian' in the popular view means pretty much a picturesque version of 'Victorian', with overtones of 'quaint' and 'theatrically squalid'.

Yet no fewer than 10 of Dickens's 14 and a half novels are set substantially or wholly before Victoria mounted the throne, and two are set when her grandfather George III occupied it. Dickens lived very much in the past. He imported memories of all his most intense experiences from the time, not of Victoria, but of George IV and William IV. These include his observant, impressionable childhood; adolescence in the blacking warehouse as a 'labouring hind [an archaism Dickens uses when emotionally overwrought; it means a farm-worker with connotations of near serfdom]'; and young adult's agony, sighing after Maria Beadnell, his first love and the model years later – by which time she had grown stout and garrulous – for Flora Finching in *Little Dorrit*.

The institutions, or more general sources of misery, that Dickens illuminates, excoriates, ridicules – the work house; beadles; thieves' dens; overcrowded, insanitary and jerry-built housing; viciously run and remotely situated

The Marshalsea Prison in Southwark, where Dickens's father was consigned after being arrested for debt.

boarding schools for unwanted children; the Marshalsea; the Circumlocution Office – are taken by today's public as absolutely representative of the Victorian Age. Yet they are more typical of the pre-Victoria one. And by the latter half of the Queen's reign most had been tackled, many reformed, some even abolished.

Dickens as novelist was uninterested in events outside England, let alone Great Britain. The Irish potato famine, the lesser-known Scottish one, the Highland clearances – none gets a look-in, however indignant Dickens is feeling. Even Chartism, which affected London, he only refers to very, very obliquely. As a journalist he was more *engagé*, in his magazine *All the Year Round* supporting Italian unification, for instance.

He was no socialist. A radical, certainly. But that is different. He knew all about mobs, as *Barnaby Rudge* testifies. Though an efficient dispenser of charity, he neither subscribed to anyone else's political programme nor had a substantial one of his own. Just a few soupy feelings, vapid as one of his own *Bleak House* fogs, only warmer. People should be nicer to each other, and jolly, and merry ... then the world would go right.

This, where the fount of power is concerned, approaches paternalism. Mind you, there are worse things. Millenary visions of the state's withering away following a dose of heavy-handed dictatorship by the proletariat for one, as the hundred million and counting victims of 20th-century Communist regimes might well agree, had they survived their murderers.

Dickens is so far true to his own beliefs that his genuinely benevolent characters are copybook paternalists: Mr Brownlow (*Oliver Twist*); the Cheeryble brothers (*Nicholas Nickleby*); John Jarndyce (*Bleak House*). One cannot imagine them having the nous to build up a fortune, as opposed to spending it. The specific exception, according to Dickens, is Magwitch (*Great Expectations*). And we are asked to believe that he, long a recidivist vagrant, has made good by way of agri-business. More a case of thumping good luck.

In Victorian Britain the sinews of prosperity were flexed by unsentimental, penny-pinching types like Scrooge before his conversion, the narrow-visioned Bounderby (*Hard Times*) and the emotional capon Mr Dombey. Dickens himself became prosperous, but he couldn't match businessmen. Novelists, however successful, seldom do.

A 1912 Dickens centenary penny stamp (top left), designed by, among others, H Rider Haggard. World sale proceeds (projected at 10,000,000, bringing over £5,200.000 in today's money) were meant to benefit Dickens's descendants.

Young Scrooge (above), conjured up by the Ghost of Christmas Past, an illustration by Honor Appleton.

Dickens was primarily a feeler, not a thinker. And feelers have longer-lived mass appeal, provided their emotions click with those of posterity. Today's public still responds to Dickens. For his melodramatic, self-pitying artistic persona is in some ways very modern. His real life character too, in that regard. Whenever he got involved in a dispute he considered himself the injured party. This comes out both in the strongly autobiographical *David Copperfield* and in Dickens's day-to-day business dealings with publishers, or social relations involving fellow literary figures.

It is an attitude that appeals hugely to today's self-styled victims. And his famous whine about being brought into contact with common people, when a child labourer in Warren's Blacking Warehouse, is, though unfashionably disparaging of the great unwashed, in its egotism very like the currently popular misery memoirists. As Anthony Powell frequently remarked, an almost invariable ingredient of the best seller is self-pity.

Dickens had that in spades. And he certainly knew how to turn out best sellers.

A Charles Dickens Timeline

No writer as careless about dates and timeframes as Dickens can be discussed as a historian without inducing a smile in the reader. The driest, stodgiest recounting of actual past events, such as the Mouse's on Edwin and Morcar in *Alice in Wonderland*, is a model of cogent and judicious analysis in comparison. As well – almost – treat Dickens's historical grasp as write up Jane Austen's obsession with social justice or P G Wodehouse's tragic insight (apologies to the American novelist Peter De Vries there, it being his coinage).

The qualification 'almost' is important, however. If one judged by the passage on Jingle in the 'Characters' section of *Pickwick Papers* or the first two paragraphs of the 'Story Commentary' to *Little Dorrit*, one would be tempted to say that Dickens, like Alice, 'had no very clear notion how long ago anything had happened'. Contrariwise, as to what had happened, provided it affected him, he possessed total recall. In the broad sense of concern with life's passing and feel for one's lost childhood then youth, Dickens has as firm a grasp, not just of Time's forelock but of his entire mane, as any English novelist ever.

What of his two historical novels, his apologists will ask? What of *A Child's History of England*? First the two historical novels, *Rudge* and *A Tale*. As novels they are satisfactory. As evocations of the historic, rather than author's, past – less so. With the great practitioners of the genre, Mary Renault, say, or Alfred Duggan, long-gone eras are rendered wholly convincing, perhaps at the expense of characterisation. With Dickens, his highly pungent characters, and especially their individual speech patterns, rather drown out the sound of a grandfather clock's slow, majestic ticking, arthritic whirring and musical chimes, things which, if historical novels are to work, must be a steady background leitmotif, Wagnerian in its persistence.

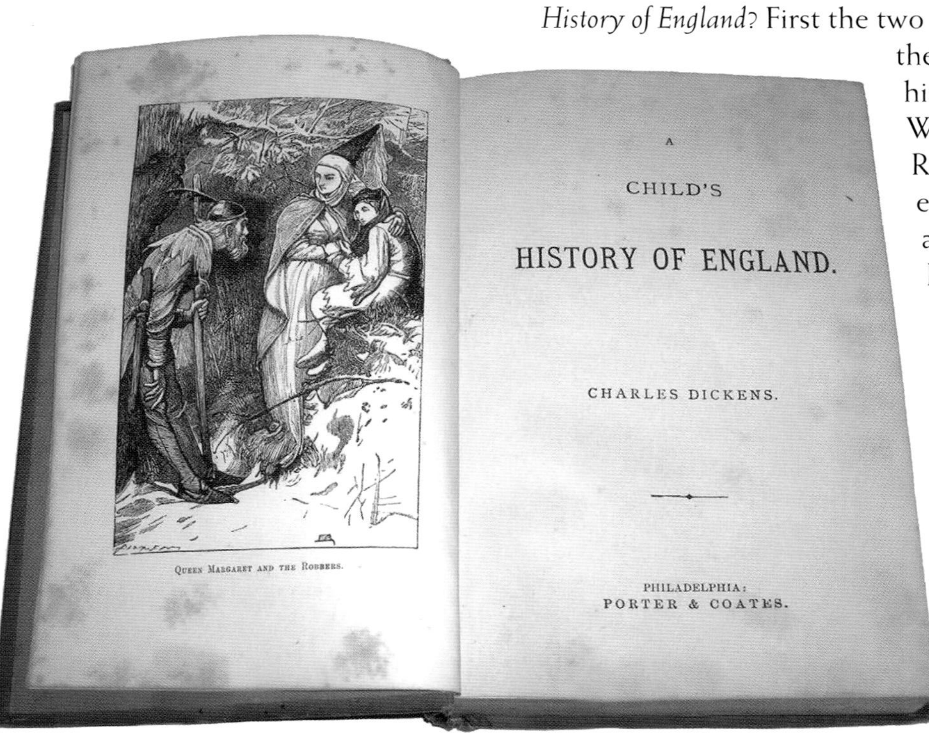
A
CHILD'S
HISTORY OF ENGLAND.
CHARLES DICKENS.
PHILADELPHIA:
PORTER & COATES.

Queen Margaret and the Robbers.

A Child's History of England, *published in book form in three volumes between 1852 and 1854.*

Dickens composed *A Child's History* between 1850 and 1853. He at first intended it for domestic consumption, that is, his own brood. His chief purpose, he had much earlier claimed, was to protect his eldest son Charley against High Tory influences (in which case, why send Charley to Eton?). But he soon laid it before the public via his magazine *Household Words* (where, however, it was no very great draw), publishing it in instalments between late January 1851 and early December 1853. He brought out a book version in a three-volume edition between 1852 and 1854.

It makes the most marvellous reading: a strong story line (history furnished that, however), backed up with stupendously colourful set pieces and seasoned with plenty of Dickens's editorialising comments. These consisted mostly of digs against the Church during coverage of the Middle Ages, for instance. But they also featured highly characteristic gems like the following (on Edward III's reign): 'The Order of the Garter (a very fine thing in its way, but hardly so important as good clothes for the nation) also dates from this period.' No king but Alfred the Great comes well out of Dickens's account. Oliver Cromwell emerges as the country's top ruler.

As with Max Beerbohm's remarks in *Zuleika Dobson* about the history muse Clio's attitude to Herodotus, what one likes – and rightly likes – in Dickens is just what prevents him from being a good historian.

Dickens lived in Chatham in the Medway Valley from the age of five until he was ten years old; this engraving dates from the mid-1820s (below).

1780–1810

Charles Dickens

Britain and Ireland

1780
Gordon Riots (*Barnaby Rudge*)

Continental Europe

1789
French Revolution erupts
(*A Tale of Two Cities*)

1792
French Revolution worsens with Paris September Massacres
(*A Tale of Two Cities*)

Rest of the World

1788
Transportation of criminals to Australia starts
(see 'Dickens Abroad')

1807
Slave trade abolished (see 'The Making of Dickens' and *Pickwick Papers* and *Dombey and Son* 'Story Commentaries')

1811–1820

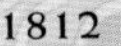

1812
Charles Dickens born on edge of Portsmouth, Hampshire

1817
Charles Dickens and family move to Chatham (2 Ordnance Terrace, then 18 St Mary's Place)

1812
Paddle steamer *Comet* plies Glasgow–Greenock, Europe's first profitable mechanised water-transport system
('Steam … was in its infancy' – *Great Expectations*)

Regency instituted due George III's madness; Prince Regent, aped by Mr Turveydrop (*Bleak House*), becomes George IV 1820

1816
Byron leaves England, stays in Switzerland and settles in Italy; Dickens, a debunker of the Byron legend, was yet all too ready to visit these countries a generation later

1812–1814
War of 1812: British burn White House, Washington DC; Americans crush British New Orleans (see 'Dickens Abroad')

1821–1825

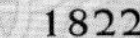

1822
Charles Dickens and family move to 16 Bayham St, Camden Town, London

1824
Charles Dickens's father arrested for debt and sent to Marshalsea Prison (*Little Dorrit*)

Charles Dickens and family move to Johnson St, Somers Town, London

Charles Dickens toils at blacking warehouse (*David Copperfield*)

1822
Royal Academy of Music opens; Charles Dickens's sister Fanny joins 1823

1825
Stockton and Darlington Railway opens, ushers in railway era (*Dombey and Son*)

1821
Dostoevsky, Dickens's chief Russian disciple, b

1824
Charles X, last legitimist King of France, succeeds brother Louis XVIII but is overthrow in July Revolution of 1830 (*Pickwick Papers*)

1823
Demerara slave revolt, 3rd biggest in Colonial-era Caribbean, involves 1,100–1,200 insurgents
(*Pickwick Papers*)

1780–1810

1811–1820

1821–1825

1826–1830

1827–1828
Charles Dickens works as solicitor's clerk

1828–36
Charles Dickens reports law courts' and Parliament's proceedings

1827
Canning's ministry replaces Lord Liverpool's (*Pickwick Papers*)

1829
Catholic Emancipation Act ends persecution people like Haredales (*Barnaby Rudge*)

1830
William IV succeeds George IV

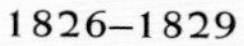

1826–1829
Prince (Hermann) von Pückler-Muskau visits Britain and Ireland (model for Count Smorltork – *Pickwick Papers*)

1828
Tolstoy, like Dostoevsky a Dickens admirer, born

1827
ar Allan Poe, his 'The Raven' inspired Dickens's Grip (*Barnaby Rudge*), self-publishes *Tamerlane and Other Poems*

1826–1830

1831–1835

1831–1832
Charles Dickens and family move to Margaret St, Marylebone

1832
Charles Dickens and family move to 18 Bentinck St, Marylebone

Charles Dickens becomes full-time journalist

1833
Charles Dickens's first story appears ('A Dinner at Poplar Walk')

1834
New Poor Law introduces workhouses (*Oliver Twist*)

Robert Peel (*Oliver Twist*) briefly succeeds Melbourne (*Pickwick Papers*) as prime minister

1831
'Canut' revolt in Lyons, first industrial workers' rising, foreshadows 1848 overthrow King Louis-Philippe of the French, which delighted Dickens

1835
Hans Christian Andersen (Dickens's future house guest) publishes first major works

1833
Slavery in most British possessions abolished (*Pickwick Papers*, also *Dombey and Son* 'Story Commentary')

1831–1835

1836–1840

1836
Charles Dickens marries Catherine Hogarth

Charles Dickens's first book, *Sketches by Boz*, and first chapters of first novel *Pickwick Papers*, published

Charles Dickens becomes full-time freelance writer

1836–1839
Charles Dickens edits magazine *Bentley's Miscellany*

1837
Dickenses move to 48 Doughty Street, Bloomsbury (now Charles Dickens Museum)

Sister-in-law Mary Hogarth dies, devastating Dickens

1838
Charles Dickens investigates Yorkshire schools for unwanted children for *Nicholas Nickleby*

1839
Dickenses move to 1 Devonshire Terrace, near Regent's Park

1836
Prime Minister Melbourne sued for 'crim con' (*Pickwick Papers*)

1837
Queen Victoria succeeds William IV

1840
Queen Victoria marries Prince Albert (promoter with Dickens of Victorian Christmas)

1838
Parts of *Pickwick Papers* translated into Russian, allegedly influencing Nikolai Gogol, who moved to Rome where he read Dickens assiduously

1840
Philadelphia publishers Lea & Blanchard (see 'Dickens Abroad') issue *Tales of the Grotesque and Arabesque* by Edgar Allan Poe (who, pot-calling-kettle-black, questions Dickens's sanity in reviewing *The Old Curiosity Shop*)

1836–1840

Charles Dickens

Britain and Ireland

Continental Europe

Rest of the World

1841–1845

Charles Dickens

1842
President Tyler receives Charles Dickens at White House on latter's first American tour

1844–45
Dickenses in Italy

Britain and Ireland

1840s
Railway boom starts (*Dombey and Son*)

1842
Chancery Six Clerks' Office (*Bleak House*), Marshalsea Prison (*Little Dorrit*) abolished

1845–1849/52
Irish potato famine (see 'The Making of Charles Dickens')

Continental Europe

1842
Nikolai Gogol in Moscow publishes *Dead Souls* (officialdom imposing the less subversive title *The Adventures of Chichikov*), some say inspired by *Pickwick Papers*

Rest of the World

1845
Poe's poem 'The Raven' published; earns him 'only' $9 (say $1,025/£650 now, a lot for a poem in a periodical today)

1846–1850

Charles Dickens

1846
Charles Dickens briefly (Jan–Feb) edits *Daily News*, though continuing to contribute thereafter

Dickenses reside Lausanne, on Lake Geneva in Switzerland, Jun–Nov

1847–57
Charles Dickens active in running Urania Cottage, refuge for 'fallen women'

Britain and Ireland

1850–1859
Charles Dickens edits, half-owns and contributes to topical-cum-fiction magazine *Household Words*

1850
Court of Chancery hearings speeded up; filing of claims replaces old cumbersome procedure (*Bleak House*)

Continental Europe

1849
Dostoevsky's sentence for subversion (death by firing-squad), despite last-minute amelioration to four years Siberian hard labour, easily trumps Dickens's Marshalsea and blacking factory shame as grim sources of artistic inspiration

Rest of the World

1846
Washington Irving, friend of Dickens from 1842 US tour, signs innovative 12 per cent royalty deal with publisher

1851–1855

Charles Dickens

1851–1857
Charles Dickens resides at Tavistock Hous[e] Tavistock Square, Bloomsbury

1853
Charles Dickens's second Italian-Swiss trip gives first public readings, doing so for charity from *A Christmas Carol*

1854
Charles Dickens studies life in the raw at Preston, Lancs (*Hard Times*)

1855
Charles Dickens agitates against official incompetence on behalf of Administrative Reform Association (*Little Dorrit*)

Britain and Ireland

1852
Great Ormond Street Children's Hospital ope[ns] Charles Dickens publicises it in *Household Wo[rds]*

1855
Lord Palmerston, last Prime Ministerial target of Di[ckens's] satire (*Little Dorrit*), forms first of his two ministr[ies]

Continental Europe

1851–1852
Louis-Napoleon dictatorial President of Fran[ce] then Emperor (1852–1870) as Napoleon II[I] (*Little Dorrit*)

1855
Reformist Alexander II succeeds reactionar[y] Nicholas I as Tsar of Russia, giving hope to inventors like Daniel Doyce (*Little Dorrit*)

Rest of the World

1852
Uncle Tom's Cabin by Harriet Beecher Stowe published; Charles Dickens lauds it in *Househ[old] Words*, though privately critical and previous[ly] satirical about anti-slavery agitators (Mrs Jellyby in *Bleak House*)

1841–1845 1846–1850 1851–1855

1856–1860

1856
Charles Dickens buys Gad's Hill Place, Kent, but moves in during following year

1857–1858
Charles Dickens's relationship with Ellen Ternan brings his marriage to an end, Dickens and Catherine separating

1858–1870
Charles Dickens's commercial readings from his works

1859–1870
Charles Dickens editor and majority shareholder literary magazine *All the Year Round*

1856–57
Whitewash Board of Enquiry into Crimean War mismanagement goads Dickens into penning furious *Household Words* articles in August 1856 and March 1857

1858–59
Anglo-French tiffs thought to have inspired Dickens's French Revolution setting for *A Tale of Two Cities*

1860
Abraham Lincoln's election as US President brings nearer secession of South, which Charles Dickens supports in Civil War

1856–1860

1861–1865

1865
Charles Dickens in Staplehurst train crash; spends two hours helping fellow-passengers but also hides identity of Ellen Ternan, his travelling companion

1864
Charing Cross station opens, London, terminus for Folkestone boat train at time of Staplehurst crash

1861
Dostoevsky's novel *The Insulted and Injured* appears; certain characters and plot twists suggest not just *The Old Curiosity Shop*'s influence but *Barnaby Rudge*'s

1861–65
American Civil War; Charles Dickens later, when in US, acquires photos of its battlefields, lends them to Queen Victoria; though publicly pro the South, the loser, he privately thinks both sides culpable

1865
The young Henry James, reviewing *Our Mutual Friend* in the newly founded (but still published) American magazine *The Nation*, calls it 'poor with the poverty … of permanent exhaustion'

1861–1865

1866–1870

1866/1867
Charles Dickens settles Ellen Ternan in a cottage at Slough, Berkshire, also renting a bolt hole there for himself, but next year installs her at a house he has procured her in Peckham, SE London

1870
Charles Dickens dies of a stroke on 9 June; buried Westminster Abbey

1870
Legislation introduces primary education on a national scale in Britain, something dear to Dickens's heart in principle, if less so when carried out unfeelingly (*Hard Times*)

1870
French Second Empire ends, defeated by Prussia

1868
President Johnson of USA impeached, stops some Charles Dickens Boston readings (see 'Dickens Abroad')

1868
Transportation to Australia ceases (*Great Expectations*)

1870
Bret Harte, who Dickens once invited to contribute to *All the Year Round*, on hearing of his death dashes off a poem 'Dickens in Camp', about a reading from *The Old Curiosity Shop* involving Little Nell which moves rough Californian gold-diggers.

1866–1870

Charles Dickens

Britain and Ireland

Continental Europe

Rest of the World

Charles Dickens's World

How truly cosmopolitan was Dickens? He scatters his characters across nearly every continent. A glance at the map of the world suggests he was more a citizen of it than most of his generation. A closer look reveals this to be a superficial judgement. He set no action in Africa, Asia and South America, though he plonked down some of his human creations there. Antarctica he touched not all, for his glacial Wilkie-Collins-dramatic-collaboration *The Frozen Deep* concerns the Arctic. The US part of North America he noticeably disparaged but hugely enriched himself by visiting. The Canada part he regarded as a bolt hole from the US. His attitude to Australia is discussed elsewhere, but that continent was to him a sideshow at best.

The Church of Santa Maria del Rosario, Venice, by James Holland, 1843 (left).

Old State House, Boston, built in 1713, restored in 1747 after a fire, and then again in 1910 (below).

Europe on the face of it fares better. But the places he spent time at or in – well-known towns or cities in France, Italy and Switzerland, the standard tourist destinations of his day – were the same ones twice or many times more. His first trip abroad ever, that of 1837, he took in Belgium, but we know next to nothing about it. For the very good reason that Dickens, the most loquacious of men about his heart's innermost secrets, chose not to tell. He passed through Germany, but only on his way to Switzerland. Eastern Europe, the Balkans, Iberia, Scandinavia he ignored.

This may seem unfair. He succumbed to neither of the world-view sicknesses that beset most Britons in the nineteenth century: vainglorious imperialism on the one hand, 'Little Englander' insularity on the other. He pokes fun in *Little Dorrit* at the Bleeding Heart Yard residents' tendency to get across their meaning to foreigners via a *fortissimo* pidgin or Pancks's repeating *'altro'* (sole word in his foreign vocabulary) to Cavalletto to demonstrate his mastery of the language of Dante and Petrarch. But Dickens also, by nominally attacking Lord Decimus Tite Barnacle, in reality savages Palmerston – or so it is usually said – as the father of jingoism, that cretinous subspecies of the *genus imperiale*.

Charles Dickens's London

1. Cleveland Street: Here Dickens lived 1815–17 and 1829–30
2. Bayham Street: Dickens lived here as child; Bob Cratchit (*A Christmas Carol*) as adult
3. Gower Street: Dickens's mother ran a school at their home here
4. Johnson Street (now Cranleigh Street): Dickens lived here as child/youth
5. Margaret Street: Dickens lived here as child/youth
6. Bentinck Street: Dickens lived here as child/youth
7. Chelsea, St Luke's: Dickens married Catherine Hogarth here
8. Furnival's Inn, High Holborn: The newly married Dickens and Catherine lived here
9. 48 Doughty Street: The newly married Dickens and Catherine lived here
10. 1 Devonshire Terrace (near Regent's Park): The newly married Dickens and Catherine lived here
11. Tavistock House, Tavistock Square: Dickens lived here in prosperous maturity
12. Goswell Street (now Road): Pickwick's lodgings
13. Farringdon Street: Site of Fleet Prison, where Pickwick held
14. Dulwich: Pickwick retired here
15. Saffron Hill: Fagin's lair hereabouts
16. Jacob's Island, Rotherhithe: Bill Sikes cornered here
17. Golden Square: Ralph Nickleby's house
18. Soho, say Manette Street: Dr Manette's residence (*A Tale of Two Cities*)
19. Tower Hill: Quilp's residence (*The Old Curiosity Shop*)
20. Bevis Marks: Brasses' residence (*The Old Curiosity Shop*)
21. Clerkenwell: Gabriel Varden's residence (*Barnaby Rudge*); Venus's shop (*Our Mutual Friend*)
22. Newgate Prison: Stormed by rioters (*Barnaby Rudge*); condemned cell later held Fagin
23. Cornhill: Dodson & Fogg offices here (*Pickwick Papers*); Scrooge's counting-house hereabouts
24. Monument: Mrs Todgers's boarding-house nearby (*Martin Chuzzlewit*)
25. Leadenhall Street: Site of shop Sol Gills's based on (*Dombey and Son*)
26. Buckingham Street: David Copperfield's rooms here
27. Norwood: Carker's villa (*Dombey and Son*); Dora Spenlow's home (*David Copperfield*)
28. Blackheath: Salem House here (*David Copperfield*)
29. Faraday Building, Queen Victoria Street: Doctors' Commons here (*David Copperfield*)
30. Lincoln's Inn: Court of Chancery and Tulkinghorn's rooms here (*Bleak House*)
31. Clare Market (near Kingsway, just east of Covent Garden): Probable site of Tom-all-Alone's (*Bleak House*)
32. Drury Lane Gardens (kids' playground), Drury Lane: Churchyard here held 'Nemo'; Lady Dedlock died at its gates (*Bleak House*)
33. Marshalsea, Borough: Dickens's father held here 1824; William Dorrit also
34. Harley Street: Merdles' house here (*Little Dorrit*)

35. Temple: Pip's rooms here (*Great Expectations*)
36. Hammersmith: Pockets' residence (*Great Expectations*)
37. Petersham: Site of Hawk-Verisopht duel (*Nicholas Nickleby*)
38. Maids of Honour Row, Richmond Green: Estella acquired social polish here (*Great Expectations*)

- Twickenham: Meagleses' house here (*Little Dorrit*)
- Houghton Place, Ampthill Square: Here Dickens kept putative mistress Ellen Ternan
- Windsor Lodge, Linden Grove: Here Dickens kept putative mistress Ellen Ternan

42 York Road (now; was Maiden Lane): Noddy Boffin's 'Bower' here (*Our Mutual Friend*)

Charles Dickens's Britain

1. Alderbury, Wiltshire: Blue Dragon (*Martin Chuzzlewit*) based on Green Dragon here/George Hotel, Amesbury
2. Barnet, Hertfordshire: Artful Dodger ensnared Oliver Twist here
3. Bath, Avon: Pickwick visited; Sam attended 'swarry'
4. Blundeston, Suffolk: Model for Blunderstone (*David Copperfield*)
5. Brighton, Sussex: Little Paul schooled here (*Dombey and Son*)
6. Broadstairs, Kent: Dickens summered here often
7. Bury St Edmunds, Suffolk: Pickwick stayed Angel Hotel, tricked by Jingle
8. Canterbury, Kent: Here David Copperfield educated, lodged with Wickfields
9. Chalk, Kent: Dickens and Catherine honeymooned here
10. Chatham, Kent: Dickens lived here as child
11. Chertsey, Surrey: Mrs Maylie's house here (*Oliver Twist*)
12. Chigwell, Essex: Near here rioters burnt the Warren; Maypole Inn based on Ye Olde King's Head? (*Barnaby Rudge*)
13. Cobham, Kent: Leather Bottle inn, Tupman's bolt-hole on losing Rachael Wardle (*Pickwick Papers*)
14. Cooling, Kent: Reckoned model for Pip's village (*Great Expectations*)
15. Corby, Northamptonshire: Rockingham Castle, model for Chesney Wold (*Bleak House*)
16. Dover, Kent: Aunt Trotwood's cottage nearby (*David Copperfield*)
17. Gad's Hill, Kent
18. Greta Bridge, North Yorkshire/County Durham: Dotheboys Hall nearby (*Nicholas Nickleby*)
19. Henley-on-Thames, Oxfordshire: Towpath upstream reckoned where Headstone assaulted Wrayburn (*Our Mutual Friend*); Anglers' Inn where Lizzie nursed Wrayburn (*Our Mutual Friend*) based on Red Lion here
20. Huntingdon, Cambridgeshire: Oliver Twist's home town?
21. Hurley Lock, Berkshire: Here Headstone drowned Riderhood and self (*Our Mutual Friend*)
22. Ipswich, Suffolk: Pickwickians visited
23. Warwick, Warwickshire: Dombey proposed to Edith after Castle visit
24. Leamington Spa, Warwickshire: Edith and Mr Dombey first met here
25. Lincolnshire Wolds: Location of Chesney Wold (*Bleak House*)
26. Liverpool: Main UK port for New World; Dickens, Martin Chuzzlewit used it
27. Maidstone, Kent: Alleged model for Muggleton (*Pickwick Papers*)
28. Pewsey Down, Wiltshire: Probable location Pecksniff's (*Martin Chuzzlewit*)
29. Portsmouth, Hampshire: Dickens born environs; Crummles troupe played (*Nicholas Nickleby*)
30. Preston, Lancashire: Coketown (*Hard Times*)
31. Rochester, Kent: Pickwickians visited; Miss Havisham resided (Rochester's Restoration House model for Satis House); *Edwin Drood*'s setting (Cloisterham)
32. Rockingham, Northamptonshire: Dedlock Arms (*Bleak House*) based on Sondes Arms
33. St Albans, Hertfordshire: Bleak House overlooked Abbey
34. Salisbury, Wiltshire: Here John Eastlake regaled Tom Pinch (*Martin Chuzzlewit*)
35. Sandling, Kent: Model for Dingley Dell (*Pickwick Papers*), nearby Cob Tree Hall is Manor Farm
36. Slough, Berkshire: Dickens kept Ellen Ternan here
37. Tewkesbury, Gloucestershire: Pickwickians toped (Royal) Hop Pole (Hotel), slept/sang thereafter
38. Tong, Shropshire: Little Nell ended here
39. Towcester, Northamptonshire: Pickwickians, rival editors met Saracen's Head here
40. West Malling, Kent: Other original Muggleton (*Pickwick Papers*)? Pickwickians drank Blue Lion (based on The Swan?)
41. Windsor, Berkshire: Esther Summerson raised here (*Bleak House*)
42. Yarmouth, Norfolk: Peggottys lived here (*David Copperfield*)

AN
Accurate MAP
OF
ENGLAND and WALES
WITH
The Principal ROADS from the best
AUTHORITIES
THE NORTH SEA OR GERMAN OCEAN
THE ENGLISH CHANNEL
Straits of Dover
FRANCE
I of WIGHT
RIVER THAMES
Humber River
LONDON

Charles Dickens's World

1. Halifax, Nova Scotia, Canada: Dickens attended legislature state opening 1842
2. Saint John, New Brunswick, Canada: Edmund Sparkler born here (*Little Dorrit*)
3. Quebec City, Quebec, Canada: Dickens visited 1842
4. Montreal, Quebec, Canada: Dickens directed garrison theatricals here 1842
5. Kingston, Ontario, Canada: Dickens visited 1842
6. Toronto, Ontario, Canada: Dickens visited 1842
7. Niagara Falls: Dickens and Catherine viewed 1842
8. Boston, Massachusetts, USA: Dickens feted 1842; did readings 1867–68
9. New York City, New York, USA: Dickens feted 1842 at 'Boz Ball'; did readings 1867–68
10. Baltimore, Maryland, USA: Dickens visited 1842 trip
11. Buffalo, New York, USA: Dickens visited 1842 trip
12. Cincinnati, Ohio, USA: Dickens visited 1842 trip
13. Columbus, Ohio, USA: Dickens visited 1842 trip
14. Louisville, Kentucky, USA: Dickens visited 1842 trip
15. Philadelphia, Pennsylvania, USA: Dickens visited 1842 trip
16. Richmond, Virginia, USA: Dickens visited 1842 trip
17. Washington DC, USA: Dickens visited 1842 trip
18. West Point, New York, USA: Dickens visited 1842 trip
19. Cairo, Illinois, USA: Original of Eden (*Martin Chuzzlewit*)
20. Barbados: Walter Gay posted here, sought here by Sol Gills (*Dombey and Son*)
21. Guyana: In Dickens's day 'Demerara': slave revolt here in 1823; Jingle migrated (*Pickwick Papers*); Fred Trent employed (*The Old Curiosity Shop*)
22. Antwerp, Belgium: Blandois found Clennam Sr's will codicil (*Little Dorrit*)
23. Paris, France: Here Sydney Carton stood in for Charles Darnay (*A Tale of Two Cities*); Dickens visited 1844–63; Dombeys honeymooned; Lady Dedlock bored by (*Bleak House*)
24. Boulogne, France: Dickens and family stayed here 1853, 1854, 1856
25. Calais, France: Clennam confronted Miss Wade, Tattycoram (*Little Dorrit*)
26. Condette, near Boulogne, France: Dickens kept putative mistress Ellen Ternan here 1862–65
27. Dijon, France: Carker, Edith rendezvous (*Dombey and Son*)
28. Marseilles, France: *Little Dorrit* opens; Blandois, Cavalletto imprisoned in
29. Milan, Italy: Dickens visited 1845, again with Augustus Egg, Wilkie Collins 1853
30. Rome, Italy: Dickens visited 1845, 1853; Dorrits stayed, William and Frederick dying there
31. Genoa, Italy: Dickens and family resided 1844–45; Dickens revisited with Augustus Egg, Wilkie Collins 1853
32. Florence, Italy: Dickens and Catherine visited 1845, Dickens revisited with Augustus Egg, Wilkie Collins 1853
33. Naples, Italy: Dickens and Catherine visited 1845, Dickens revisited with Augustus Egg, Wilkie Collins 1853
34. Venice, Italy: Dickens visited 1845; Dorrits stayed; Dickens revisited with Augustus Egg, Wilkie Collins 1853
35. St Petersburg, Russia: Doyce negotiated use his invention here (*Little Dorrit*)
36. Great St Bernard Pass, Switzerland: Dickens visited 1846; Dorrits reached Italy via, met Gowans

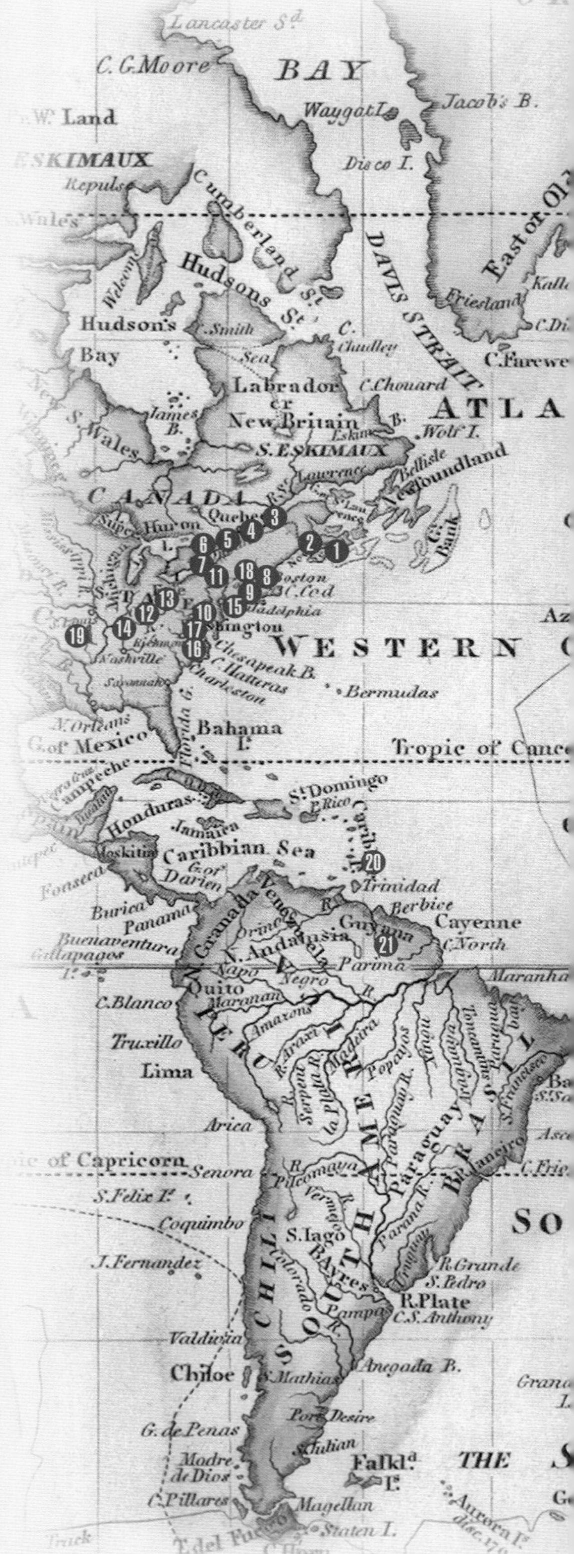

37. Lausanne, Switzerland: Dickens and family resided 1846; Dick revisited with Augustus Egg, Wilkie Collins 1853
38. Martigny, Switzerland: Dickens visited 1853, Dorrits met Gow
39. Cairo, Egypt: Pip with H Pocket's firm (*Great Expectations*)
40. The Cape, South Africa: John Harmon lived at till father died (*Mutual Friend*)
41. Sri Lanka (then 'Ceylon'): Neville and Helena Landless childre here (*Edwin Drood*)

China: Walter and Florence Gay voyaged hither (*Dombey and Son*); Arthur Clennam traded here (*Little Dorrit*)

India: Ben Allen, Bob Sawyer East India Co. surgeons Bengal (*Pickwick Papers*); Julia Mills married nabob (*David Copperfield*)

Botany Bay, Australia: Magwitch (*Great Expectations*), Artful Dodger (*Oliver Twist*), Brooker, Squeers (both *Nicholas Nickleby*) transported here

45 Australia, general: Alice Marwood transported to (*Dombey and Son*); Em'ly, Dan Peggotty, Mrs Gummidge, the Micawbers, Martha Endell and Mr Mell (all *David Copperfield*) emigrated here from UK

46 Tasmania, Australia (then 'Van Dieman's Land'): Augustus Moddle fled here from Cherry Pecksniff (*Martin Chuzzlewit*)

Collectable Dickens

Dickens published a huge amount and in very different formats. Furthermore, book production was immensely various in his day. It involved not just black-and-white or coloured illustrations but variations in the black-and-white, from the lightly drawn illustrations of early Phiz to the heavy-set figures of Stone and Fildes in the 1860s, with commensurate differences in reproduction techniques.

There were commonly bindings in a range that extended from calf (including full green, half plum, half red, half tan, half tan polished), through morocco to cloth (in blue, brown, dark green, pink, purple, red). Luxurious touches might include a gilt, marbled or sprinkled edge to each page; gilt (as opposed to plain black) lettering for titles; and endpapers in a choice of colours (e.g. olive) or patterns (e.g. marbling). Spines might involve banded gilt on broad bands.

Gentlefolk amassing libraries often got books bound to their specifications and embellished inside by book plates showing the owner's coat of arms, some of them genuine grants. Numerous Dickens volumes dating from his lifetime contain just such features. For the broader market there were de luxe editions, 'middling' ones, cheap ones. And, in Dickens's case, not just differences in quality but in the sheer number, reflecting his novels' enduring popularity.

Such was Dickens's swift and lasting impact on the book trade that even spin-offs of his works cobbled together by obscure hacks now fetch

respectable sums, for instance *The* [Pickwick] *Illustrations*, by Thomas Onwhyn (1837), currently priced at £200. This is not much less than a first edition of *Pickwick Papers* proper, current price £275. (All mentions of Dickens works in this section refer to prices extant in June 2011, also to first editions unless stated otherwise.)

The standard practice as regards a single work of fiction in book form in Dickens's early manhood was to bring the title out in three volumes. An *Oliver Twist* in this format can fetch as much as £3,750. A *Nicholas Nickleby* in two volumes has been advertised for £500. Dickens's signature may boost a title's value by not far off 100 per cent. A *Martin Chuzzlewit* so adorned had a recent asking price of £895; one without, £500.

Bleak House, *first and indeed grimmest of Dickens's 'Dark Period' novels, came out in the usual monthly serialised part-work format between the very end of February 1852 and the beginning of September 1853. Dickens usually supplied each number with three or four chapters. Complete sets of part-work versions of his novels are collectors' items.*

Since nearly all Dickens's novels first appeared in a magazine serial format, some one-volume book editions (a rather later development than the three-volume kind) signalled their 'superiority' by incorporating more illustrations. Two examples from such an edition of *Dombey and Son*, containing 12 extra plates by Phiz over and above the standard 38, were recently on offer, one for £900, the other for £995. Two other copies of the same work, each with only the original 38, were also available, one for £400, the other for £500.

A complete set of the Nonesuch Dickens *published in the late 1930s. The Nonesuch Press, founded in the early 1920s and still going, has produced beautiful editions of timeless classics.*

Master Humphrey's Clock *was a weekly magazine edited by Dickens and, as it turned out, written entirely by him too. It appeared from 4 April 1840 to 4 December 1841, whereupon the Clock was, as it were, wound up. (Master Humphrey himself, an old codger with a small circle of old codger-ish friends given to telling stories, had failed to hold the public's interest.) A complete set of numbers of the magazine named after him is nonetheless very desirable to bibliophiles.*

Dickens novels fetching four-figure sums are rarer. *Bleak House* is a notable exception, two copies being recently put on the market in the US for $1,999.95 (£1,214.74) and $2,650 (£1,609.57). A *Hard Times* for £1,000 and a *Great Expectations* for £2,000 are other examples, the latter an interesting case since it is a second edition but the first in one volume. It also contains illustrations, which the original versions, whether periodical-publication or in book form, did not.

The later an edition of Dickens, the cheaper – usually. And sets of his complete works are very often less expensive than a good-condition first edition of a single work, even when quite lavishly bound. The exception is the Nonesuch Dickens complete works of 1937–38. The asking price there is £15,000, though for that you get all the desirable features mentioned as regards Nonesuch in this book's bibliography, together with full morocco bindings in various colours topped off by gilt titles and gilt top edges to the pages.

A Christmas Carol beats all Dickens's other titles pricewise. It was arguably more Dickens's brainchild than any other work inasmuch as he oversaw its production as well as gestation. He had it beautifully bound in red cloth (on the rare surviving copies usually faded to a ruddy brown) and gilt titles both on the cover and spine plus floral panelling to the boards. To begin with he chose green-coated endpapers. These during the printing process got replaced by yellow ones. The half-title he had set in blue, the title page in red and blue. He commissioned four hand-coloured illustrations by John Leech and priced the whole at 5 shillings (the equivalent sum then of 25p today and in value today over £30). Five shillings was far too high for so short a book then, hence his slender profit. But so would £30 be today.

Oliver Twist, *or* The Parish Boy's Progress, *published in 1838 in three volumes by Richard Bentley, the owner of* Bentley's Miscellany, *under the author's pseudonym 'Boz'; it included 24 steel-engraved plates by Cruikshank. The original binding seen here is by the Chelsea Bindery.*

Nonetheless the current asking price is £4,500. And a unique presentation copy signed on New Year's Day 1844 by the author (with the words 'from his affectionate friend') to the actor William Macready was expected to make £200,000 when auctioned by Sotheby's

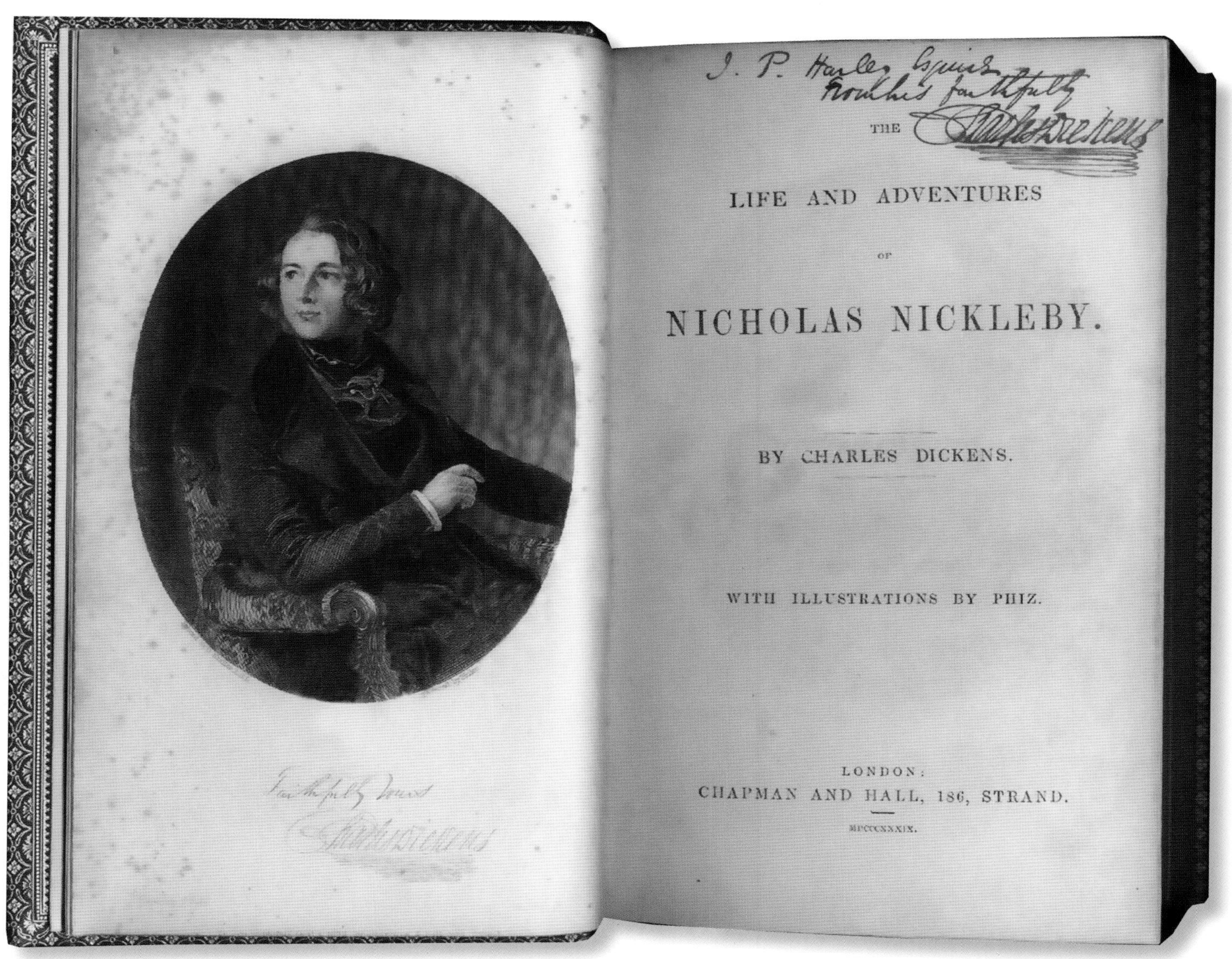

THE

LIFE AND ADVENTURES

OF

NICHOLAS NICKLEBY.

BY CHARLES DICKENS.

WITH ILLUSTRATIONS BY PHIZ.

LONDON:
CHAPMAN AND HALL, 186, STRAND.
MDCCCXXXIX.

An exceptionally rare signed presentation copy of Nicholas Nickleby *in the first 1839 edition published by Chapman and Hall.*

in London in October 2010. In the event it fetched £181,250. Back in 1996 another copy of the same work went for $160,000 in New York (say £104,000 then). In February 2009 an *Oliver Twist* signed by the author to his fellow novelist William Harrison Ainsworth fetched $229,000 (say just over £160,000 at the then $/£ exchange rate).

Factoring in inflation gives the equivalent of $230,000 today for the 1996 sale price (just under £140,000) and $240,000 for the 2009 one (nearly £146,000). The Dickens first editions market seems to be more or less holding up. This despite suggestions that the rise of the internet has weakened it. Odd reasoning. The ability to advertise the sale of a rare volume worldwide, using sophisticated visual aids, rather than obliging potential buyers to visit a sale room in person to inspect it, should boost, not restrict, the market. On the other hand, Sotheby's overestimate of the October 2010 sale figure by roughly 10 per cent may indicate an unpredictable market.

Pickwick Papers

The Posthumous Papers of the Pickwick Club

Monthly serial, April 1836 to November 1837
Book published 1837

Pickwick, wholly inexperienced, tries driving a four-wheel chaise.

A NOTE ABOUT THE CHARACTER IMAGES

Dickens's characters have been imagined by illustrators over and over again, and these pages include many such interpretations. One important source, from which fifty of the images are drawn, is a set of cigarette cards published by the tobacconists Cope Bros & Co in 1903; the same company also produced another, less interesting, set of Dickens character cards in 1939.

Characters

Allen, Arabella Friend of Emily Wardle spending Christmas at Manor Farm, Dingley Dell, Kent.

Allen, Ben(jamin) Arabella's brother; medical student; places Arabella with their aunt to frustrate suitors other than his friend Bob Sawyer; he and Bob later settle in Bengal as surgeons to the East India Company.

Ayresleigh Middle-aged fellow inmate with Pickwick of debtors' place of remand.

Bamber, Jack Long-time Inns of Court habitué.

Bantam, Angelo Cyrus Bath Master of Ceremonies.

Bardell, Martha Pickwick's landlady; takes Pickwick's hint that he is about to employ Sam Weller as preliminaries to a marriage proposal. Played by Hermione Baddeley in the 1952 film.

Mrs Bardell, by Kyd.

Bardell, Tommy Mrs Bardell's young son.

Betsy Mrs Raddle's maid.

Blotton Sometime member of Pickwick Club; expelled for presuming to question Pickwick's scholarship over an old stone with carved letters Pickwick has found in Kent.

Boldwig, Captain Suffolk smallholder.

Bolo, Miss Pickwick's whist partner at Bath Assembly Rooms.

Buzfuz, Serjeant Counsel for Mrs Bardell in her lawsuit. Played by Donald Wolfit in the 1952 film; Peter Bull in the 1965 New York musical *Pickwick*.

Clarke, Susan Second wife of Tony Weller.

Cluppins, Elizabeth Friend of Mrs Bardell.

Craddock, Mrs Pickwick's Bath landlady.

Crushton, Hon Mr Friend of Lord Mutanhed.

Serjeant Buzfuz.

Dodson Attorney; with partner Fogg acts for Mrs Bardell on speculative basis in suing Pickwick.

Dowler Ex-army officer; meets Pickwick on his trip to Bath.

Dubbley Ipswich special constable.

Emma Maid to Mr Wardle.

Fitz-Marshall, (Capt) Charles Jingle's alias in Suffolk.

Flasher, Wilkins Stockbroker; invests Sam Weller's legacy from his stepmother.

Fogg Attorney; partner of Dodson.

Goodwin Mrs Pott's maid.

Groffin, Thomas Juryman in *Bardell v Pickwick*.

Grummer, Daniel Ipswich special constable.

Gunter Friend of Bob Sawyer.

Gwynn Girls' school mistress.

Harris Bath greengrocer avid for grand families' custom.

Hopkins, Jack Medical student.

Humm, Anthony Evangelical.

Hunter, Mrs Leo Pretentious hostess; makes much of Pickwick as her star guest. Played by Joyce Grenfell in the 1952 film.

Hutley, John, aka Jem, aka Dismal Jemmy Actor; Job Trotter's brother.

Jackson Clerk to Dodson & Fogg.

Jingle, Alfred

A penniless adventurer and actor, the latter then a despised calling such that even an obscure sawbones in an unsmart regiment (Dr Payne) advises his friend Dr Slammer not to condescend to fight a duel with Jingle once his profession is revealed. But Jingle is wonderfully impudent, plausible, articulate, inventive and enterprising. His idiosyncratic speech, technically anacoluthon, involves machine-gun-fire bursts: 'smart chap that cabman – handled his fives [fists] well; but if I'd been your friend in the green jemmy [shooting-coat] – damn me – punch his

Alfred Jingle, by Kyd.

head – 'cod ['God'] I would – pig's whisper [very swiftly] – pieman too – no gammon [nonsense].' Alfred Jingle was played by Laurence Olivier (see also *David Copperfield*) in a 13 May 1938 Henry Irving centenary memorial performance at the Lyceum Theatre, London; by Anton Rodgers in the 1963–65 London musical *Pickwick*.

Dickens may have intended Jingle as a take-off of Byron. Proof:

- he is a poet, or claims to be ('Jingle' a snide reference to Byron's more slapdash verse)
- he claims to have been also a man of action, taking part in the July Revolution; this occurred in France in 1830, three years into the future from May 1827, as Dickens in a footnote observes (thus blaming on Jingle's mendacity his own carelessness); Byron, a would-be man of action, ineffectually championed Greek independence from the Turks
- the typical late-Byron love affair, involving a high-born beauty of Latin extraction, is burlesqued in Jingle's account of a Spanish grandee's only daughter who takes poison for thwarted love of him, her jealous (hence incestuously-inclined) father impeding any match then committing suicide from remorse, conceivably over his illicit urges; Byron had put incest on the sexual map by first sleeping with his half-sister then failing to keep mum about it
- Byron was often harassed over money; Jingle's poverty is constantly underlined
- Jingle's speech pattern reproduces Byron's breathless style in his letters and journals down to the very dashes

Jingle has his sinister side. On a first reading, and in the 1952 film, his con man act is comic. A later reading brings out his Iago-like lies about Wardle and Tupman to Rachael Wardle; the risk to Winkle of being killed in a duel after Jingle borrows his evening clothes and quarrels with Slammer; Jingle's brutal exploiting of Rachael Wardle's thirst for affection followed by his mercenary repudiation of her; his responsibility for the emotional castration of Tupman that results. Jingle plays tricks on Pickwick throughout the rest of *Pickwick Papers*, but eventually gets thrust in the same debtors' prison that Pickwick enters voluntarily. Even there he retains a look of Byronic melancholy, judging by Phiz's illustration. Pickwick later pays Jingle's debts and his passage to Demerara, now Guyana, in South America.

Jinks Nupkins's clerk.

Joe (the 'Fat Boy') Wardle's servant; sleeps a lot, indeed victim of what doctors now call obesity hypoventilation ('Pickwickian') syndrome; catch-phrase 'I wants to make your flesh creep'.

Lowten Perker's clerk.

Magnus, Peter Neurotic coach companion of Pickwick.

Mallard Serjeant Snubbin's clerk.

Martin, Mr Groom to Arabella Allen's aunt.

Fat Boy Joe.

Martin, Tom Inmate with Pickwick of Fleet Prison.

Mary Housemaid; marries Sam Weller.

Miller Whist-playing friend of Wardle.

Mivins Fellow inmate of Pickwick in Fleet Prison.

Mutanhed, Lord Young sprig of nobility at Bath.

Muzzle Footman to Nupkins.

Namby Sheriff's officer.

Neddy Fleet Prison functionary.

Noddy Friend of Bob Sawyer.

Nupkins, George Ipswich magistrate.

Nupkins, Mrs His wife.

Nupkins, Henrietta Their daughter.

Payne, Dr 43rd Regiment Medical Officer; a real 43rd (Monmouthshire) Regiment of Foot existed between 1748 and 1881.

Pell, Solomon Insolvency Court attorney.

Perker Pickwick's attorney re *Bardell v Pickwick*.

Phunky Junior counsel.

Samuel Pickwick (above) and below, by Kyd..

Pickwick, Samuel

General Chairman Pickwick Club (PC), not an exclusive St James's sodality like White's or Brooks's but a typically 19th-century group of convivial souls who meet regularly on hired premises to tipple, smoke, exchange sporting anecdotes and play billiards under the pretext of debating and literary discussion. After Pickwick has travelled round England for over a year the Club is split by quarrels and dissolved. Far from being a caricature benevolent-John-Bull type, Pickwick is as varied a character as Dickens was ever to produce, though lighter-sketched. He is the presiding spirit among the four individuals whose adventures constitute such plot as there is of *Pickwick Papers*. He has a scientific bent. (He has conducted research into tittlebats – not bats but small fish or 'tiddlers'.) Pickwick can be censorious, chiefly of Winkle's pretended expertise in handling a gun and skating. The carved stone episode suggests Pickwick has a streak of vanity, for he gets a commemorative portrait of himself painted and hung in the club. Where does Pickwick's money come from? He is said in court to possess 'considerable independent property' and be retired from business. Pickwick's unworldliness makes past business success unlikely. Yet Pickwick does say late in the book that he has spent most of his life making money. We must accept this, though his largesse, embracing even the trickster Jingle, makes him the first of Dickens's implausibly soft-hearted commercial successes. Dickens gives us a later glimpse of Pickwick's financial affairs. An agent at Liverpool owes Pickwick a favour from when he was in business and will gladly arrange Jingle's employment out in Demerara on Pickwick's recommendation. Liverpool had been Britain's greatest slave-trading port. Most commerce in Demerara would have rested on slave labour, which was not abolished till 1833, two years after the final events in *Pickwick Papers*. So it's possible that Pickwick derives at least some of his wealth from slavery. And if your business dealings primarily involve the unfree, whose motivation and emotions are of no account and who cannot make use of the law, you will know little of human psychology or legal procedure among the free. Pickwick, who demonstrates just such defects, may well be one of those types who are benevolently avuncular to their intimates but batten on human misery off-stage. Pickwick was played by Nigel Stock (see also *A Tale of Two Cities*) in the 1985 BBC televisation; Harry Secombe in the London and New York productions of the musical *Pickwick*.

Pott Editor, *Eatanswill Gazette*.

Pott, Mrs His wife; fancies, and is fancied by, Winkle.

Price Inmate of Sheriff's officer's place of remand.

Raddle, Mr Pusillanimous husband of Mrs Raddle.

Raddle, Mrs Mary Ann Bob Sawyer's landlady.

Rogers, Mrs Mrs Bardell's subsequent tenant.

Roker, Tom Fleet Prison turnkey (gaoler).

Sanders, Susannah Friend of Mrs Bardell.

Sawyer, Bob (more formally Robert) Medical student; friend of Bob Allen.

Simmery, Frank Stockbroker friend of Wilkins Flasher.

Simpson Ex-horse chaunter (dealer in worthless or 'nobbled' horses), now a 'leg' (racecourse betting cheat); inmate of Fleet Prison.

Skimpin Junior counsel.

Slammer, Dr Gregarious but irascible surgeon to the 97th Regiment; challenges Winkle to a duel via an intermediary since he believes Winkle is the person who cut him out with rich widow

Bob Sawyer.

at a ball the night before (it was actually Jingle). A 97th Regiment really existed – 'The Earl of Ulster's' – after a subsidiary title of George III's second son Frederick, Duke of York; it was an infantry body formed in 1824.

Slurk Editor of rival newspaper to Pott's.

Smangle Fleet Prison inmate.

Smauker, John Angelo Bantam's footman; asks Sam Weller to a 'swarry' (soirée).

Smithers Girls' school boarder.

Smorltork, Count Guest of Mrs Leo Hunter at her fête champêtre.

Smouch Helps Namby arrest Pickwick.

Snodgrass, Augustus

One of the trio touring England with Pickwick, his guardian while a minor; of a poetic turn; marries Emily Wardle and buys a small farm at Dingley Dell 'more for occupation than profit'.

Snubbin, Serjeant Pickwick's advocate in *Bardell v Pickwick*.

Snuphanuph, Dowager Lady Old lady at Bath.

Stareleigh, Mr Justice Judge in *Bardell v Pickwick*.

Stiggins Evangelical.

Tappleton, Lt Slammer's second in near-duel.

Tomkins, Miss Bury St Edmunds girls' school headmistress. Played by Hermione Gingold in the 1952 film.

Trotter, Job Jingle's servant.

Trundle Marries Isabella Wardle.

Tuckle Footman; chairman at servants' 'swarry' at Bath.

Tupman, Tracy

Another of the trio who tour England with Pickwick; stout but susceptible; provides comic love interest, wooing middle-aged Rachael Wardle; later retires to lodgings in Richmond and never again attempts matrimony.

Wardle Yeoman farmer; host to Pickwick and friends at Manor Farm, near Rochester; brother of Rachael.

Wardle, Emily Wardle's elder daughter; marries Snodgrass.

Mr Stiggins.

Wardle, Isabelle Wardle's younger daughter.

Wardle, Rachael Spinster sister of Wardle; prised apart from Tupman by Jingle using insinuations worthy of Renaissance intrigue; eloped with by Jingle on his supposition that she has money; 'ransomed' from Jingle for £120 (say £15,000 today).

Watty Bankrupt (ex-)client of Perker's.

Weller, Sam

Boots (shoe-shine boy) at the White Hart inn in the Borough (Southwark, southeast London); taken on by Pickwick as his valet; gets Pickwick out of scrapes, offering pithy observations on life adorned with colourful similes the while, making him and Pickwick prototypes of the Jeeves-Wooster relationship; his naming an 'artful dodge' the trick Jingle plays on Pickwick at Bury St Edmunds foreshadows Dickens's coinage 'the Artful Dodger' in *Oliver Twist*. Played by Roy Castle in the New York production of the musical *Pickwick*.

Weller, Tony Sam's coachman father (George Robey in the 1952 film).

Whiffers Coachman at Bath servants' 'swarry'.

Wicks Clerk to Dodson & Fogg.

Winkle, Nathaniel

Son of Birmingham wharfinger (owner or manager of a wharf); favours green shooting coat, but no sporting type; more aesthetically inclined, since he designs the uniform he proposes the Pickwick Club should adopt; Winkle on marrying abandons sporting costume and becomes a City of London agent for his father, commuting from Dulwich, where he settles 'not half a mile' from Pickwick's new residence.

Sam Weller (above) and Tony Weller (below).

Winkle Sr Nathaniel's father; eventually accepts his son's secret marriage to Arabella.

Witherfield Middle-aged maiden lady Pickwick encounters at Ipswich.

Wugsby, Mrs Colonel Pickwick's whist opponent at Bath.

Zephyr, The Fleet Prison inmate.

Pickwick Papers

Story Commentary

Pickwick Papers was Dickens's maiden venture into novel-writing. It is extremely entertaining, even funny, arguably more so than anything he ever wrote again. But it is episodic, even picaresque (a literary convention involving disconnected adventures, usually on the open road), hence rather disparaged by literary pundits.

There are picaresque elements in Dickens's other early novels (*Oliver Twist*, *Nicholas Nickleby*, *The Old Curiosity Shop*), but they are usually less overwhelming. Eventually Dickens outgrew the habit. It was a genre which at literature's highest level he more or less killed off single-handedly.

Mr Pickwick as portrayed by Harold Copping.

In his Preface to the 1867–68 'corrected' edition of *Pickwick*, Dickens relates how the project took shape. He was 22 or 23. His *Sketches by Boz* inspired William Hall, of the publishers Chapman & Hall, to suggest he compose a series of adventures to match illustrations by Richard Seymour. They were to involve sporting types who go shooting, fishing and so forth but come croppers through their ineptitude. Dickens forcefully turned this trite idea on its head, proposing that the illustrations arise from the text rather than the other way round. He carried his point, a remarkable achievement for a nobody, as he then still was.

So much for *Pickwick*'s genesis. Now to the story. After the Pickwick quartet resolve to tour England, Pickwick takes a cab to meet his friends before proceeding into Kent. His inquisitiveness about the cabby's treatment of his horse leads the cabby (William Hartnell [the first Dr Who] in the 1952 film) to suspect he is an informer. For this is May 1827 and Lord Liverpool's ministry, which used spies to monitor radicals, has only recently been replaced by Canning's less repressive one. It is the first of several quite specific political allusions that Dickens scatters throughout his novels.

The cabby, incensed, sets upon Pickwick and his friends. The crowd, persuaded that the Pickwickians are informers, support the cabby. The Pickwickians are rescued by a stranger, Alfred Jingle. Whatever his faults as subsequently revealed, this is greatly to his credit. Or is it? For he rescues them only to prey on their purses. It is a classic Dickens out-of-the-frying-pan-into-the-fire incident, repeated in *Oliver Twist* when the Artful Dodger ensnares Oliver.

Jingle is one of Dickens's masterpieces. Yet he appears in *Pickwick Papers* only intermittently. Dickens had hoped he would attract many more readers. This didn't happen, hence Dickens inventing Sam Weller, a more winning personality. Then again, like Frankenstein's monster, Jingle might have overwhelmed his creator unless firmly restrained. Dickens may also have feared he would elbow aside the other characters (rather as Toad does his fellow river-bank residents in *The Wind in the Willows*). Dickens never resuscitated the personality type in later novels, despite its offering rich dramatic possibilities.

Sam Weller (above) and Tony Weller (below), both by Kyd.

The Pickwickians and Jingle take a coach to Rochester. After the business involving the ball and aborted duel, Jingle and the Pickwickians part. They encounter him again at the Kentish town of Muggleton, two miles from Dingley Dell. The occasion is a cricket match. They all get drunk and Wardle invites Jingle to stay at Manor Farm. This gives Jingle the opportunity to detach Rachael Wardle from Tupman (no very hard task, be it said).

The newly formed couple elope. Wardle and Pickwick give chase but their carriage overturns. They eventually trace the errant pair to a Southwark inn. Here Dickens introduces Sam Weller, who so boosted readership figures (from an early print run of about 400 to, eventually, 40,000) as to be the saviour of the *Pickwick Papers* publishing project. Sam is every bit as articulate and witty as Jingle. Nor is he much less poor. But unlike Jingle he more or less knows his place.

The Pickwickians next attend the Eatanswill parliamentary election. By now Pickwick is showing a little more nous, suggesting, when confronted by a mob, to do what the mob does, and when asked what to do if there are two mobs, saying to shout with the largest. His uncharacteristically worldly advice here may derive from experience of the 1823 Demerara slave uprising.

The criticism that Pickwick changes personality from innocent to canny stung Dickens into retorting that with Pickwick, as with any other man who has something 'whimsical about him', his idiosyncrasies strike people first, his solider qualities only emerging on

better acquaintance. An unconvincing defence: Pickwick soon reverts to innocent.

Hearing that two men sounding like Jingle and Trotter recently travelled to Ipswich, Pickwick and Sam go there too. Pickwick and Sam are bamboozled by Trotter into invading a girls' school at night. Pickwick also attends a *battue* (game-bird shooting party), his subsequent arrest giving him the opportunity of unmasking a further attempt at confidence trickery by Jingle.

Dickens fast-forwards us three months to Christmas, spent at Dingley Dell. Winkle, forgetting Mrs Pott, falls for Arabella Allen. Pickwick next has to cope with a law suit for breach of promise (to marry) brought against him by Mrs Bardell. It comes to trial on Valentine's Day, 14 February.

It is often said that Dickens based *Bardell v Pickwick* on the action for 'crim con' (criminal conversation, or adultery) brought in 1836 by the Hon George Norton against Lord Melbourne, then Prime Minister, over Norton's wife Caroline. This is a distortion. The Melbourne trial did, however, furnish Dickens with superbly comic material in the form of notes of staggering banality by Melbourne to Caroline. They included 'How are you?...', or 'No House [of Lords sitting] today: I will call after the levée ... ' Counsel for Norton had an uphill struggle, arguing that they exhibited great affection because lacking the salutation 'My Dear Mrs Norton' and suggesting that their very lack of ardour concealed 'latent love'. So too in *Bardell v Pickwick*, Serjeant Buzfuz strains to inject sinister intent into Pickwick's notes to Mrs Bardell such as 'Dear Ms B. – Chops and Tomata [*sic*] sauce ... ' on the grounds of its having 'no date whatever, which is in itself suspicious'.

Fat Boy Joe by Harold Copping (top), and by Kyd (above).

Nonetheless, the jury in *Bardell v Pickwick*, more gullible than its real life counterpart in *Norton v Melbourne* (Melbourne got off), finds for the plaintiff, setting damages at £750 – half what Dodson & Fogg had initially demanded, but still about £95,000 today, a hefty sum. Pickwick is so indignant that he refuses to pay and goes to prison as a debtor. But before that he travels with his three friends to Bath. There he experiences the dying embers of the great ceremonial gatherings of *ton*, fashion etc. for which Bath had been famous over the preceding century. He also travels to Bristol and its environs, where he helps Winkle secure the affections of Arabella Allen.

On Pickwick's entering prison the tone of *Pickwick Papers* changes drastically. Dickens, recalling his father's imprisonment for debt, grips the bit firmly between the more crusading of his teeth and devotes several chapters to the cruelty and pointlessness of imprisonment for debt, the unnecessary complexity of the law as regards debt and the unfeeling rapacity of attorneys and court officials who prosper through those laws. Because of the contrast with the sunlit scenes played out earlier, these episodes are oddly harrowing, more so even than their equivalent in *Little Dorrit*.

Soon Mrs Bardell is thrust in the Fleet Prison too, ensnared by Dodson & Fogg's cunning. The lawyer Perker suggests to Pickwick that he pay Mrs Bardell's costs and his own in exchange for a statement by her that she drops the suit and that the business has been got up not by her but by Dodson & Fogg. Pickwick will thus be free from the constraint on his freedom, also the imputation of obstinacy to his character – all for around £150 (some £20,000 today).

Pickwick is won round, pays his and Mrs Bardell's way out of prison, lends Jingle money with which to emigrate, launches the reconciliation process whereby Winkle *père* accepts his son's secret marriage, and retires to Dulwich, where he hosts the wedding of Snodgrass and Emily Wardle.

Serjeant Buzfuz, by Kyd.

Oliver Twist

Monthly serial, 1837 to 1839
Book published 1838

'Lots were cast who should walk up ... and ask for more; ... it fell to Oliver Twist.' (Ch II), by Harold Copping.

Characters

Anny Attendant with Martha on the dying Sally.

Barney Jewish accomplice of Fagin and Sikes.

Bates, Charley Artful Dodger's associate; later reforms; becomes a Northamptonshire grazier. Played by Jack Wild (see also below, Dodger, The Artful) in Lionel Bart's 1960 musical *Oliver!*

Bedwin, Mrs Mr Brownlow's housekeeper. Played by Anna Massey (see also *David Copperfield* and *A Tale of Two Cities*) in a 2007 televisation.

Bet/Betsy Fellow prostitute with Nancy.

Blathers Bow Street Runner.

Brittles Servant 'boy' (though past 30) to Mrs Maylie.

Brownlow

Friend in the distant past of Oliver's father Edwin Leeford and one-time fiancé of Edwin's sister (who had died on the morning of their intended wedding); victim while browsing at bookstall of handkerchief-lifting by Artful Dodger when latter accompanied by Oliver; Oliver wrongly suspected but set free on bookstall keeper's testifying that another boy committed the theft; Brownlow takes Oliver home but Oliver abducted by Nancy on Fagin's behalf; Brownlow later frustrates Monks's plotting against Oliver, extracts his confession and adopts Oliver. Played by Frank Middlemass (a sometime Dan Archer in *The Archers*) in the 1985 televisation; James Villiers in the 1994 Sam Mendes-directed London revival of Lionel Bart's 1960 musical *Oliver!*; Edward Fox in the 2007 televisation.

Bumble

Parish beadle (minor official), later master of the workhouse where Oliver is born. Played by Harry Secombe in the 1968 musical Oliver!

Charlotte The Sowerberrys' maid; adores Noah Claypole. Played by Diana Dors in David Lean's 1948 film.

Bumble the beadle.

Chitling, Tom Ex-short-sentence prisoner associate of Fagin.

Claypole, Noah

Charity boy but senior apprentice to Mr Sowerberry, hence superior to Oliver, whom he bullies; later with Charlotte decamps to London, taking with them Sowerberry's cash; soon involved by Fagin in petty crime, also set by Fagin to spy on Nancy when she confers with Rose Maylie and Brownlow; by turning King's evidence, ensures Fagin's conviction.

Corney, Mrs, later Mrs Bumble

Matron of workhouse where Oliver is born; marries Bumble and later sells evidence of Oliver's origins to Monks, who destroys it. Played by Miriam Margolyes in the 1985 TV serialisation.

Crackit, Toby Housebreaker associate of Bill Sikes.

Dawkins, Jack/John Real name of the Artful Dodger.

Dick Childhood companion of Oliver's at Mrs Mann's.

Dodger, The Artful

See Dawkins. Played by Anthony Newley (sometime husband of Joan Collins) in David Lean's 1948 film; the pop musician Phil Collins (then aged thirteen) in the Lionel Bart musical *Oliver!*; and Jack Wild in the 1968 film *Oliver!*, for which he got an Oscar nomination; voiced by Davy Jones (sometime member of the '60s pop group The Monkees) in a 1974 full-length cartoon; played by Davy Jones in the 1963 Broadway production of the musical *Oliver!*; voiced by Billy Joel (as a dog) in *Oliver & Company*, for which see under Fagin.

Duff Bow Street Runner.

Fagin

For Fagin's role in the story, see 'Story Commentary' below. Played by, among others: Lon Chaney in a 1922 silent film version; Alec Guinness in David Lean's 1948 film; Ron Moody (see also *A Christmas Carol* and *David Copperfield*) in the original 1960 London production of the musical *Oliver!*, for which he was nominated for an Oscar for Best Actor and won a Golden Globe award for Best Actor – Motion Picture Musical or Comedy; Max Adrian in the 1962 televisation; Roy Hudd in the 1977 revival of the musical *Oliver!*; George C Scott in a 1982 Australian-made film; Eric Porter in the 1985 televisation; Jonathan Pryce and (among others) Russ Abbot (who replaced Rowan Atkinson early in the run of the 2009–11 revival of the musical *Oliver!*) in the 1994 London revival of the musical *Oliver!*; Richard Dreyfuss in a 1997 Disney-produced made-for-TV film; Ben Kingsley in the 2005 film

The Artful Dodger (above) and Fagin (below).

directed by Roman Polanski and scripted (with help from Charles Dickens) by Ronald Harwood; Timothy Spall in the 2007 televisation; Griff Rhys Jones in the 2009–11 London revival of the musical *Oliver!*; voiced by Dom DeLuise (as a human) in a 1988 Disney cartoon *Oliver & Company*, involving mostly dogs and a cat (Oliver).

Fang Magistrate bent on convicting Oliver of theft.

Fleming, Agnes Oliver's mother. Played by Lysette Anthony (see also Dombey and Son) in the 1985 televisation.

Fleming, Rose Oliver's aunt; marries Harry Maylie. Played by Lysette Anthony in the 1985 televisation; Keira Knightly in the 1999 one.

Gamfield Sweep who nearly takes Oliver on as an apprentice to climb chimneys.

Giles, Mr Butler-cum-steward to Mrs Maylie.

Grannett Overseer at Oliver's workhouse.

Grimwig Friend of Brownlow.

Kags Convict in Jacob's Island warehouse where Sikes turns up while evading the law.

Limbkins Chairman of board of workhouse where Oliver lives from age nine.

Lively Street-seller acquaintance of Fagin.

Losberne Mrs Maylie's neighbourhood surgeon (but charitably called 'doctor' by locals; 'surgeon' then meant not the paladin of the operating theatre we know today, more plain sawbones, whereas 'doctor' signified someone medically better qualified; Dickens sometimes calls Losberne surgeon, sometimes doctor).

Mann, Mrs Superintendent of branch workhouse where Oliver reared till aged nine. Played by Julie Walters in the 1999 televisation.

Martha Attendant with Anny on the dying Sally.

Maylie, Harry Mrs Maylie's son; marries Rose Fleming.

Maylie, Mrs Benevolent and rich old lady who has adopted Rose and takes in Oliver after he is found wounded on her doorstep.

Monks

Oliver's half-brother by their father's first wife; 'real' name in the novel Edward Leeford. Played by Julian Rhind-Tutt in the 2007 televisation.

Nancy

Former child thief in Fagin's gang, long since a prostitute, to which trade

she claims Fagin drove her; spies on Fagin's conference with Monks, hence learns of Rose Maylie's existence; drugs Sikes with laudanum so that she can give word of Oliver to Rose; Sikes's moll, she insists on returning to him after telling Rose about Oliver's kinship with Monks, despite Rose's offer to care for her. Played by Kay Walsh in David Lean's 1948 film; Ruthie Henshall in the 1994 London revival of the musical *Oliver!*

Sally Old pauper who on her deathbed tells Mrs Corney that she stole gold articles from Oliver's dying mother at time of his birth; dies before she can say what; they are in fact a locket and gold ring, evidence of Oliver's mother's identity; these are redeemed from the pawnbroker that Sally had placed them with by Mrs Corney, using the pledge ticket she has stolen from the dying Sally, then bought from Mr and Mrs Bumble (the latter formerly Mrs Corney) by Monks, who destroys them.

Sikes, Bill

Housebreaker and thief; claims Fagin started him on crime; murders Nancy after Fagin tells him she has betrayed him then accidentally hangs himself when fleeing from justice. Played by Robert Newton in David Lean's 1948 film; Oliver Reed in the 1968 film *Oliver!* directed by his uncle Carol Reed.

Bill Sikes.

Slout Master of the workhouse where Oliver is born.

Sowerberry Undertaker to whom Oliver is apprenticed. Played by Barry Humphries in the 1960 musical *Oliver!*

Sowerberry, Mrs Mr Sowerberry's wife.

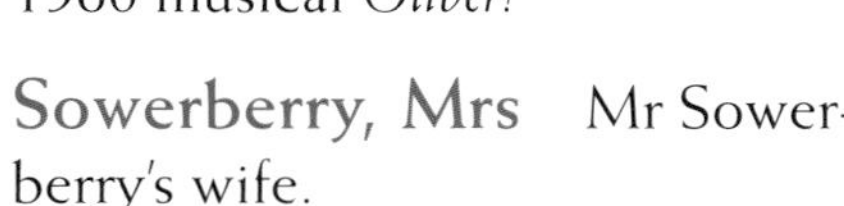

Twist, Oliver

Boy hero. Played by Jackie Coogan in a 1922 silent film; Mark Lester in the 1968 film adaptation of the musical *Oliver!*, which won his director Carol Reed an Oscar.

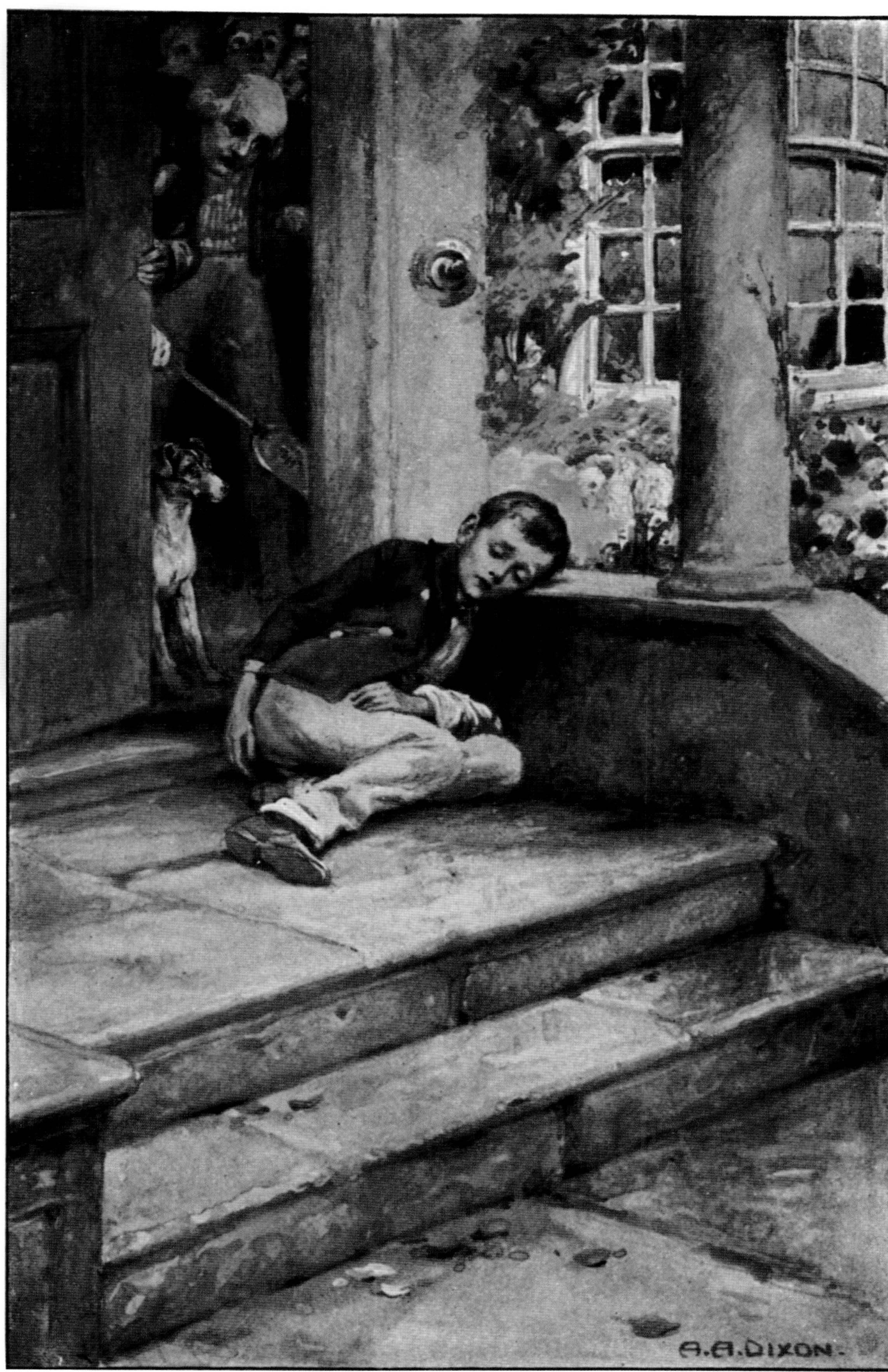

'. . . he sank down against one of the pillars', an illustration by Arthur Dixon (left).

Opposite: Another illustration by Arthur Dixon (below left), and a movie poster for the 1922 silent film (below right).

Oliver Twist

Story Commentary

Sir Robert Peel, by John Linnell.

This was Dickens's first novel with a coherent thread. Its immediate inspiration was the 1834 Poor Law, which had been passed by Melbourne's ministry. Dickens hated that law as inhumane. He has a dig in *Oliver Twist* not at Melbourne, however, but at his successor as Prime Minister Sir Robert Peel, making Mr Grimwig complain of orange peel as 'the poor surgeon's friend', i.e. its slipperiness. (Sir Robert was known as 'Orange Peel' for his ginger hair and Protestant leanings over Ireland.)

The 1834 Poor Law confined 'sturdy paupers' (healthy poor) inside local-taxpayer-funded institutions called workhouses. It was specifically decreed that such places should be less attractive than life outside, otherwise the poor would flock to them. This would cost the local rate-payers more. (Rates were the council, or local, taxes of their day.)

Oliver's workhouse is certainly no Eden. He is half-starved there, all he gets to eat being gruel, and precious little of that, plus two onions a week and a lump of bread on Sundays. Oliver is a foundling, born out of wedlock to a good-looking girl who dies minutes later, before she can even give him a name. So the task falls to Mr Bumble, who often doles out such labels to abandoned infants.

Bumble, having used up the alphabet's previous letters on other foundlings, has come to T, hence 'Twist'. Dickens does not tell us why 'Oliver'. And he refuses, he says from prudence, to tell us the town where Bumble is beadle. Dickens does let drop that it is about 75 miles from London, and that it is more or less on a river substantial enough to have once made building a large factory on its bank worthwhile. Further, we are told that when Oliver goes to London to seek his fortune he travels along a high road via Barnet.

A look at the map shows the most likely candidate among thoroughfares to be what is now the A1. Advancing 75 miles up it we hit Huntingdon, which thus fits the bill, especially since 'Oliver', after Oliver Cromwell, Huntingdon's most famous son, is the likeliest boy's name to occur to Bumble, a man very mindful of civic prestige. And it would have appealed to Dickens, who was no great lover of kings.

Dickens tells us that Oliver has 'a good sturdy spirit'. Here he errs. A more tearful young hero it is impossible to conceive. Oliver may snivel a lot, but he has much to snivel about. He is essentially passive, however, and this diminishes his hero status. Even his famous request for more (gruel) comes

Mr Bumble, by Kyd.

about because the other workhouse boys have cast lots as to who should take the step, and Oliver has 'won'.

On arriving in Barnet (his running away from Sowerberry's is his one show of initiative) he is accosted by the Artful Dodger, lead thief in the boy gang of pickpockets presided over by Fagin, an adult 'fence', or receiver of stolen goods. The Dodger stands Oliver a meal and inveigles him into entering Fagin's central London lair. (Fagin has another, in the East End.)

Fagin is, as well as a fence, a former thief, though now self-promoted to a managerial role organising other thieves. Dickens also tells us that Fagin is a Jew, rubbing it in rather by referring to him as 'the Jew' over and over again.

The Artful Dodger introduces Oliver to Fagin, from an engraving by Cruikshank.

This, and Fagin's nefarious calling, has got Dickens into hot water with various champions of Jewry both then and since. On one current website forum that discusses Jewish dietary laws, even mention of the words 'Dickens' or 'Fagin' is banned.

Actually Fagin was a name Dickens lifted from his boyhood comrade, Bob Fagin, fellow child labourer in Warren's Blacking Warehouse. It is true that Fagin can be a Jewish name. Numerous Ashkenazi (Central and East European-origin) Fagins have settled in Western Europe or America from what are now Belarus and the Ukraine. But their doing so would have come much later, after the 1880s Russian pogroms (Jew-bashing exercises tacitly encouraged by the Tsarist authorities).

By contrast, in the 1830s Irish settlers in London were already numerous. Fagin is a variant of Fagan, a fairly common Co Dublin name, perhaps also of Fegan, which is found in Dublin, Co Louth and Co Armagh. So the original, Bob Fagin, of fiction's most famous Jewish hate figure is more likely to have been Irish — a piquant curiosity of literature. It was ungrateful of Dickens to pervert Bob's name in this way. Bob had been very kind to him when he was learning how to stick labels on blacking pots. But novelists have to be heartless, picking the metaphorical pockets of their friends and acquaintances for names, traits, tricks of speech, gestures, physical peculiarities. In that sense Dickens himself was the artfullest of dodgers.

The fictional Fagin, though Jewish ethnically, is either assimilated or appallingly lax in observance. He keeps a decidedly non-kosher establishment. The moment we are introduced to him he is described as cooking sausages. Even supposing these are for his gang to eat, he ought not to handle them. And later he consumes a saveloy, or sausage stuffed with brains. *Feh*. When finally arrested and put in the condemned cell, he drives away with curses 'venerable men of his own persuasion' who have 'come to pray beside him'. They even renew 'their charitable efforts', but he beats them off. The phrases in quotes are Dickens's own words and by stressing that Fagin is a bad apple among an otherwise wholesome crop should go far to acquit him of blanket anti-semitism.

Fagin's purpose for Dickens is a literary one. He embodies criminal intelligence. Sikes, all criminal muscle, will never do in that department. That is why Fagin is depicted as a Jew. It's the quickest way to signal that he's brainy, which is of course just as much a stereotypical Jewish characteristic as his long hair, beard and large nose, though not one that Dickens's detractors in the matter of Fagin seem greatly bothered by.

And Fagin provides Oliver with something Oliver has never known before: kindness. He calls him 'My dear', feeds him, clothes him, gives him shelter.

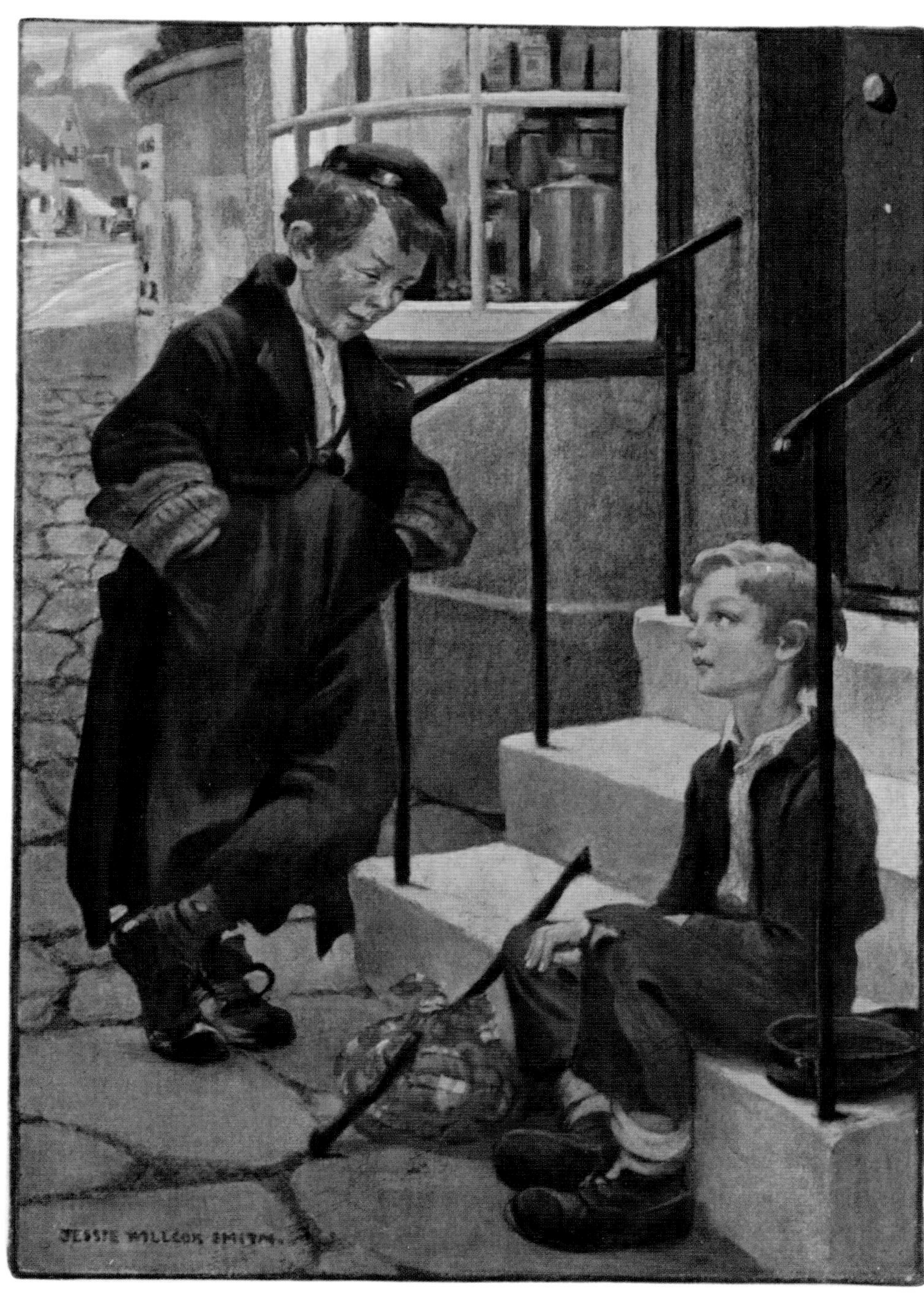

Oliver's first meeting with the Artful Dodger, an illustration by Jessie Willcox Smith.

That Fagin's kindness has ulterior motives is for the moment beside the point. To begin with it seems eminently avuncular. His establishment is almost a burlesque of a seedy tutor's in a boys' public school presided over by an eccentric unmarried housemaster.

Fagin, then, is true to one Jewish tradition, education, albeit a warped sort. He takes a distinctly didactic line when recruiting Noah Claypole to the thief's profession. He gives his boys detailed tuition in the art of pick-pocketing, first 'wipes', or handkerchiefs, then more valuable items, like notecases, pocketbooks, snuffboxes and watches. (Mind you, a silk handkerchief could be worth 5/-, or over £30 today, and rate a sentence of seven

The Artful Dodger, by Kyd.

years' transportation.) Fagin does so, moreover, via the most progressive technique, that is, play acting. No book learning by rote with him; it's all pure practical exercises. He is a natural teacher, instilling such professional pride in his pupils that when the Dodger is finally arrested Charley Bates laments that his full list of thefts is not better known, so as to earn him a high place in the Newgate Calendar, the criminals' hall of fame of its day.

Oliver is next made to accompany the Dodger on a pick-pocketing expedition and after the incidents involving Mr Brownlow is taken under his wing. Oliver's very fetching looks, here as elsewhere in the book, promote his being cosseted. It is one of life's unfairest truths (not, however, made explicit by Dickens) that the pretty spark more sympathy than do the plain. Oliver's attractions extend to speech. He has an unaccountably pure diction for a workhouse boy, though it is true that under the rules of the time he would have been given some kind of education there. But had he looked and sounded like Noah Claypole, an ugly long-limbed hobbledehoy, who says 'yer' for 'you' and 'creetur' for 'creature', no one would have spared him a second glance, not if he were one of the lost Princes in the Tower.

And Oliver is, it turns out, a child of privilege, if not at princely level. Oliver's true father has left Oliver money, thereby completely changing Oliver's position in life, even if the money is not immediately to hand. This is not the only stroke of capricious fortune. The chance of Oliver's father's friend Brownlow encountering Oliver now, when neither knows the other's identity, is millions-to-one. That much is novelist's licence. What is stretching that licence is for Oliver, after his recapture by Fagin's followers, to be made to accompany Bill Sikes in burgling the very house where his mother's sister Rose just happens to live.

Worse, the means to explain this second, colossally long-shot coincidence are actually to hand. For Dickens quite soon tells us that Oliver's hateful half-brother Monks has commissioned Fagin to turn Oliver into a thief, so that Oliver will breach the terms of his father's will leaving him all the family property provided he leads a blameless life. Yet Dickens doesn't tell us that till well after the attempted burglary. And there is no indication that Sikes or Fagin knows, at the time, that the house to be burgled is occupied by a close relative of Oliver's. Monks could have told them. It is a glaring plot defect. In Dickens's defence, it arises from the rapid output conditions under which he had undertaken to write the novel.

The main denouements, involving Nancy's murder, Bill Sikes's death, Fagin's arrest and the breaking up of his gang, are too well known from the numerous films and stage adaptations to need detailed repeating here. The fates of the small fry deserve a glance.

The Artful Dodger is convicted. Monks dies in a distant New World jail (possibly one in the West Indies, where he has, or has had, an estate). Noah Claypole, a free pardon from the Crown in his hand for having informed against Fagin, sets up as a professional grass, but on the pettiest of scales. The Bumbles sink into poverty. But not before Mr Bumble has uttered the second immortal quotation in all of *Oliver Twist*'s 180,000 or so words (the first being Oliver's 'Please, sir, I want some more.'). The words are: 'the law is a [*sic*] ass'.

The occasion is Brownlow's confronting Bumble and his wife with having destroyed evidence of Oliver's parentage. Bumble tries to shuffle off the blame on his wife. Brownlow tells him that is no excuse since the law supposes his wife acts under his direction. (The concomitant to this was that a woman's property in those days became entirely her husband's on marriage.) Bumble's memorable excoriation of the law, as spelt out above, rounds off the episode.

Mr Brownlow, by Harold Copping.

It sums up Dickens's own attitude: bend the law to your own conception of right and let due process go hang. He has Mr Losberne, first, throw dust in the eyes of the Bow Street Runners investigating the attempted burglary of Mrs Maylie's house; second, lean on her servants to drop their earlier half-formed assertions that they recognise Oliver as the nocturnal intruder; and, third, conceal the bullet he has drawn from Oliver's arm, a major item of Crown evidence. Brownlow acts as a vigilante in browbeating a confession from Monks. *Oliver Twist* is a highly successful novel and has been a huge hit as a musical and films. It nonetheless tells a partisan story, and one that is quite as much shocking for legal irregularities by 'good' characters as it is for criminal behaviour by wicked ones.

Nicholas Nickleby

Monthly serial, 1838 to 1839
Book published 1839

'Does no other profession occur to you ... ?' ... 'No,' said Nicholas ... 'Why ...' said Mr Crummles ... 'The stage.' (Ch XXII).

Characters

Adams, Capt Verisopht's second in latter's duel with Sir Mulberry Hawk.

Belvawney, Miss Actress with Crummles's company.

Blockson, Mrs Charwoman to the Knags.

Borum family Minor patrons of provincial drama.

Bravassa, Miss Actress with Crummles's company.

Bray, Madeline Daughter of Walter Bray; marries Nicholas. Played by Anne Hathaway in the 2002 film.

Bray, Walter Peevish, impoverished former spendthrift.

Brooker Former clerk of Ralph Nickleby's; has a criminal record.

Browdie, John

Yorkshireman initially hostile to Nicholas since jealous of his fiancée 'Tilda's flirting with him; later Nicholas's friend, lending him a sovereign (£1, say £125 today) after Nicholas leaves Yorkshire for London; honeymoons in London, where he releases Smike from imprisonment by Squeers, who has snatched him off the street and locked him in a room at Snawley's house preparatory to hauling him back to Yorkshire.

Cheeryble, Charles

Merchant; employs Nicholas. Played by Timothy Spall in the 2002 film.

Cheeryble, Frank Nephew of brothers Charles and Ned, in whose firm he eventually becomes a partner; marries Kate.

Cheeryble, Ned Brother/business partner of Charles.

Chowser, Colonel Militia (equivalent of Territorial Army [National Guard in USA] today) officer; minor guest of Ralph Nickleby's.

Crowl Selfish acquaintance of Newman Noggs.

Crummles, Ninetta, aka 'The Infant Phenomenon' Vincent Crummles's actress daughter. Played by Hermione Baddeley in a 1927 Lyric Theatre, Hammersmith, production.

Crummles, Vincent

Actor-manager; later emigrates to America. Played by Stanley Holloway in the 1947 film; Nathan Lane in the 2002 one.

Curdle, Mr Portsmouth amateur man of letters; insists on the dramatic unities.

Curdle, Mrs His wife; patroness of Portsmouth drama.

David The Cheerybles' butler.

Folair, Augustus Pantomime actor with Crummles's company; addressed as 'Tommy' by his colleague Mr Lenville. Played by Timothy Spall in David Edgar's two-part play of 1980 at the Aldwych, London.

Gazingi, Miss Actress with Crummles's company.

George Friend of Kenwigs.

Gregsbury MP with whom Nicholas tries half-heartedly to get work as a secretary.

Gride, Arthur

Usurer associate of Ralph Nickleby's, though on smaller scale; tells Ralph of his desire to make Madeline Bray his wife in return for cancelling an old debt of her father's, asking for Ralph's help as a more forceful character in negotiating with Walter; Ralph, another long-standing creditor of Walter's, agrees in return for substantial payment; Gride, through legal loophole and clever counsel, escapes punishment for unlawful possession of will benefiting Madeline but is murdered by burglars some years later.

Grudden, Mrs Assistant stage manager of Crummles's company.

Hawk, Sir Mulberry

Elderly baronet and rake; Ralph Nickleby's go-between in ensnaring Lord (Frederick) Verisopht; after Nicholas gashes his (Hawk's) face, recuperates in France, giving out that he has contracted erysipelas; his influence over Verisopht wanes, especially when he hints at the revenge beating he has arranged for Nicholas; he and Verisopht quarrel when drunk; Verisopht, taunted beyond endurance by the more articulate Hawk, strikes Hawk; they fight a duel; Hawk shoots Verisopht dead; Hawk flees to France, lives abroad for some years then returns to England and is thrust in prison for debt, dying there.

'Johnson, Mr' Nicholas's stage name when with Crummles's company.

Kenwigs Ivory-turner tenant of same house as Noggs, though better off.

Kenwigs, Susan His wife; niece of Lillyvick.

Kenwigs, Morleena The Kenwigs's eldest daughter.

Knag, Miss Madame Mantalini's forewoman; acquires Madame Mantalini's business.

Knag, Mortimer Brother of above.

La Creevy, Miss

Kate and Mrs Nickleby's landlady. Played by Athene Seyler (see also *A Tale of Two Cities*) in the 1947 film.

Mrs Kenwigs and the four little Kenwigses, by Jesssie Willcox Smith.

Ledrook, Miss Actress with Crummles's company.

Lenville Tragic actor with Crummles's company; becomes jealous of Nicholas's acting success so writes him an insulting note then tries to humiliate him before the assembled company.

Lenville, Mrs Actress with Crummles's company.

Lillyvick Water-rate collector, which reflects glory on his niece Mrs Kenwigs; marries Henrietta Petowker, who soon leaves him for a bottle-nosed half-pay captain.

Linkinwater, Tim The Cheerybles' book-keeper; eventually marries Miss La Creevy.

Lumbey The Kenwigs's doctor.

Mantalini, Madame Dressmaker; employs Kate Nickleby.

Mantalini (originally Muntle), Alfred

Madame Mantalini's much younger husband; his extravagance ruins them; ends up working a mangle in a low laundry establishment between Seven Dials and Soho. Played by Cyril Fletcher in the 1947 film.

Alfred Mantalini.

Nickleby, Kate

Nicholas's sister, as beautiful as she is virginal. Like her brother (see 'Story Commentary' below) she is given to high-flown oratory. Her speech of reproach and self-justification to Mrs Wititterly (Chapter XXVIII) uses such sophisticated devices as anaphora (repetition for dramatic effect: 'Is it possible ... ? Is it possible ... ? Is it possible ... ?'). Declamation clearly runs in the blood of the Nicklebys, emerging in debased form via Mrs Nickleby's rambling and inconsequential discourse, though even that as, say, a filibuster in the US Senate, would have had its uses. Played by Sally Ann Howes in the 1947 film.

Nickleby, Mrs Mother of Kate and Nicholas; said to have been based by Dickens on his mother.

Nickleby, Nicholas

Said in real life to have owed something to Henry Burnett, husband of Dickens's musical elder sister Fanny and a person Dickens may well have rather disliked, which would account for Nicholas's less attractive personality traits (see 'Story Commentary'); Dickens's illustrator Phiz perhaps also used Burnett as a model; 'very nearly' 19 when the story opens, though earlier said by Dickens, referring to when their father was alive, to have been about 19 then – another muddle arising from the haste of Dickens's serialised publication schedule. Played by Nigel Havers in the 1977 BBC televisation.

Nickleby, Ralph

Uncle/brother-in-law to the preceeding; also chief villain. By now, his third novel, Dickens handles villains more maturely. (The flaws in Nicholas's character mentioned in the 'Story Commentary' below show that Dickens can now also create more 'rounded' heroes.) Ralph is certainly avaricious. But towards his niece Kate he experiences some dim feeling of near-warmth. He is capable of remorse over past actions. He does not, before committing suicide, write a will leaving his money away from Nicholas's branch of his family, even though someone with his business experience would have known that his dying intestate would mean his property passed to his next of kin. So at the end of his life he may be said to have shown family feeling of a kind, over and above his mild warmth towards Kate, if only by default. Played by Cedric Hardwicke in the 1947 film; Christopher Plummer in the 2002 one.

Newman Noggs (above).

Noggs, Newman

Ralph Nickleby's factotum; once kept his own (fox) hounds, i.e. had been of at least yeoman farmer or squireen status, presumably in the Barnard Castle area of Co Durham, since he tells Nicholas they know him there. Played by Bernard Miles in the 1947 film; Tom Courtenay (see also *The Old Curiosity Shop* and *Little Dorrit*) in the 2002 one.

Petowker, Henrietta Actress at the Theatre Royal, Drury Lane; her status with the Kenwigs circle consequently high, an interesting case of showbiz-connexion snobbery at a time when actors were mostly despised.

'Phib' (Phoebe) Fanny Squeers's maid.

Pluck One of Hawk's two sycophants.

Price, 'Tilda Fanny Squeers's friend; fiancée then wife of John Browdie.

Pugstyles One of Gregsbury's constituents.

Pyke Other of Hawk's two sycophants.

Scaley Dun (debt-collector); enters the Mantalinis' establishment to enforce payment of debts of a little over £1,527 (say nearly £200,000 today).

Simmonds, Miss Seamstress at Madame Mantalini's.

Sliderskew, Peg Gride's housekeeper.

Smike

Drudge at Dotheboys Hall; treated kindly by Nicholas, hence hero-worships him and accompanies him on his adventures, including the acting episode; stage name when with Crummles's company 'Mr Digby'; falls in love with Kate and pines away from melancholy when it becomes clear she prefers Frank Cheeryble.

Smike.

Wackford Squeers.

Mrs Squeers.

Snawley

Stepfather to two boys he places with Squeers; later rents Squeers lodgings in his London house and conspires with Ralph Nickleby and Squeers to reclaim Smike from Nicholas's household on the false grounds that Smike is his son, thus perjuring himself.

Snevellicci, Miss Leading actress in Crummles's company; keen on Nicholas.

Snevellicci, Mr Bibulous actor; father of above.

Snobb, The Hon Mr Minor guest at Ralph Nickleby's dinner party involving Kate.

Squeers, Fanny

Wackford's daughter; falls in love with Nicholas.

Squeers, Mrs

Wackford's wife. Played by Sybil Thorndike (see also *Bleak House*) in the 1947 film; Beryl Reid in the 1973 BBC televisation of the pop musical *Smike*.

Squeers, Wackford

In real life said to have been at least partly based on one William Shaw, at whose school, Bowes Academy, many boys were so malnourished they went blind; headmaster and proprietor of Dotheboys Hall, near Greta Bridge, Yorkshire (that part of it formerly called the North Riding), though Greta Bridge is now in Co Durham; one-eyed, ignorant and cruel, indeed a virtual flagellant; his instruction technique, crudely self-serving though it may be (he teaches the verb 'clean' and noun 'winder' – window – by ordering a boy to go and wash it) and although tainted by poor spelling, nonetheless foreshadows such modern 'practice-related activities' as the Montessori Method. Having taken part in Ralph Nickleby's conspiracy, he is sentenced to seven years' transportation for unlawful possession of the stolen will benefiting Madeline Bray. The Dotheboys pupils rise in revolt – they for the most part abandon the school and the school itself eventually fades from local memory. Played by Ben Kingsley in David Edgar's two-part play of 1980.

Squeers, Wackford 'Junior' Played by Timothy Spall in David Edgar's two-part play of 1980.

Tix Dun; Scaley's partner.

Trimmers Philanthropist friend of the Cheeryble brothers.

Verisopht, Lord Frederick

Aristocratic client of Ralph Nickleby's. Dickens at this stage of his career was clueless about titles. The 'Lord Frederick Verisopht' nomenclature can only refer to a younger son of a duke or marquess. Even in the 1830s such people would have been unlikely to have had enough money of their own to attract Ralph Nickleby's intense interest. But Dickens quite soon in the novel calls him instead Lord Verisopht, implying he possesses a peerage (and probably a fortune too), rather than being a younger son with a courtesy title or mere 'handle' to his name. On the other hand Lord (Frederick) Verisopht (as it will be best to call him) is an advance on Lord Mutanhed in *Pickwick Papers*. Though naïve, he is not a complete idiot. True, he lacks the Nickleby wordiness, for he sucks the gold knob of his cane when in company out of sheer inability to think of anything to say (a habit Dickens bestows on Dick Swiveller in *The Old Curiosity Shop*, though Swiveller is articulate; also one that P G Wodehouse borrowed for his more tongue-tied aristocrats). Nor is Verisopht wholly contemptible. Indeed he is the only member of Ralph Nickleby's gang of crooks, debauchees, sycophants and dupes who shows Kate Nickleby anything approaching politeness. And he disapproves of Hawk's treatment of Nicholas in regard to Kate. Played by Timothy Bateson in the 1947 film.

Westwood Hawk's second in his duel with Verisopht.

Wititterly, Henry Husband of Julia W.

Wititterly, Julia Socially ambitious resident of Cadogan Place; employs Kate Nickleby as live-in companion.

Nicholas Nickleby

Story Commentary

Mrs Nickleby, a poor and foolish widow with two teenage children, Nicholas and Kate, leaves Devon, their former home, for London, where her late husband's brother Ralph lives, in the hope of getting his help. Ralph, a wealthy usurer operating out of Soho, grudges any such help, though he does let them use a decrepit house of his in the City (now London's business district, but then also residential). He finds Nicholas school-mastering work under one Wackford Squeers in Yorkshire and Kate work with a dressmaker who is one of his money-lending clients. But he also uses Kate's charms to help win business from susceptible clients of his such as Verisopht.

Nicholas becomes disgusted by Squeers's brutal management of Dotheboys. When Squeers flogs for presuming to run away an especially pathetic inmate, the mildly retarded Smike, an ex-pupil whose family have long abandoned him, Nicholas in turn thrashes Squeers. Nicholas decamps from Dotheboys, is followed by Smike, joins with Smike in seeking their fortunes and returns temporarily to London. Here he quarrels with his uncle and again leaves London, this time lest his presence jeopardise Kate's prospects as Ralph's protégée.

He falls in with Vincent Crummles and is invited to join Crummles's troupe of travelling players. At this point, sorry to say, a less attractive side to Nicholas emerges. His affected speech, for instance. Understandable in an ex-schoolmaster? Ah, but he was one too briefly to have been infected that way. No, Nicholas is naturally orotund. Of Smike, for instance, he says 'I would that I knew on whom he has the claim of birth: I might wring something from his [i.e. Smike's father's] sense of shame, if he were dead to every tie of nature.'

Standard speech in a Victorian melodrama juvenile lead, you may say. Perhaps. But at Portsmouth, where Crummles's troupe are playing, Nicholas betrays something worse: a tendency to laugh up his sleeve at the pathetic pretensions of his obscure hams of fellow actors, made worse by his snootiness towards their social status. He declines to help Miss Snevellicci get up an audience for her benefit night. 'Oh dear me,' he says prissily, 'I shouldn't like to do that' and 'I must decidedly object to making one of the canvassing party.' Yet he has been ready enough to join Crummles's troupe in the first place, earning money as a sort of literary adviser to it, as well as actor.

Mr Squeers and a new pupil in an illustration by Harold Copping.

In the scene where he and Lenville thrash out their differences before the other actors Nicholas both assaults Lenville and insists that Lenville apologise for his insulting note of the night before 'humbly and submissively'. This rubbing his antagonist's nose in it is ungentlemanly. Nicholas is even patronising about the faithful Smike, referring to him as 'the most grateful ... affectionate creature that ever breathed', words more apt for a dog. Mrs Squeers may have been a grasping child-tormentor, but was onto something in calling Nicholas 'stuck-up'.

On the other hand he turns out a superb actor, though with no training (rather like Dickens himself). Crummles was no great actor-manager in the way Dickens's friend Macready turned out to be, but he could spot talent.

(The outer story of Ken Russell's 1971 film *The Boy Friend* – within which is the original Sandy Wilson story – echoes plot elements from Nicholas's time with Crummles's company, chiefly the London theatre manager seeing the show, his being identified by the cast as a London theatre manager and the cast playing to him rather than to the rest of the audience – or, in the case of cues, to each other. The final scene of the Russell film was even shot outside a Portsmouth theatre.)

Nicholas, summoned back to London by Noggs, overhears Hawk and members of his set publicly and coarsely bandying his sister Kate's name about. Nicholas demands Hawk's name, implicitly so that he can challenge him to a duel. Hawk refuses, saying that for all he knows the young man may be an errand-boy. (We saw in *Pickwick Papers* the importance duellists attached to what the Germans call in regard to dynastic marriage *Ebenbürtigkeit*, or equality of birth, here operating when two parties agreed to try and kill or wound each other as part of the aristocratic code of honour.) Hawk, still refusing to disclose his identity, then jumps into his carriage, Nicholas mounts the step so as not to lose his quarry and Hawk strikes him with a whip. Nicholas seizes the whip and strikes Hawk, gashing his face. Hawk loses control of the horse, which bolts along the pavement and overturns the carriage.

Nicholas breaks off relations with Ralph and after subtly, delicately, but nonetheless in blunt actuality importuning Charles Cheeryble in the street, gets taken up by Charles and his brother Ned, who make him assistant and successor in expectancy to their aged book-keeper Tim Linkinwater with an immediate annual salary of £120 (say £15,000 today), low-rent tied housing and a loan to furnish it with.

The Cheerybles proclaim themselves self-made. Charles Cheeryble even confesses (or boasts) that he was barefoot (he later amends this to 'almost barefoot') when they first sought their fortunes. But they are ludicrously implausible businessmen. They give money away to unfortunates right and left, employ Nicholas without even asking if he knows book-keeping, let alone requiring references, and propose making Tim Linkinwater a partner on no better grounds than his long service in a purely clerkly capacity. Dickens was sufficiently aware of this to insist in his preface to *Nicholas Nickleby* that the Brothers Cheeryble were drawn from life. He had indeed met a pair of factory-owning brothers called Grant, in Manchester, who Dickens scholars accept as having inspired the Cheerybles. One would nonetheless like to audit the Grants' accounts to see if they matched the Cheeryble profligacy with money.

At the Cheerybles' counting-house Nicholas one day catches sight of a mysterious but beautiful girl, an object of the Cheerybles' charity. He has seen her before, in an employment agency, and is strongly attracted to her. He gets Newman Noggs to sniff out her whereabouts and circumstances, for to begin with he doesn't even know her name.

Here we glimpse another slightly repellent aspect of Nicholas's character. Being presently told by Noggs that the girl he is so interested in is called

Cecilia Bobster, he can hardly repress his distaste for so unromantic a surname. But Dickens has the last laugh against Nicholas by arranging for Noggs to contrive a clandestine tryst between Cecilia and 'Nick' (as Noggs, alone of the book's characters, calls him). This involves the standard romantic paraphernalia of nocturnal setting, threatened discovery (it is feared by Cecilia's stern and brutal widower father) and lament by the lady that she may lose her reputation in consequence – only for it to be revealed that Miss Bobster is the wrong girl. Noggs has blundered.

Wackford Squeers, by Kyd.

Nicholas looks pretty foolish at this point too. One suspects that Dickens finds his hero too priggish and has brought him down a peg. Further signs that Dickens does not wholly approve of Nicholas are, that when Charles Cheeryble commissions him as go-between to bring regular financial help to Madeline Bray and her father, Nicholas rationalises his breach of duty to Charles in neglecting to disclose his own amorous interest in Madeline by a self-deceiving concern lest this hamper Charles's philanthropy. In fairness to Dickens, he makes plain in the preface that he is aware of Nicholas's imperfections, ascribing them to Nicholas's impetuosity and inexperience of life.

Madeline, a latecomer to the cast of characters, is now moved by Dickens centre-stage. Arthur Gride applies for her hand in marriage. A grotesque figure, Gride is also unconvincing in his senile lust. Not that senile lust didn't exist then (nor has it been extinguished yet). Only Dickens at this stage didn't handle sexual passion well, though he made good the deficiency in his very next novel, *The Old Curiosity Shop*.

What Dickens does show superbly is the self-centred petulance of such as Walter Bray, Gride's opposite number inasmuch as he is the proprietor of the luscious piece of goods (Madeline) that Gride is proposing to take off his hands for a fat price. At all events, Bray, since he *is* self-centred, agrees to Gride's and Ralph Nickleby's terms for handing over his daughter to be trussed in holy matrimony to the repulsive Gride, pawed, drooled over and penetrated in the sweaty intimacy of the marriage bed then subjected to petty slights and annoyances out of it, in the latter case due to Gride's miserly habits.

Newman Noggs learns of the impending marriage but, ignorant that Nicholas's fancy is for Madeline, does not immediately alert Nicholas. At their next meeting Madeline's name comes up in conversation as the true object of Nicholas's admiration. Aghast, Noggs reveals the plot to marry her to Gride. Nicholas, forced to act alone by the absence of the Cheeryble brothers on business abroad, tries to dissuade first Madeline from marrying Gride then Gride from marrying Madeline, high-handedly pledging the Cheerybles' wealth to buy off the latter. In neither case does he succeed.

Nicholas appears again at the Brays' next day when the wedding is about to take place. He is accompanied by Kate, whom he has brought to try and persuade Madeline to make her home with the Nicklebys pending the return of the Cheeryble brothers to England. Ralph and Gride oppose him but are overborn. Walter Bray drops dead. The wedding now need not go ahead, since Madeline's sole motive for sacrificing herself to the aged goat

Gride is to secure to her father the wherewithal to pass his last years in comfort. Nicholas takes Madeline away, his sister acting as her chaperone, and fires a parting shot at Ralph by informing him that a £10,000 investment of his (say £1,250,000 today) has been lost.

Smike, long ailing, has by now become so ill that on medical advice the Nicklebys arrange for him to go to Devon, whose clean air and wholesome sea breezes may counteract what is implicitly tuberculosis, then the sort of A-list killer that cancer is today. The Cheerybles give Nicholas leave to accompany Smike.

Gride on returning home with no bride discovers his housekeeper Peg Sliderskew has decamped with many of his most secret papers. These include a stolen will making an heiress of Madeline Bray and whoever marries her. It is an added reason, over and above Gride's lust, for his making her his bride, indeed a neat device of Dickens's for explaining why, if Gride is so keen on young girls, he hasn't already bought one off the shelf from some other indigent father.

Gride is terrified that if he reports the theft of his papers he will go to prison as a receiver in regard to the will benefiting Madeline. Ralph offers Squeers £100 (say £12,500 today) if he will trick Peg into handing the will over, whereupon he, Ralph, will burn it. Ralph's motive here is pure malice against Nicholas, who he rightly suspects of hoping to marry Madeline. Certainly the will, whether executed or otherwise, would not benefit Ralph directly. Squeers does trick Peg out of the document but before he can take it to Ralph is knocked senseless by Noggs, who has accompanied Frank Cheeryble on a rescue party to the Lambeth garret where Peg has sequestered herself and her stolen papers.

Down in Devon Smike drifts gently off to his death, but not before he experiences (as Nicholas then thinks) a vision of the man who took him all those years ago to Dotheboys and consigned him to Squeers. It turns out to have been no vision (see further below).

Ralph Nickleby meanwhile is reeling from the loss of his £10,000. He had placed it overnight with a bank, which fails, as banks not infrequently did then, and without compensating depositors. (Prudent men, long vilified as misers before modern bank guarantees were instituted, thus had good reason to keep their wealth at home, and to hide evidence of it by dressing shabbily if they wished to avoid being robbed and murdered; eccentric loners were sometimes thought to be secretly rich in consequence, as happens with Nell's grandfather in *The Old Curiosity Shop*.)

Ralph is also prey to insomnia and lack of concentration. He has begun to suspect Noggs, his factotum, of disloyalty – a slowness of apprehension suggesting his faculties have been waning for some time. Charles Cheeryble calls on Ralph to offer him help from Nicholas but is rebuffed. Ralph tours London calling on his various confederates in wickedness – Snawley, Squeers and Gride – but finds them absent from their usual haunts or, in the case of Gride, terrified of being seen speaking to him. By now gravely perturbed, Ralph calls on the Cheeryble brothers. They tell him that Squeers has been remanded in custody for possession of the stolen will and that Snawley, in return for immunity from prosecution, has confessed his part in the forgery of papers asserting his, Snawley's, paternity of Smike.

Ralph defies the Cheerybles to prove a link between him and Snawley or Squeers. He visits Squeers, who refuses to prop up their conspiracy. Ralph returns home to brood on his difficulties. Tim Linkinwater calls on him and takes him once more to the Cheerybles. Brooker is with them and reveals to Ralph that Smike was Ralph's son and is now dead. It turns out that, some 20 or more years before, Ralph had secretly married the rich sister of one of his spendthrift clients, the secrecy being necessary since under a clause in her father's will she had to marry with her brother's consent or lose her inheritance, whereas the brother, needing money, would only assent if richly rewarded, something Ralph refused to arrange. Smike, the product of Ralph's marriage, had therefore to be hidden.

'Miss Squeers [,having] made up her mind that she would take a personal observation of Nicholas the very next day, went accidentally into the schoolroom to get a pen mended: where, seeing nobody but Nicholas presiding over the boys, she blushed very deeply, and exhibited great confusion.' (Ch IX).

Ralph and his wife had lived apart to avoid arousing any suspicion in her brother and as a result grew estranged. She had eventually left Ralph for a younger man and Ralph had followed them to exact revenge. He had meanwhile entrusted Brooker with care of Smike, a name Brooker gave him. Brooker, resentful of ill treatment he had suffered at Ralph's hands, had deposited Smike with Squeers and told Ralph he had died. Brooker had paid Smike's school fees for six years, doing so as insurance against the time when he might gouge compensation out of Ralph. He had then left the country (i.e. was transported for criminal activity), having long left Ralph's employ. Only many years later did he return to England, first seeking out Ralph in the hope of extracting money, then spying on Nicholas and Smike down in Devon to check the identity of the latter (the occasion Smike glimpsed him).

Ralph has sat motionless throughout this recital. He now smashes the room's only lamp and takes a hurried departure. The Cheerybles, apprehensive because of Ralph's unaccustomed passivity, send to his house to enquire how he is. Ralph commits suicide, hanging himself from a hook beside the very ceiling trap-door that had so terrified Smike when as a child he had been kept in that self-same garret.

Meanwhile Nicholas tells Kate of his love for Madeline and she tells him of Frank's proposing marriage to her. Brother and sister agree that, being poor, they cannot abuse the Cheerybles' confidence by Nichols's wooing Madeline in earnest or Kate's accepting Frank's proposal. The Cheerybles dismiss these scruples, Frank marries Kate and Nicholas marries Madeline, recently promoted heiress through the recovered will (that of her maternal grandfather) leaving her £12,000 (say £1,500,000 today). Nicholas invests his wife's money in Cheeryble Brothers and in a few years is promoted to partner.

The first number of *Nicholas Nickleby* (as usual with Dickens's novels, published in serial form) sold 50,000 copies and sales never dipped much subsequently.

The Old Curiosity Shop

Weekly serial, 1840 to 1841
Book published 1841

Little Nell cossets Grandfather, their saviour Mrs Jarley behind them on her caravan, an illustration by Jessie Willcox Smith.

Characters

Barbara Maid to the Garlands; wooed and won by Kit Nubbles.

Brass, Sally

Sampson Brass's sister. Played by Jill Bennett in the 1975 film (a musical), released in the UK under the same title as the book but in the USA as *Mr Quilp*.

Brass, Sampson

Quilp's dishonest lawyer. Played by David Warner in the 1975 film.

Cheggs, Alick Market gardener; marries Sophy Wackles.

Cheggs, Miss Alick's sister.

Chuckster

Clerk to Witherden; takes dislike to Kit Nubbles, constantly calling him 'Snobby', an early meaning of 'snob' that signifies less a person attaching excessive value to rank and titles than one in lowly circumstances who is suspected by his social superiors of presuming above his station.

Codlin, Thomas/Tom/Tommy Partner in Punch and Judy show with Short.

Edwards, Miss Pupil-teacher at Miss Monflathers's girls' school.

Garland, Abel Pupil articled to Witherden.

Garland, Mr Father of above; lives at Abel Cottage, Finchley; Dickens said he had based the Garland husband and wife on a Mr and Mrs Albert Russell with whom he had lodged as a boy when his father was imprisoned for debt in the Marshalsea.

George Surname-less man-of-all-work to Mrs Jarley, who he eventually marries. Played by Windsor Davies in the 1975 film.

George, Mrs Friend of Betsy Quilp.

Grandfather

Nell's mother's father; dealer in curios (as antiques were called in those days, though perhaps his stock is better described by the French word *brocante*,

Tom Codlin.

signifying junk); tries to build Nell a nest egg by gambling, thus losing even that small capital which he started with and borrowing ever more from Quilp in consequence; has an odd habit of addressing Nell using 'thee' and 'thou' as if he were a Quaker (but since he does it to nobody else he can't be). Played by Michael Hordern in the 1975 film; Derek Jacobi (see also *Little Dorrit*) in the 2007 ITV adaptation.

Grinder Itinerant showman.

Groves, Jem/Jemmy Landlord of inn where Grandfather's gambling mania revives.

Harris, 'Trotters' or 'Short' Codlin's partner.

Harry Schoolboy protégé of Marton.

Jarley, Mrs

Proprietor of Jarley's Waxwork. Played by Zoë Wanamaker in the 2007 ITV adaptation.

Jerry Itinerant showman handling performing dogs; his feeding routine with his dogs echoes Squeers's with his pupils in *Nicholas Nickleby*.

Jiniwin, Mrs Mrs Quilp's mother.

Jowl Gambler; initially referred to by Dickens as Mat, but by his confederate List as Joe.

List, Isaac Gambler.

'Marchioness, The'

'Slavey' (put-upon maid of all work) in Brasses' house.

Marton Rural schoolmaster; accommodates Nell and her grandfather.

Monflathers, Miss Girls' school headmistress.

Nell(y), Little

The story's heroine, if a child created and nurtured by its author purely to be killed off can be so designated.

Nubbles, Kit (formally Christopher)

Friend and pupil of Nell's (she gives him writing lessons); employed by Garlands as servant at £6 annual wages (say £725 today).

Nubbles, Mrs Kit's widowed mother.

Quilp, Daniel

Dwarf with a variety of business interests: marine merchant, rent-collector, usurer, wharfinger (see Winkle, Nathaniel, in *Pickwick Papers*); lives at Tower Hill hard by the Tower of London; believes his wife to nurture a *tendresse* for Fred Trent, thus in Quilp's eyes retroactively justifying his long-standing ill treatment of her; Dickens is said to have based Quilp on a donkey-jobbing Bath dwarf

Harris (above) and Quilp (below).

called Prior, who beat both his wife and beasts. Played by Anthony Newley in the 1975 film; Trevor Peacock in the 1979 BBC televisation scripted by the novelist William Trevor; Tom Courtenay (see also *Little Dorrit*) in both the 1995 Disney televisation and the 1998 BBC Radio 4 broadcast.

Quilp, Betsy, *née* Jiniwin Quilp's bullied wife.

Scott, Tom Quilp's servant boy.

Short See Harris.

Simmons, Henrietta Friend of Betsy Quilp.

'Single gentleman, the' Mysterious lodger at the Brasses'. Played by James Fox in the 1995 Disney televisation.

Slum Styled by Dickens a poet, but copywriter more accurate; composes advertising puffs for the likes of Mrs Jarley.

Swiveller, Dick (more formally Richard)

Friend of Fred Trent; his irrepressible good spirits, gift of repartee, habit of reciting snatches of verse and ingenious way with creditors prefigure P G Wodehouse's young men about town; he even has that most Wodehousian of pecuniary resources, an aunt from whom he expects a remittance (she later leaves him £125 a year [say about £16,000 today]); becomes Sampson Brass's clerk. Played by David Hemmings in the 1975 film.

Trent, Fred Nell's brother; three years before the story opens had gone out to Demerara; gets involved with the crooked gamblers Groves, Jowl and List in some way that Dickens fails through cryptic use of language to explain properly; goes abroad and lives 'by his wits' as Dickens puts it, presumably by gambling again, but gets involved in a brawl and is found drowned in the Seine as it passes through Paris.

Trent, Nell(y) See Nell, Little.

Vuffin Showman running a collection of freaks.

Wackles, Jane Sophy's younger sister.

Wackles, Melissa Sophy's elder sister.

Wackles, Mrs Widowed mother of the Wackles sisters.

Wackles, Sophy Girl in whom Dick Swiveller has been showing languid interest; she accordingly encourages Cheggs.

West, Dame Grandmother of Harry (the appellation 'Dame' Smith, Jones etc. even in 1840 was old-fashioned but survived in country districts; it was not a title in the way 'Dame Jane Snooks DBE', the famous actress, is).

William, Sweet Card trick magician.

Witherden Notary.

The Old Curiosity Shop

Story Commentary

This is an odd novel, the oddest Dickens ever wrote. Why the title? The shop itself plays no real part in the plot except very early on as grotesque backdrop to Little Nell's night fears. (And Dickens tells us in one of the book's last paragraphs that after Nell's death it was pulled down, so that the 'real life' tourist shop of that name in Portugal Street, off Lincoln's Inn Fields in the London West Central district, can have no genuine link with the original.)

Then there's the clumsy way the story gets told. It starts with an unnamed first person narrator, who soon bows out, Dickens reverting to the third person. There is Dickens's failure to give names to Nell's grandfather, his brother the 'single gentleman', Mr Garland's brother the 'bachelor' and 'The Marchioness', this last a sobriquet Dick Swiveller bestows on the Brasses' 'slavey'. Given the very tight timetable Dickens was working to, which is discussed further below, this may in the first three cases be no more than Dickens's fear, if he assigned each pair the same surnames, of spoiling the plot by revealing kinship between the 'single gentleman' and Grandfather on the one hand, and between Mr Garland and the 'bachelor' on the other.

Yet he couldn't jettison the blood tie since no other device would plausibly explain the interest the 'single gentleman' has in Nell and her grandfather, also the 'single gentleman' discovering their whereabouts by his learning it from Mr Garland's brother via Mr Garland. The trouble is, anonymous characters make the bits of plot they inhabit as dramatically barren as those brain-teasers where you must compute which of a farmer's three sons owns what number of the family's cows using scraps of mathematical data.

The historical reasons for these various imperfections are straightforward. The framework for the story was the periodical *Master Humphrey's Clock*. In it, a 'host', Master Humphrey, or a guest narrator (Pickwick on one occasion, Sam Weller on another) reeled off a series of short yarns. Dickens found that this injured sales, which had started at around 70,000 copies but after two more weeks dropped to around 50,000. He quickly abandoned the format, expanding a short piece of his about a lost little girl into a long-ish novel, but in a still more makeshift way than was usual with him at that point in his artistic development, though he did make notes to prevent glaring plot inconsistencies.

The imperfections touched on above and below do not constitute a fatal flaw, more bits of dramatic litter. And commercially the expanded story was

'The Marchioness', by Kyd (above).

'The Marchioness' and Dick Swiveller, by Harold Copping.

a huge success, for towards the end sales hit 100,000 copies a week. But by now you'd think Dickens was experienced enough to avoid such purely technical mistakes.

Then there is Little Nell. Is she the heroine? She doesn't do much. Like Oliver Twist she is a child. Or rather, Dickens keeps calling her that, which isn't quite the same thing. She is even more passive than Oliver. Her function in Dickens's day was to look fetchingly pathetic; arouse concupiscence in such of her fellow male characters as are in their sexual prime; spark lachrymose sympathy in her fellow female characters (and such male ones as are past, or yet to enter into, their sexual prime), also in the reading public; fade away; then, finally, die.

Because modern readers are less susceptible to Dickens's tear-jerking, the most emotionally important of the above five purposes, getting the public to have a really good blub, is not nowadays fully attained. Nell thereby loses much of her artistic value. To us the real action is not with her and her grandfather on their wanderings, getting ever further from London, but back in London. It is as if Dickens's inventiveness wanes once he leaves his beloved city.

What then is the point of Nell? Well, as touched on above, she constitutes Dickens's first very cautious fumblings in the direction of sex. The age of consent for girls in those days was 13, Nell's age, that is, on the threshhold of puberty or even a bit over it. Thirteen could make you the legitimate (if rather shameful) target of male carnal interest. So Nell is not a genuine child any longer. She sometimes talks as if younger, but most of the time conducts herself in solemn fashion as if much older, or even as if some preternaturally exalted individual such as a royal. Dickens, normally rather good in his handling of child characters (boys mostly, however), falters here.

Certainly Nell from the word go is subjected by other characters to sexual speculation, in the sense both of wondering and calculating. First Quilp, presumably jocularly (but you never know with a personality like his), suggests she marry him. Then her brother Fred puts her forward for his friend Dick Swiveller's consideration as a wife. So far it is at worst in mildly questionable taste. But darker elements intrude. When Quilp visits Grandfather (Chapter IX) to tell him he will lend no more money since it's become clear the loan will be spent on gambling, he launches into the most lubricious encomium on a young girl in all literature to that date. (And even into our time, for the overwritten prose and self-congratulatory tone of Vladimir Nabokov in *Lolita* – 'look what a clever juggler with the English language I am, and it's not even my mother tongue' – disqualify that meretricious novel from proper comparison.)

Daniel Quilp, by Kyd.

Take this by Quilp: 'Ah … what a nice kiss that was [of the parting caress Nell's grandfather has given her before shooing her out of the room] – just upon the rosy part … ' And Quilp casts 'an admiring leer' after her, only to continue 'Such a fresh, blooming, modest little bud … so beautifully modelled, so fair, with such blue veins, and such a transparent skin.'

Marcel Proust's central character, Charles Swann, in *A la recherche du temps perdu* calls an episode in Balzac's *Les Illusions perdues* involving the homosexual Carlos Herrera 'the *Tristesse d'Olympio* [a celebrated poem by Victor Hugo about lost love] of pederasty'. The speech by Quilp above is the moppet-molester's equivalent. When Grandfather takes Nell away from London, it is fairly obviously because he sees in Quilp a threat to her virginity.

A high-falutin theory woven around Nell is that she symbolises 'thanato-erotism', or in plain man's words the morbid interplay of death and desire which so bewitched the Victorians. If so, Dickens doesn't work it out. It doesn't stop his further gropings in the murky closet of non-vanilla sexuality. Take the relationship Quilp has with his wife Betsy. The first thing Dickens has Betsy do is tell her circle of chattering housewives how sexually alluring Quilp is, and how none of them could resist him if he 'chose to make love to them'. (To 'make love' to a woman in 19th-century usage didn't mean intercourse, more extravagant compliments; 'coming on to', or 'hitting on' her, if you like.)

Little Nell in an illustration by Harold Copping.

Can Quilp possibly be attractive? Physical shortcomings like his have their admirers. And his actual face, at any rate in the illustrator Phiz's first depiction of him, is well moulded. It is also highly sensual and splendidly swarthy, belonging to the sort of man some women melt over as being 'dark and dirty'. His smallness of stature needn't have stopped him being well-endowed down south. As for his brutality, Dickens gives us a strong hint that he has a sado-masochistic relationship with his wife.

But Quilp, however potent in the boudoir, is a bit of a duffer in the counting house. He hasn't bothered to find out what Nell's grandfather's assets or income are before advancing him loans. Luckily, the old man possesses real property in the form of The Old Curiosity Shop, and Quilp in foreclosing takes possession of both it and the stock, quickly selling off the latter. (He has previously discredited Kit Nubbles with Nell's grandfather by falsely blaming Kit for having revealed Grandfather's gambling mania.) So Grandfather must find alternative accommodation and, by now rather senile, steals away with Nell the day Quilp is due to empty the premises of its contents.

Unfortunately, Grandfather has no destination in mind. He and Nell drift, falling in with Punch and Judy showmen headed for a race meeting and through them encountering other fairground folk. The passage in Chapter XIX on dwarves and giants is among the funniest, but to modern minds 'sickest', that Dickens ever wrote, foreshadowing Diane Arbus's photographs, only in prose.

Along with the Fagin episodes in *Oliver Twist*, it is so politically incorrect as would make publishing it today for the first time risky. Yet Dickens could only hint at Nell's sexual allure (Codlin fancies her but never at the time goes beyond protestations of friendship, though much later in the book he claims he loved her). And Dickens could only hint at the Quilps' S &

Dick Swiveller, by Kyd.

M marriage. They are themes people today would barely turn a hair at (or, if they did turn any hairs, wouldn't dare admit it). Each age has its taboos, and the 21st century's hypersensitivity towards ethnic minorities and the deformed while being relatively blasé about consensual sexual cruelty is in its way as quaint as the 1840s' reverse attitude.

At the races Nell concludes Codlin is getting too interested in her for comfort and with her grandfather escapes from him and his mountebank associates. Grandfather is becoming more of a burden, his mind and soliloquies full of apprehension that he may be incarcerated as a madman, then chained and whipped. Though in 1840 this sort of treatment might still have been meted out to very obstreporous inmates of the more laxly regulated asylums, it was mostly on the way out. But a confused old man such as Grandfather would not have been familiar with current psychiatric developments. And the real effect in any case is to intrude further dark sexual overtones. Grandfather now addresses Nell as 'you', however, rather than 'thou'. His debility of mind has at least cleared the cobwebs from his vocabulary.

Meanwhile, back in London, Quilp maliciously encourages Dick Swiveller to try and marry Nell, persuading him that her grandfather is secretly rich, though Quilp himself reckons otherwise. He also gets the hard-up Dick a job with Sampson Brass as law clerk, so as to keep an eye on him. Dick makes friends of a sort with Sampson's sister Sally and alone of the Brass household is able to manage an eccentric but well-to-do lodger. This lodger, the 'single gentleman' (as he remains known throughout the book), is very anxious to trace the whereabouts of Nell and her grandfather. They are respectively his great-niece and brother, though neither we nor the other characters are made aware of this yet.

For their part Nell and her grandfather get put up by a village schoolmaster. Scarcely have they arrived than the latter takes Nell to visit his favourite pupil, who is dying and indeed expires shorty after their arrival. A small boy with but a single relative, and that his grandmother, he constitutes pretty clearly the blueprint for what Dickens has in store for Nell.

This signalling so blatantly by Dickens of the denouement to the entire novel makes one wonder if his creative powers weren't temporarily flagging. Evidence? He most unusually repeats himself almost word for word in introducing the schoolmaster, first describing the latter as 'a pale ... man, of a spare and meagre habit [meaning outward appearance, not customary behaviour]' then 10 lines later saying 'he looked pale and meagre'. Dickens's prodigal facility with language meant that though he often spun out descriptive or editorialising passages to pad his material, he very seldom slipped up to the extent of actually saying the same thing twice in identical words. But on this occasion he was turning out material only two weeks ahead of the printers' schedule and the 16–17 pages he wrote each week varied between short and long chapters such that, as he said at the time, 'I hadn't room to turn'. Yet he downed tools at one point to revisit his childhood haunts of Chatham and Rochester. In anyone else it would have been irresponsible. In him it reflected pure strain. That the infelicity above is its sole literary evidence says much for his professionalism.

Little Nell meets Mrs Jarley; illustration by Arthur Dixon.

Nell and her grandfather leave the schoolmaster then encounter Mrs Jarley. The latter employs Nell to compere her waxwork exhibits. Dickens throws off his sentimentalising and grows satirical again, describing how Mrs Jarley, to attract a more select public, refashions the waxwork of a murderess to resemble the philanthropist Hannah More and that of Mary Queen of Scots to resemble Lord Byron.

Mrs Jarley is mostly kind to Nell, but in making her sleep among the waxworks (for better security of her stock-in-trade) re-awakes the morbid fancies Nell had suffered in the curiosity shop. Notable among these are visions of Quilp, who Nell has recently glimpsed in physical form late at night in the town where the waxworks are shown (from circumstantial evidence thought to have been Warwick). This makes the third time in three successive novels that Dickens has confronted a child character far from London with an adult persecutor the child has supposed is still in London: Oliver and Fagin when at Mrs Maylie's, Smike and Brooker when down in Devon. The dramatic force wears thin in consequence.

The 'single gentleman' leaves London for where Nell and Grandfather were last seen, taking Kit Nubbles's mother with him as proof of his bona fides to Nell and her grandfather, who are not familiar with his appearance but do know her. Meanwhile Nell's grandfather plunders Nell's savings to gamble with, each night losing his entire stake to List and Jowl. Nell prevents him robbing Mrs Jarley, but only by insisting that they leave her and press on. Nell develops fever from getting soaked in heavy rain, they pass through what sounds from Dickens's description like the Black Country around Birmingham (which Dickens visited while writing *The Old Curiosity Shop*) and fall in with the schoolmaster again.

The schoolmaster's new place of employment is not named in the book, but was based by Dickens on Tong, in Shropshire, as Dickens himself later revealed. Its picturesqueness in Dickens's description almost overwhelms the narrative, but at least provides Nell with employment as a tour guide in the local church, building on her experience as a waxworks compere. Dickens now devotes some elaborate passages to Nell's impending death, involving what to our minds involve heavy hints by a local lad likening her to an angel.

Back in London, Sampson Brass frames Kit Nubbles for theft to gratify Quilp's malice. Frivolous grounds for involving oneself in conspiracy? Yes. Then, as now, it was a grave crime. But Brass's attorney practice is so thin that Quilp is virtually his sole source of revenue. He must obey Quilp's every wish. And being dishonest, he has no scruples.

Dickens's description of Kit's wrongful imprisonment is marvellous. Take the 'turnkey' (gaoler). He is no monster. That would be too crude. By now Dickens has begun to deploy rather more nuanced minor characters as well as major ones. 'The man [the turnkey] was not naturally cruel or hard-hearted. He had come to look on felony as a kind of disorder, like the scarlet fever ... : some people had it – some hadn't – just as it might be.' Pathos, leavened by irony. And a further irony is that many people today view felony as just that – a disorder.

What transforms brilliance to genius is Dickens's pulling the rug from under our feet in the chapter's last few paragraphs by a burlesqued literary allusion. Kit is told by the prison warder that while he is in custody a pint a day of porter (the dark beer with creamy head) will be supplied him by a well-wisher.

Who is the well-wisher? He adds a message: 'Drink of this cup, you'll find there's a spell of its every drop 'gainst the ills of mortality. Talk of the cordial that sparkled for Helen [of Troy]! *Her* cup was a fiction, but this is reality (Barclay and Co.'s). If they ever send it in a flat state, complain to the Governor. Yours R. S.' The quotation involving 'mortality', 'cordial' and 'Helen' is from 'Drink of This Cup', by the poet and friend of Byron, Thomas Moore (1779–1852). The 'R.S.' is Dick Swiveller.

Kit is not imprisoned long. 'The Marchioness' tells Dick Swiveller she has overheard the Brasses plotting to frame him for theft, and at Quilp's behest. Confronted by Messrs Garland and Witherden and the 'single gentleman', Sampson Brass confesses, though Sally stays tight-lipped. Quilp is hunted down but falls in the Thames and drowns. Kit is freed. His release coincides with, perhaps nourishes, his awakening sexuality, for he and the pretty maidservant Barbara now embark upon a series of necking sessions, a reprise of Sam Weller's with his maidservant inamorata Mary in *Pickwick Papers*.

The 'single gentleman' then hastens to Shropshire with Garland as companion and Kit as lieutenant to rescue his brother and great-niece Nell from their penurious rustication. He arrives too late. Nell has died. Her grandfather, at first unaware of her death then mad with grief then reverting to a childish denial of it, follows her to the grave next spring.

Sally Brass escapes formal punishment, but degenerates into a scavenger for food scraps in the London gutters. Sampson Brass is convicted of fraud and perjury and struck off the attorneys' register. His confession saves him from transportation. Instead he is shackled and put to working a prison treadmill, in Victorians' eyes a less degrading punishment. After serving his sentence, implicitly a five-year one or thereabouts, he joins Sally in scavenging. An inquest on Quilp's death judges him to have committed suicide. He is 'left to be buried' at a crossroads with a stake through his heart. This was the traditional protection against suicides becoming 'revenants' or vampires.

Sampson Brass, by Kyd.

Dick Swiveller, inheriting a private income, pays for 'The Marchioness' to be educated. Six years later, by which time she is 19, he marries her. Her age at the time of the main story is thus 13, exactly Nell's. And once educated, hence of bourgeois status, she effectively assumes the heroine function that Nell could never properly undertake, while Dick, initially a bohemian buffoon, becomes by inheriting an annuity bourgeois also, and by his help to Kit then educating 'The Marchioness' graduates to hero status.

It remains only to say a little more about 'The Marchioness'. Dick before educating her gives her a name, 'Sophronia Sphynx', thus establishing the first of those options over her that he cashes in on marrying her, by which time she is good-looking and good-humoured and has shown by her educational attainments that she possesses a good mind. Her origins remain mysterious. Dickens tells us Quilp is thought to have been involved. One construes this as his fathering her on some unmarried woman.

Why 'The Marchioness' as sobriquet, though? Dickens doesn't say, either directly or through Dick Swiveller. And why should the latter choose such an esoteric label, deriving from the peculiar form which the wife of that high-ranking sort of peer a marquess is known by?

The answer lies in a clue buried 100 pages back. The first time the 'single gentleman' hurries down to the country to ferret out Nell, his air of 'money-no-object' urgency persuades the rustics with whom she has recently mingled that she is the lost daughter of a high nobleman, such as a prince, duke, earl, viscount or baron. The sole noble rank missing from that list is marquess. 'Sophronia', under her nickname 'Marchioness', supplies this earlier deficiency, thus symbolically stepping into the moribund Nell's shoes as another lady of make-believe high birth.

Sales of *The Old Curiosity Shop* in serial form (the magazine *Master Humphrey's Clock*) reached six figures. The *Clock* sold at 3d (1.5p, or £1.53 today) for the weekly version and, for the monthly one, a shilling (5p, or £6.25 today), generating for the publishers Chapman and Hall a projected turnover equivalent to at least £7.5 million a year nowadays. Dickens had become by far the hottest literary property in Britain, probably the world.

Barnaby Rudge

Weekly serial, 1840 to 1841
Book published 1841

Squire Geoffrey Haredale, his house the Warren a blackened ruin after firing by rioters, kills Sir John Chester.

Characters

Akerman Chief gaoler at Newgate, in the City of London, then Britain's leading prison.

Benjamin Sim Tappertit's subordinate at meeting of the 'Prentice Knights secret society.

Chester, Edward

Chief male love interest; eventually marries Emma Haredale.

Chester, John (later Sir John)

Father of above; opposes Edward ('Ned' to him) marrying Emma since her family is Catholic and not well-off; temporarily parts them by poisoning the minds of each against the other; provokes Edward into leaving the family dwelling; later placed by a grand kinsman as MP for a 'close borough', the kinsman, its proprietor, dictating who it elects to Parliament, and is knighted.

Cobb, Tom Maypole Inn regular and local post-office manager.

Dennis, Ned

Ex-hangman; one of the Protestant fanatic Lord George Gordon's keenest supporters; his craven pleading for mercy once condemned to death for rioting is among the best scenes in the book.

Daisy, Solomon Maypole regular and Chigwell parish clerk.

Gashford

Lord George's secretary, having apostatised from Catholicism and joined the extreme Protestant cause; exercises great influence over Gordon.

Gilbert, Mark Ex-apprentice; lieutenant to Sim Tappertit.

Gordon, Lord George

Leader of the 1780 riots against the Catholic Relief Bill (which would have softened the harsh penalties imposed on people simply for being Catholic, such penalties being a relic of the 16th century, when Catholic-Protestant religious strife had dominated public life); a historic character, being youngest son of the 3rd Duke of Gordon and President of the Protestant Association; eccentric even by the generous standards of the British aristocracy; depicted by Dickens as a blue-blooded semi-imbecile reflection of Barnaby Rudge, talking to himself, waving a great gold-knobbed stick (even when on horseback), easily led and prey to a succession of disconnected enthusiasms; the real Gordon converted to Judaism and Dickens's version talks of having dreamed he was a Jew shortly after being introduced to us.

Grip.

Grip

Raven; Barnaby Rudge's companion ('pet' will hardly do, Grip talking more sense than Barnaby); performs an important dramatic function in uncovering at the height of the riots valuables looted by Hugh; inspiration for Edgar Allan Poe's 'The Raven' (Poe met Dickens on the latter's first trip to America in 1842) and named after a pet raven Dickens kept in real life.

Grueby, John

Lord George's associate-cum-servant; sacked at height of riots for emphasising Barnaby Rudge's mental incapacity, this being a sensitive point with Lord George since in his more lucid moments he knows he tends that way too; later helps rescue Haredale from mob.

Haredale, Emma

Marries Edward Chester.

Haredale, Geoffrey

Chigwell local squire and younger brother of Emma's murdered father Reuben; lives at house called the Warren, formerly one of consequence with an accompanying estate; now both house and estate are in decline; of a Catholic family, presumably recusant stock (i.e. having clung to their faith since before the Reformation); at the height of the riots arrives from London too late to save the Warren from destruction by a mob under Hugh and Ned Dennis but discovers Barnaby Rudge's supposedly dead father alive and skulking on the premises, instantly realising that he must therefore have murdered his, Geoffrey Haredale's, brother Reuben 27 years before; escorts Rudge Senior to prison; goes abroad to avoid rioters but returns and kills Sir John Chester in what some commentators (and Dickens himself, too hastily) call a duel but is really an affray, having flared up in the heat of the moment rather than being arranged with all the gentlemanly paraphernalia of seconds, choice of weapons and attendant surgeons that your true duel demanded.

Hugh

Maypole Inn servant; strong and fleet of foot but a lout; John Chester's bastard by a woman (Mary Jones, it is later revealed to us) hanged at Tyburn for petty theft by the executioner Ned Dennis; Chester establishes ascendancy over Hugh by force of personality alone, since at that point neither man knows of their kinship; Hugh later joins the Protestant Association, in which he serves shoulder to shoulder with Ned Dennis; presiding spirit in riots, hence arrested and condemned to death; even on the point of execution he betrays neither fear nor remorse, thereby, though less nobly, prefiguring Sydney Carton in *A Tale of Two Cities*.

Langdale Catholic distiller and vintner, based on a real person.

Lion, The Landlord of an inn called the Black Lion in London's Whitechapel, so called because he has got his own features incorporated in the lion on the inn sign.

Miggs

The Vardens' servant; calls Mrs Varden 'mim' instead of 'mum' or 'ma'am' and Mr Varden 'Mr Warden', the other side of the coin of the old Cockney habit of turning 'Ws' into 'Vs' ('Vest End' for 'West End'); on her rejection by Sim, whom she adores, becomes increasingly bitter, is dismissed by the Vardens and ends as a female 'turnkey' (prison wardress).

London, Lord Mayor of Does nothing whatsoever to help Haredale and other Catholics during riots, just wrings his hands and laments that they have committed the inconvenience of being Catholic; the best depiction of an appeaser in all literature; the Lord Mayor at the time of the real Gordon Riots was Brackley Kennett, who for his pusillanimity was convicted of criminal negligence and fined £1,000 (up to £200,000 today).

Parkes, 'Long' Phil Maypole regular.

Peak Sir John Chester's servant.

Barnaby Rudge.

Rudge, Barnaby

Idiot; forerunner of Julia Mills in *David Copperfield* in his taste for whimsy ('when I talk of eyes the stars come out. ... If they are angels' eyes, why do they look down here and see good men hurt, and only wink and sparkle all the night?'); joins the rioters, though clueless as to what their cause is all about; does at least keep himself clean and spruce between bouts of rioting, unlike most rioters.

Rudge, Mary Barnaby's mother.

Rudge, Mr Barnaby's father; formerly the Haredales' steward and supposedly murdered at the same time as Reuben Haredale; in fact he himself had murdered Reuben and dressed a corpse he found in his own clothes to escape detection; after discovery by Haredale is jailed.

Stagg Blind owner of a subterranean boozing den and skittle alley where Sim Tappertit holds his 'Prentice Knights meeting.

May your
Christmas be
as bright as
Dolly Varden's
smiles.
DOLLY VARDEN
"Barnaby Rudge."

Tappertit, Simon/Sim

Gabriel Varden's live-in apprentice, as which he makes a duplicate key of the front door to let himself out at night with and preside over a meeting of the 'Prentice Knights, whose name he later changes to The United Bull-Dogs, becoming their President also; a leading rioter; in love with Dolly Varden.

Varden, Dolly

Gabriel Varden's very pretty daughter and a visitor since infancy to the Warren; her name since has been borrowed for, among other things, a cake and a faux 18th-century costume (recognisable by the shallow dish-shaped hat which surmounts the whole and is secured by a broad ribbon round the wearer's chin).

Varden, Gabriel

Locksmith; lives in Clerkenwell, on the western edge of the City of London; very decently proposes after the first outbreak of rioting to save Sim Tappertit and spirit him out of London; Sim refuses; Varden refuses the rioters' demands that he pick locks of Newgate Gaol to gain them admittance, he having fashioned the locks in the first place; they storm the place anyway.

Varden, Martha

Gabriel's wife and Emma Haredale's former foster-mother; pores over the *Protestant Manual* (probably *The Protestant's Manual or Reasons for the Reformation*, a propagandist work along the lines of Foxe's *Book of* [Protestant] *Martyrs*, itself one of the most effective propaganda works of the Reformation, indeed of all time).

Willet, John

Runs Maypole Inn near Chigwell in Essex.

Willet, Joseph/Joe

His son, and so bullied by him that he runs away and enlists as a soldier; loses an arm in the War of American Independence, where he is involved in the defence of Savannah, Ga., the war's one incontestable British triumph; marries Dolly Varden.

Dolly Varden by William Frith, c.1842–49 *(above).*

A Christmas card featuring Dolly Varden (above left).

Barnaby Rudge

Story Commentary

Barnaby Rudge is the runt of the litter among Dickens's novels. Yet it also had the longest gestation. Dickens had agreed with his then publisher John Macrone to write *Gabriel Vardon, The Locksmith of London*, generally reckoned the blueprint of *Rudge*, as far back as May 1836. He certainly produced two chapters in 1839, long before he started full-time on the novel at the very end of January 1841.

But runt it principally was. It sold disappointingly: 30,000 a week in the periodical *Master Humphrey's Clock*, less than a third of *The Old Curiosity Shop*

John (later Sir John) Chester disports himself in society, an illustration by Fred Barnard.

peak figures. It is seldom filmed; its most recent television adaptation was a BBC one of 1960 with Timothy Bateson as Sim Tappertit. (Bateson had possibly the longest Dickens association of any actor ever: he played Lord Verisopht in the 1947 film of *Nicholas Nickleby* and landed a cameo role as a cleric in the 2005 Polanski film of *Oliver Twist* nearly 60 years later; see also *A Christmas Carol*, *David Copperfield* and *Bleak House*.)

Stagg rests after trying to extort money from Barnaby's mother, another fine illustration by Fred Barnard.

Barnaby Rudge suffers in most people's eyes by comparison with Dickens's other historical story of mob violence, *A Tale of Two Cities*. Yet to the discerning, notably the great Mrs Gaskell specialist Alan Shelston, it rates higher.

With good reason. Take Sim Tappertit. As head of the 'Prentice Knights secret society he is much more convincing in his chip-on-shoulder malevolence than the insufficiently limned M and Mme Defarge of *A Tale*. He even looks like a French Revolution *sansculotte*, not just in Dickens's detailed description but in illustrations, especially Harry Furniss's to the Edwardian-era editions.

Further, in Dickens's hands – as dextrous here as at any time in his career – Sim's absurdity makes his sinister side all the stronger. (A point worth remembering today: Kim Jong Il of North Korea may look a joke, but his nuclear weapons aren't, especially when the finger on the red button is so palsied.) Thus Sim's addressing his master as 'G. Varden' when intoxicated by his rioting is both fatuous yet chilling, reminiscent of that self-important language with which revolutionaries often cut their victims down to size before liquidating them altogether.

Dickens modulates the tone of *Barnaby Rudge* unusually well. His almost lyrical description of London in 1775, each house with its garden, each street with its trees, goes entirely against the squalor and claustrophobia of that city in his mainstream novels. Yet he is ready a few chapters later to remind us how dangerous 18th-century London was, especially after dark, with minimal street lighting, no police force (the watch 'utterly inefficient'), and more cut-purses, footpads, highwaymen, jailbirds, bravos, resurrectionists, housebreakers, cracksmen, skulkers, prowlers, occasional ex-pat rapparees and the odd shore-leave picaroon than you could shake a stick at.

BARNABY RUDGE.

THE MURDERER ARRESTED [*By G. Cattermole*

"Villain!" cried Mr. Haredale. "You, Rudge, double murderer and monster, I arrest you in the name of the God who has delivered you into my hands."—*Barnaby, chap. lvi*

'The murderer arrested' by George Cattermole.

The action of *Barnaby Rudge* drags a bit to start with, a lethargy that was to continue in *Rudge*'s immediate younger brother, *Martin Chuzzlewit*. Even when the plot throws up every likelihood of a duel, that godsend to writers of period romance, Dickens goes and calls it off. Perhaps a duel was too precious a dramatic property to be squandered early in the story. Yet we are over 100 pages into the story. *Barnaby Rudge*'s sluggish sales figures come as no surprise.

But there are compensatory gems. Miggs's revealing at the height of the riots that she has poured beer down the muzzle of Gabriel Varden's blunderbuss to disable it from harming her adored Sim Tappertit. And there's John Chester, as good an embodiment of insolent, witty, cynical insouciance as anything in Oscar Wilde's plays.

After the breaches between the two fathers, Johns Chester and Willet on the one hand, with their respective sons, Edward and Joe on the other, Dickens whisks us forwards five years to the 19th of March 1780. Lord George Gordon at last makes his appearance. Though a contemptible figure, he is more subtly so than Lords Mutanhed or even Verisopht. He thus paves the way for the blue-bloods of Dickens's mature period, by which time Dickens was hobnobbing with real live aristocrats and had found they weren't all as cretinous as in youth he had supposed.

Barnaby and his mother, to whom Stagg in their rustic retreat delivers some mysterious threat, evade him and head up to London. There Barnaby joins the crowd of Protestant Associationists gathering in St George's Fields, south of the Thames. The crowd moves on Parliament. Barnaby gets taken in hand by Hugh, already of NCO equivalent under Sim Tappertit as Captain. MPs reject the Association's petition to drop the Catholic relief measure and the crowds menacing the Houses of Parliament become still more restive. Hugh and Barnaby slip away and hole up at the Boot, a den of ne'er-do-wells off Tottenham Court Road.

Hugh lets drop to the hangman Ned Dennis that he and Tappertit are planning an expedition to attack the Haredales at the Warren out near Chigwell. Gashford appears and eggs them on. The rioters under Hugh and Dennis march to Chigwell and first loot the Maypole then break into and burn down the Warren.

Barnaby Rudge, left to guard the Boot since Hugh fears he will side with the Haredales if accompanying the rioters to Chigwell, is arrested by soldiers and jailed. He is taken before the magistrate Sir John Fielding, blind half-brother of the novelist Henry Fielding and like Lord George a historic personage. He is condemned to death. He receives a free pardon, coaxed from the authorities by Gabriel Varden.

BARNABY RUDGE.
THE MAYPOLE [By G. Cattermole
Built in the days of King Henry the Eighth; it had many gable ends, huge zig-zag chimneys, and its windows were diamond-pane lattices.—Barnaby, chap. i

'The Maypole' by George Cattermole.

Gabriel's lovely daughter Dolly and her friend Emma Haredale are imprisoned by the rioters and threatened with rape by Hugh and Sim Tappertit. A feebly managed scene. Dickens's highly graphic descriptions of violence to property meant he would have had to be equally detailed over sexual violence. Yet 1840s readers would not have swallowed rape. So after a bit of bosom-heaving by the two girls and some heavy breathing by their assailants, forcible sex gets shelved.

By now well into his stride, Dickens doesn't let up on his larger theme. It comprises the arbitrariness of rioters; their folly in breaking the law openly, before witnesses, tempered only by their determination to intimidate any who would testify against them in subsequent criminal proceedings; their readiness to betray each other; the way they are easily influenced by a cunning manipulator like Gashford; their preference for settling old scores against individuals they can see, strike and torment over enthusiasm for an abstract cause, here Protestantism, as against an equally abstract target, here Catholicism; their pathetic gullibility faced with anyone canny enough to wear a badge suggesting sympathy, here a blue cockade (sported by Sir John Chester, who in a wonderful scene takes it off once the rioters have passed by and folds it away for use in the next tricky confrontation); their swigging alcohol to lend them Dutch courage; their delight in rape and looting on the side, with arson to maintain fervour.

Change the cause and target a bit, multiply the cunning manipulators, narrow the focus of the mob's violent hatred and you see how riot morphs to revolution. *Barnaby Rudge* is the dress rehearsal for *A Tale of Two Cities*, but, as with some stage dramas, turns in a better performance than does the first night. And it surely influenced Dostoevsky's *The Devils*, generally recognised as the archetype of every attempt since at what stirrers-up-of-trouble call 'direct action'. (See also 'Dickens Abroad'.)

A Christmas Carol

Published 1843

'In came Bob [Cratchit] . . .[with] Tiny Tim upon his shoulder.' (Stave Three), an illustration by Jessie Willcox Smith.

Characters

Christmas Past, Ghost of

Mixture in appearance of child and elderly gentleman, like the late Quentin Crisp, though more gorgeously attired; conjures up Scrooge's youthful experiences. Voiced by Whoopi Goldberg in the same 1997 cartoon *A Christmas Carol* that Tim Curry voiced Scrooge in; Gary Coleman in the 2003 made-for TV film.

Christmas Present, Ghost of

A jovial personage, but with his serious side, as indeed the original Jove had; manifests himself to Scrooge in a robe open to his navel and surrounded by a Fortnum & Mason-like cornucopia of Yuletide provender; addresses Scrooge as 'man', like a South African or West Indian. Played by Edward Woodward in the 1984 made-for TV film; William Shatner in the 2003 one.

Christmas Yet to Come, Ghost of

Shrouded in black, its eyes alone visible, it completes Scrooge's psychological collapse.

Cratchit, Belinda Daughter to Bob Cratchit.

Cratchit, Bob

Scrooge's clerk; earns 15 shillings (75p) a week (say £4,875 a year today); lives in Camden Town, much as Dickens had when a child (Bayham Street to be exact). Played by Alfie Bass (see also *A Tale of Two Cities*) in a 1962 American TV musical adaptation called *Mr. Scrooge*; David Warner in the 1984 made-for TV film.

Cratchit, Martha Milliner's apprentice daughter to Bob.

Cratchit, Mrs Bob's wife. Played by Hermione Baddeley in the 1951 film; Susannah York in the 1984 made-for TV one.

Mrs Cratchit, by Harold Copping.

Jacob Marley's ghost drawn by John Leech, 1843.

Cratchit, Peter Bob's eldest son.

Dilber, Mrs Corpse-dresser.

Fezziwig, Mr The young Scrooge's boss. Played by Timothy Bateson in the 1984 made-for-TV film.

Fred Scrooge's nephew.

Joe Dealer in clothing and other oddments taken from corpses.

Marley, Jacob, Ghost of

Dead exactly seven years before the story starts, having expired on Christmas Eve; appears chain-girt to Scrooge, his erstwhile business partner; his name still visible with Scrooge's above the door of the firm's warehouse, which together with the counting-house is in the City of London, implicitly near Cornhill since Bob Cratchit slides down Cornhill for recreation on his way home. Played by Basil Rathbone in the 1954 TV musical involving Fredric March (see against Scrooge below); Alec Guinness in the 1970 film musical *Scrooge*; Michael Hordern in two TV adaptations.

Scrooge, Ebenezer

Hard-hearted merchant who becomes a warm-hearted one by the intervention of four ghosts. Played by Seymour Hicks, who made the role his own from 1901 to 1935, both in theatre and a 1913 silent film *Scrooge* (US title *Old Scrooge*), also a 1935 talkie again called *Scrooge*; Lionel Barrymore in a US Christmas Day radio dramatisation of 1934, repeated annually till 1953 apart from 1936, when his brother John Barrymore stood in, and 1938, when Orson Welles did; Ronald Colman in a 1941 gramophone recording; Alec Guinness in a BBC radio production of 1951 and annually for some years afterwards; Laurence Olivier in a 1953 radio dramatisation; John Carradine in a 1947 TV adaptation; Ralph Richardson in a 1951 one; Alastair Sim in the 1951 film (UK title *Scrooge*, US one *A Christmas Carol*), Sim also voicing Scrooge in the Oscar-winning 1971 cartoon film; Fredric March in a 1954 TV musical; Basil Rathbone (see also against Marley above) in a 1956 TV musical called *The Stingiest Man in Town* and a 1958 TV adaptation; Albert Finney in the 1970 film musical; Michael Hordern in a 1977 TV adaptation; Walter Matthau as voice-over in a 1978 TV cartoon musical called, like its 1956 predecessor, *The Stingiest Man in Town*; George C Scott in the 1984 made-for TV film; Michael Caine in *The*

Muppet Christmas Carol (1992); among others Tony Randall (1996), Roddy McDowell (alternating 1997), Roger Daltrey (1998), Frank Langella (2000), Tim Curry (2001, he having also done the Scrooge voice-over in a 1997 cartoon film), F Murray Abraham (2002) and Jim Dale (2003) in *A Christmas Carol: The Musical* (mounted annually on Broadway 1994–2003); Kelsey Grammer in a 2004 TV version of the same musical; Jim Carrey in a 2009 digitised film; Henry Winkler took the Scrooge role of Benedict Slade in the film *An American Christmas Carol* (1979), set in 1930s Depression New England; in the film *Scrooged* (1988), which also tampered with the original, a modern-day TV producer (Bill Murray) takes the Scrooge role; Ron Moody in a Cardiff New Theatre production during the 2006–07 winter season.

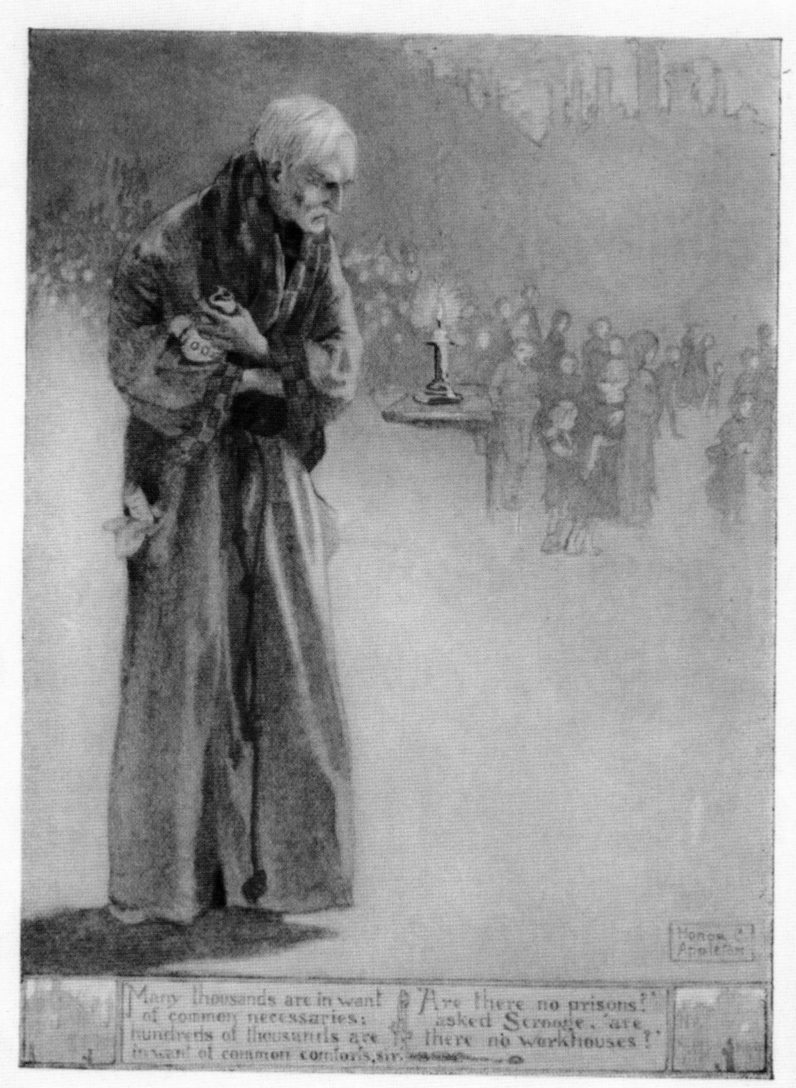

Ebenezer Scrooge, by Honor C Appleton.

Tim, Tiny

Bob Cratchit's crippled son; his origins are to be found in *Nicholas Nickleby*, where the Cheerybles' chief clerk, Tim by name, in his leisure hours thinks up treats for a crippled boy neighbour.

Tiny Tim, in a drawing by Harold Copping.

A Christmas Carol

Story Commentary

Ebenezer Scrooge, by Honor C Appleton.

One of the greatest successes of Dickens's career, and the only non-novel of his still widely read, *A Christmas Carol* started as a frankly commercial project to counterbalance the disappointing early sales of *Martin Chuzzlewit*. Dickens conceived it in October 1843 and had finished it by early December. Part of the time he had spent visiting his now married sister Fanny in Manchester, his chief purpose there being to raise funds for an educational institution to benefit working people. He gave a speech (alongside the MPs Richard Cobden and Benjamin Disraeli, a future Prime Minister) in which he pointed to ignorance as the parent of misery and crime. Ignorance and Want are the two feral children the Ghost of Christmas Present reveals to Scrooge in *A Christmas Carol*.

The action opens on a foggy Christmas Eve just after three in the afternoon, but dark already. Scrooge has a small fire. Bob Cratchit has a positively minute one, and for him to try and beg more coal from the office's only coal-box, which is kept in Scrooge's room, would be a sacking offence. Scrooge's nephew Fred drops by to wish his uncle 'Merry Christmas' but is rebuffed with Scrooge's famous catch-phrases 'Bah!' and 'Humbug!' Scrooge does at least wish him 'Good afternoon!' So far, then, he is at worst an irritable humanist. Hardly a hanging offence.

Two charitable souls also drop by. They ask Scrooge for a contribution to buying the poor some Christmas cheer. They too get rebuffed, Scrooge expressing himself a strong supporter of rugged individualism and non-intervention in economic cycles, to say nothing of his belief that deaths among the poor will decrease the surplus population. For Scrooge is pretty much a doctrinaire utilitarian. His getting the better of the philanthropists puts him in something like good humour with himself.

Page from manuscript of A Christmas Carol.

Stave I.

Marley's Ghost.

Marley was dead: to begin with. There is no doubt whatever about that. The register of his burial was signed by the clergyman, the clerk, the undertaker, and the chief mourner. Scrooge signed it; and Scrooge's name was good upon 'Change, for anything he chose to put his hand to. Old Marley was as dead as a door-nail.

Mind! I don't mean to say, that I know, of my own knowledge, what there is particularly dead about a door-nail. I might have been inclined, myself, to regard a coffin-nail as the deadest piece of ironmongery in the trade. But the wisdom of our ancestors is in the simile; and my unhallowed hands shall not disturb it, or the country's done for. You will therefore permit me to repeat, emphatically, that Marley was as dead as a door-nail.

Scrooge knew he was dead? Of course he did. How could it be otherwise? Scrooge and he were partners for I don't know how many years. Scrooge was his sole executor, his sole administrator, his sole assign, his sole residuary legatee, his sole friend and sole mourner. And even Scrooge was not so dreadfully cut up by the sad event, but that he was an excellent man of business on the very day of the funeral, and solemnised it with an undoubted bargain.

The mention of Marley's funeral brings me back to the point I started from. There is no doubt that Marley was dead. This must be distinctly understood, or nothing wonderful can come of the story I am going to relate. If we were not perfectly convinced that Hamlet's Father died before the play began, there would be nothing more remarkable in his taking a stroll at night, in an easterly wind, upon his own ramparts, than there would be in any other middle-aged gentleman rashly turning out after dark in a breezy spot—say Saint Paul's Churchyard for instance—literally to astonish his son's weak mind.

Scrooge never painted out old Marley's name. There it

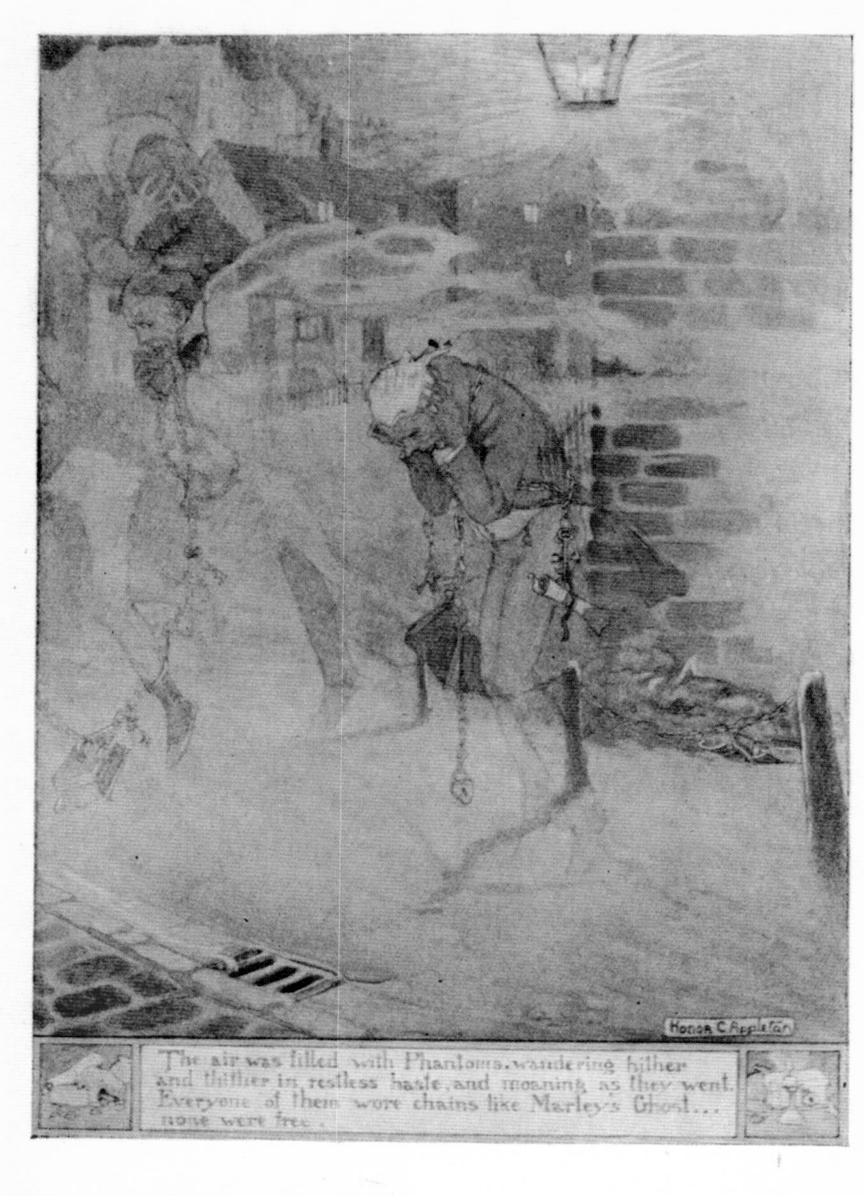

Honor C Appleton
The air was filled with Phantoms, wandering hither
and thither in restless haste, and moaning as they went.
Everyone of them wore chains like Marley's Ghost...
none were free.

Ebenezer Scrooge, by Honor C Appleton.

Scrooge lives in chambers that were once Marley's. He is the building's sole resident. He thinks he sees Marley's face in the external front-door knocker, glowing a little 'like a bad lobster in a dark cellar'. His apartment comprises a sitting-room, bedroom and lumber-room, modest accommodation for a rich man. Scrooge has a head cold, so takes gruel for supper. His state of health may explain his subsequent hallucinations, starting with the door-knocker. He now 'sees' Marley again in the old Dutch tiles representing biblical scenes that surround the fireplace.

Marley's ghost appears to Scrooge dressed in 18th-century fashion and asks if he, Scrooge, believes in him, Marley's ghost. Scrooge turns all rationalist facetiousness, suggesting his senses are no true guide to a phenomenon's really existing since they may be disordered by a faulty digestion acting on poorly cooked comestibles. His cheap pun ('You may be more gravy than grave') is an artistic blunder. The unenlightened Scrooge would no more have uttered a quip, especially a food-related one, than Mr Murdstone in *David Copperfield* would have set David a sum involving the homely element 'double-Gloucester cheeses'. (This point about Murdstone is made by George Orwell in his essay on Dickens in *Inside the Whale* as an example of how Dickens's love of domestic detail often defeated his wider novelist's purpose.)

Marley's ghost takes off a bandage round its head (tied on corpses to stop the lower jaw falling open). This causes Scrooge to lose all self-possession. He falls to his knees, hides his face in his hands and pleads for mercy. The ghost apostrophises him as 'Man of the worldly mind!' Though a bit pompous, it sufficiently expresses what each of Scrooge's ghostly visitors finds objectionable about him: less his money-grubbing than his 18th-century scepticism. For this is the 1840s and the religious revival is at white heat.

Marley's ghost tells Scrooge he will have three spirit visitors. They are his sole hope of escaping Marley's fate, which is to wander the world unable to help the afflicted. This ducks the question as to why you should care about the afflicted, which up till now Scrooge palpably has not. But applying reason to ghost stories is a barren exercise. Scrooge goes to bed and falls straight asleep.

It is past two. He wakes to hear a nearby clock strike twelve. It is pitch dark. He is alarmed lest it be daytime. To his relief he hears no noise of passers-by when he opens the window. Relief, because he is worried that if daytime has been eclipsed, payments to him due within three days of sight by the debtor will become 'a mere United States' security'. This dig by Dickens at America and its lax banking system matches the anti-American satire he was simultaneously spewing out in *Martin Chuzzlewit*.

Ebenezer Scrooge, by Honor C Appleton.

At the stroke of one Scrooge is confronted by the Ghost of Christmas Past. It takes Scrooge back to the scenes of his childhood. These include a solitary-small-boy-Scrooge left for the holidays at school. Dickens resurrects his own juvenile reading at this point, such as the tale of Ali Baba. Scrooge's sister Fan (short for Fanny, or Frances, mother of Scrooge's nephew Fred) makes her appearance. Scrooge is shown to be the product of a once-strict father (who later softens) and insensitive schooling by harsh masters. We cut to what is implicitly the young Scrooge's first employer, a fat old fellow called Fezziwig, the model of the jolly, paternalist boss so dear to Dickens's heart.

Scrooge's cold one is melting already. He wishes to say a word or two to Bob his clerk, clearly a kind word, but is unable to intervene in the vision. Next Scrooge's young love reproaches him for preferring the pursuit of wealth to her. She releases Scrooge from their engagement. Cut to a scene years later when the girl, Belle, is married to another. Her husband tells her how he has seen Scrooge that day, attending Marley's deathbed.

The Ghost of Christmas Present succeeds his brother of Christmas Past. Among his supernatural accomplishments is the ability to sprinkle from his torch incense and drops of water that dispel people's bad humour. Scrooge starts an argument with him over the Sunday shop-closing laws. The Ghost (called by now 'Spirit') disingenuously shuffles off the blame on ungenerous-minded bigots. (His supernatural powers could presumably put that right, after all.) He also attacks Scrooge's utilitarian doctrine of 'surplus population'. Scrooge has no answer to this and hangs his head in shame. The ghost transports him to a moor where miners work, probably

Scrooge buying a turkey, by Harold Copping.

those digging for tin in Cornwall, which Dickens had visited a few weeks before starting *A Christmas Carol*, then on to a light-house, then out to sea to a ship's crew. Everyone has a Christmas song on his lips. The Ghost takes Scrooge on to nephew Fred and his family circle. It grows visibly older each moment, for its lifespan extends only to Twelfth Night.

Scrooge is now confronted by the Ghost of Christmas Yet to Come. This phenomenon disdains the use of words, a gesticulating hand its sole means of communication. It shows Scrooge various acquaintances who calmly, even indifferently, receive news of his death. Then it shows him his own gravestone. Scrooge is by now a psychological wreck. He has hitherto confined himself to falling on his knees. At this point he clutches the Ghost's hand and holds up his own ones, praying to avoid the fate in store for him. The Ghost shrinks, collapses and dwindles into a bedpost.

Bob Cratchit and his family, by Honor C Appleton.

And now Scrooge wakes and finds it Christmas Day, clear bright weather, church bells tolling. He is transformed into a cheerful, merry, almost euphoric type, not far off a hysteric. The effect to thoughtful readers is disconcerting. For the odd thing is, that whereas Scrooge's reaction to the ghosts was religious (the genuflections, the praying, the clasping of hands, his accompanying the Ghost of Christmas Present in the latter's sacerdotal aspersions, or sprinklings of holy fluid), his reformed character degenerates into frenetic consumerism actuated by nothing more profound than Rotarian matiness.

He splashes out a tip of half a crown (over £40 today) on an errand boy to go and buy a prize turkey, splashes out on donating the turkey to the Cratchits, splashes out on sending the errand boy to Camden Town by cab with it, splashes out on the charitable project he spurned only the day before and drops in uninvited to his nephew Fred's, imposing himself as Christmas luncheon guest. He raises Bob Cratchit's wages, cares for Tiny Tim and becomes another Cheeryble.

Dickens would have done better to introduce something like the excellent Patrick Stewart 1999 TV film take on *A Christmas Carol*. (Stewart also gave a one-man performance of *A Christmas*

Carol in London over the Christmas of 1993–94.) Here Scrooge's coffin during the Ghost-of-Christmas-Yet-to-Come visitation is shown bearing the pregnant letters RIP (*Requiescat In Pace*, or 'May He/She Rest in Peace'). The 'RIP' suggests that Scrooge has turned Catholic by his death, or at the very least come over all High Church Anglican. And this would have made historical sense, since the High Church and Back to Rome movements were flourishing at the time.

More importantly, it would have made better artistic sense. For if you embody your Christmas message in spirit form, and make constant references to Jesus Christ's benevolent treatment of the afflicted and children, as Dickens does throughout *A Christmas Carol*, you should make your flinty-hearted central character turn over a new leaf spiritually, not just neurologically. Sudden and total reverses of character springing from a religious crisis are historically common. Anyway, Christmas is one of the two main Christian festivals.

Honor C Appleton
'Am I that man who lay upon the bed,' he cried, upon his knees. 'Good Spirit.. assure me that I yet may change
these shadows you have shown me by an altered life.. Oh, tell me I may sponge away the writing on this stone

Ebenezer Scrooge, by Honor C Appleton.

As it is, one would think Scrooge had got at psychotropic drugs and undergone his massive personality realignment that way. The upshot is that Scrooge embodies in his reformed state a materialism which is just as soulless as his old money-grubbing. The only difference is the new improved model Scrooge spraying its promiscuous shower of largesse left, right and centre like a one-man Welfare State.

A Christmas Carol is the most televised, filmed, recorded, radio-broadcast, animated, digitised, burlesqued and set-to-music work in Dickens's entire output (and almost certainly anyone else's). It is additionally by far the most often alluded to. The major examples, and the eminent actors involved, are mentioned in the 'Characters' list above. Even excluding the lesser ones, they bulk it out quite enough.

Dickens chose *A Christmas Carol* for the first of his public readings, those bravura perfomances which so dominated his later career, kicking off in Birmingham on the day after Boxing Day of 1852. Patrick Stewart in 1988 staged one-man readings in London and New York. They have been revived since. As a story, not only has *A Christmas Carol* never died, but it transcends national frontiers and artistic genres. Marcello Mastroianni appeared in an Italian film *Non è mai troppo tardi* (1953; 'It is Never Too Late') based on it. James Stewart starred in a TV Western, *The Six Shooter* (Christmas 1953), also based on it. Jack Palance played a brutal land-grabber Scrooge type in *Ebenezer* (1997), a Canadian TV Western based on it. Marcel Marceau mimed it. Benjamin Britten set it to music (*Men of Goodwill: Variations on 'A Christmas Carol'*). Thea Musgrave has turned it into an opera, first performed in 1979.

A Christmas Carol has inspired a strip cartoon, an earth-bound sci-fi novel involving zombies, a space-wide play based on the *Star Trek* cosmos and a time-travelling episode of *Dr Who*. On top of that there are annual performances by local theatre groups all over the USA and Britain, readings and recordings galore, puppet versions, a quiz show based on the story and renditions by filmdom's leading 'Toons (Bugs Bunny, Daffy Duck, The Flintstones, Mickey Mouse, Mr Magoo).

BobCratchit and his children, by Arthur Dixon.

Mr Fezziwig's Ball, by John Leech.

In the week of Christmas 2010 alone there were half a dozen or more versions plus other *A Christmas Carol*-inspired programmes shown on television. They included the Ross Kemp made-for-TV film of the year 2000 in which he plays Eddie Scrooge, a London loan shark, and that most ominous-sounding of entertainments, 'a spoof version ... screwball comedy' Radio 4 offering called *Marley Was Dead*, introduced by Jonathan Dimbleby and – to be fair – starring Ian McKellen and our old friend Patrick Stewart. The Nativity story, by contrast, hardly got a look in.

Ebenezer Scrooge, by Honor C Appleton.

Tiny Tim and his father, by Harold Copping.

Martin Chuzzlewit

Monthly serial, 1843 to 1844
Book published 1844

Pecksniff (centre) dismisses Tom Pinch (right) lest he reveal Pecksniff's advances to Mary Graham, Old Martin's (left) protégée.

Characters

Bailey or Bailey 'Junior', Benjamin/Uncle Ben/Uncle Barnwell Initially boy in Mrs Todgers's employ; later factotum to Tigg Montague.

Bevan, Dr Benevolent acquaintance of young Martin (Chuzzlewit) in New York.

Bib, Julius Washington Merryweather 'Gentleman in the lumber line'.

Brick, Jefferson *New York Rowdy Journal* war correspondent.

Buffum, Oscar Member of Bib's entourage.

Bullamy Porter at the Anglo-Bengalee Disinterested Loan and Life Insurance Company's City branch.

Choke, Cyrus (General) American real estate promoter who encourages young Martin and Mark Tapley to settle in the pest-ridden swamp of Eden; they sink Mark's savings of £37-10-6 (£37.53, or just over £4,500 today) and Martin's of just under £8 (say £975 today) in the venture, Martin characteristically allotting himself 50% equity on the grounds that, although his cash investment is under 25% of Mark's, his 'professional knowledge and ability' make up the difference; Mark sadly acquiesces; the pound sterling was then worth about five dollars, and their down payment on a 50-acre plot of land in Eden is $150, or £30 (say $18,750/£3,750 today).

Chollop, Hannibal Eden neighbour of young Martin and Mark.

Chuffey, 'Old'

Clerk to Anthony and Jonas Chuzzlewit; words of his to the effect that he knows something suspicious about Anthony's death decide Jonas to get him 'looked after' by Mrs Gamp, thus keeping him secluded and with luck, given Mrs Gamp's negligence, hastening his end; Chuffey later spills the beans about Anthony's death. Played by John Mills (see also *A Tale of Two Cities* and *Great Expectations*) in the 1994 televisation.

Chuzzlewit, Anthony

Brother of old Martin (Chuzzlewit); aged 80, says his son Jonas, though Chuffey claims he was 70 at death, a discrepancy ascribable to Chuffy's senility; senior

Bailey 'Junior' (above) and Jefferson Brick (below).

proprietor of Anthony Chuzzlewit and Son, Manchester Warehousemen; lives with Jonas 'over the shop ... somewhere behind the Post Office', i.e. St Martin's Le Grand, near the Stock Exchange in the City of London.

Chuzzlewit, George Bachelor 'cousin' (presumably of old Martin from the context); pimply and stout.

Chuzzlewit, Jonas

Son of Anthony; given the Victorians' tendency to early marriage and procreation, would normally be between 50 and 60, but Dickens calls him a young man (say 35 at most), so Anthony must have begotten him aged between 45 and 60. Played by Keith Allen, father of the pop singer Lily Allen, in the 1994 televisation.

Chuzzlewit, 'old' Martin

Well-to-do grandfather of 'young' Martin (see below), cousin to Pecksniff, patriarch of the Chuzzlewits generally; irascible and suspicious but inclined towards integrity, though it is distinctly unattractive how late in the story he promotes a false view of himself until, at a moment of his own choosing, he dazzles his circle with a revelation of his capacity for true feeling (a variant of Pecksniff's hypocrisy, really). Played by Paul Scofield in the 1994 televisation.

Chuzzlewit, 'young' Martin

Grandson of old Martin, also (ultimately) the novel's hero, though he needs first to be purged of his character defects; is, however, from the first generous; initially self-centred (rather than, as Dickens claims, selfish, the distinction being between someone who cannot see other people's point of view – a frequent failing in young people – and someone who can, but who rides roughshod over it for his own benefit); his illness in America turns him into a decent human being, Dickens's acknowledgement of an American environment's ability to instil virtue surely mitigating his satire at the American nation's expense.

Chuzzlewit, Mrs Ned Widowed sister-in-law of old Martin.

Cicero Ex-slave engaged by Mark Tapley in New York to help with luggage and render him, Mark, 'jolly'.

Codger, Miss Literary lady living in Watertoast.

Crimple (né Crimp), David Pawnbroker's clerk, later company secretary and 'resident director' of the Anglo-Bengalee Disinterested Loan and Life Insurance Company at £800 a year (say £100,000 today); absconds with its funds.

Diver, Colonel Editor New York Rowdy Journal; New York-bound shipmate of young Martin.

Dunkle, Ginery (Dr) Describes himself as 'of Troy [Missouri?]', but currently residing in the National Hotel, Watertoast.

Fips Middleman acting for a mysterious well-wisher who employs Tom Pinch at £100 a year (say £12,500 today) as a book-cataloguer in the Temple (a haunt of lawyers off Fleet Street in what is now the East Central Four district of London); the well-wisher turns out to be old Martin Chuzzlewit.

Fladdock, General Fat, tight-uniformed military figure at the Norrises' in New York.

Gamp, Mrs (Sarah/Sairah/Sairey)

Bibulous and slatternly nurse; frequently alludes to 'Mrs Harris' as friend and reference, though there is no evidence of the latter's existence; among her possessions is a large, unwieldy umbrella, whence the slang term 'gamp'.

Gander Lodger at Mrs Todgers's.

Graham, Mary Orphan; companion and adoptive daughter to old Martin.

Groper, Colonel Citizen of Watertoast.

Hominy, Mrs American authoress.

Jinkins Fishmonger's book-keeper; lodger at Mrs Todgers's.

Jobling, John Medical Officer, Anglo-Bengalee Disinterested Loan and Life Insurance Company.

Kedgick, Captain Landlord National Hotel, Watertoast, where young Martin and Mark Tapley stay when acquiring their land at Eden (itself far distant from Watertoast); arranges levée for Martin as being a public curiosity since, as Kedgick reveals to Mark Tapley when it's too late to withdraw from the Eden project, no one who's gone to Eden lives to return.

Kettle, La Fayette Prominent Watertoast citizen.

Lewsome Invalid tended by Mrs Gamp, also ex-schoolmate of John Westlock, who pays his medical and nursing costs; has supplied Jonas Chuzzlewit in the past with drugs Jonas intends using to shorten his father Anthony's life.

Lupin, Mrs

Landlady of the Blue Dragon inn in the village where Pecksniff lives; eventually marries Mark Tapley. Played in the 1994 televisation by Lynda Bellingham, the 'Oxo Mum' in the TV commercials for that substance 1983–99.

Moddle, Augustus Inmate of Mrs Todgers's boarding house; is booked to marry Charity Pecksniff but stands her up at the last minute.

Montague, Tigg

Montague Tigg (see below) reincarnated as the Anglo-Bengalee Disinterested Loan and Life Insurance Company's chairman.

Mould Undertaker instructed to arrange Anthony Chuzzlewit's funeral.

Mould, Mrs His wife.

Nadgett

'Private eye' spying on Jonas Chuzzlewit for Tigg Montague.

Norris family Acquaintances of young Martin in New York; obsessed with the British upper classes; veer between patronising amusement at 'negroes' and a conviction of their unsuitability as comminglers with whites, all the time proclaiming themselves abolitionists; in short, outwardly liberal, retrograde within.

Montague Tigg (above) and Seth Pecksniff (below).

Tom Pinch (above) and Hon Elijah Pogram (below).

Pawkins, Major Pennsylvanian acquaintance of Col Diver.

Pecksniff, Charity ('Cherry')

Pecksniff's elder daughter; after being jilted by her cousin Jonas Chuzzlewit then hearing of Tom Pinch's fight with Jonas, proclaims herself Tom's friend.

Pecksniff, Mercy ('Merry')

Pecksniff's comely younger daughter. Played by Julia Sawalha in the 1994 televisation.

Pecksniff, Seth

Architect and land surveyor, but never known to design anything subsequently erected; lives off rent-collecting and fees from pupils (whose designs he sometimes pirates, including young Martin's for a grammar school); cousin of old Martin Chuzzlewit; lives in a village 20 miles from Salisbury (which if southwards, southeastwards or southwestwards would be nearer Bournemouth, Southampton or Winchester; since it lies amidst downs is probably within the Andover-Devizes-Warminster triangle, perhaps near Pewsey Down). Played by Tom Wilkinson (also Narrator in the 1999 televisation of *David Copperfield*) in the 1994 televisation.

Pinch, Ruth Tom's sister; taken by Tom to lodgings in Islington, whose landlord happens to be Nadgett.

Pinch, Tom

Former pupil of Pecksniff, the premium having been paid by his grandmother, housekeeper to a gentleman (much as Dickens's grandmother had been to Lord Crewe); when the story opens, a drudge in Pecksniff's employ; Dickens as author falls into the same odd habit with Tom Pinch that Grandfather in *The Old Curiosity Shop* does with Little Nell, viz. addressing him in archaic language ('thee', 'thou art', 'thy'). Played by Philip Franks in the 1994 televisation; see also *Bleak House*.

Pip Hanger-on of Tigg Montague.

Pogram, Hon Elijah 'Member of Congress' (ambiguous: he could be a Senator or a Member of the House of Representatives); meets young Martin on Watertoast-bound steamer.

Prig, Betsey Fellow nurse with Mrs Gamp. Played by Joan Sims in the 1994 televisation.

Scadder, Zephaniah Front-office agent for the Eden project.

Simmons, Will/Bill Carter; gives Martin Junior lift to London's western outskirts.

Slyme, Chevy

Cousin of Pecksniff; nephew of old Martin (Chuzzlewit); joins the police force and is among the officers who arrest Jonas Chuzzlewit for murder.

Spottletoe, Mr Kinsman by marriage of Chuzzlewits.

Spottletoe, Mrs, neé Slyme Wife of above; niece of old Martin Chuzzlewit and cousin of Chevy Slyme, whose father was her father's brother (i.e. two brothers called Slyme must have married two sisters called Chuzzlewit).

Sweedlepipe, Poll (Paul) Landlord to Mrs Gamp; the unusual abbreviation 'Poll' for 'Paul' derived from Poll Green, Dickens's blacking warehouse fellow-child labourer.

Tacker Mould's assistant.

Tapley, Mark

Servant at the Blue Dragon, whose employ he is leaving when we first encounter him; insists on being 'jolly' all the time, especially when things look blackest; binds himself to Martin as latter's manservant in preparation for their voyage to America, and for no wages, a remarkable instance of an immigrant to the New World voluntarily submitting himself to unpaid labour as opposed to being taken there as a slave; gets taken on as cook of the *Screw* on his and Martin's homeward voyage from New York, his wages paying Martin's passage.

Poll Sweedlepipe (above) and Mark Tapley (below).

Tigg, Montague (see also Montague, Tigg)

Seedy friend of Chevy Slyme, whom he calls 'Chiv'.

Todgers, M (Mrs) Lodging house proprietress in City of London. Dickens does not reveal what the 'M' stands for.

Westlock, John

Disgusted ex-pupil of Pecksniff's, having paid him a £500 premium (well over £60,000 today) and £70 lodgings a year for five years (nearly £45,000 today) but having got nothing like that in value; tries to make Pinch see Pecksniff's faults; lives in Furnival's Inn, High Holborn (a former roost of Dickens), in the West Central district of London; marries Ruth Pinch.

Toppit, Miss Literary lady living in Watertoast.

Wolf Hanger-on of Tigg Montague; involved with a weekly paper.

Martin Chuzzlewit

Story Commentary

By the 1840s Dickens's pace was slackening. He still produced good solid novels. But the copious flow of the 1830s, with each successor treading on its predecessor's heels, had receded. Two years passed between the appearance of *Barnaby Rudge*, which had been fermenting for years anyway, and *Martin Chuzzlewit*. This was an eternity by Dickens's former standards.

Mr Pecksniff, by Kyd.

Another five years then elapsed before *Dombey and Son*. True, Dickens meanwhile produced lesser works, such as his *Christmas Books*. Yet the novels, his greatest gift to mankind, now lost some of the earlier fantastic sparkle and did not develop compensating weightiness till *Dombey*.

Despite the flaws in *The Old Curiosity Shop*, it was a success in consolidating Dickens's fame abroad, particularly America. (There is no proof that New Yorkers mobbed the latest ship from Britain to ask if Little Nell had died, but the legend to that effect is evidence of Dickens's transatlantic popularity then.)

Chuzzlewit, in contrast, proved disappointing both for Dickens's earnings and his reputation in America. This brings us to his two sojourns abroad, another aspect of the 1840s as they affected Dickens. The first involved the tour he undertook of America in 1842. Americans didn't like Dickens's home truths. And Dickens didn't much like their pestering of himself and was furious at their pirating of his works (which is why he makes Pecksniff pinch his pupils' designs; it's the quickest way to point out his loathesomeness). The other was the Dickens family's migrating to the Continent. Retrenchment was the aim here. Dickens had incurred heavier outgoings in Britain than even a colossus of his stature could underwrite.

How does *Martin Chuzzlewit* read today? It has its admirers, notably Peter Ackroyd. Dickens himself thought it at the time his best story yet. But it is slow to get up steam. First we meet the awful Pecksniff, his elder hoity-toity daughter, younger affected one and the now familiar victim-cum-sexual-wallflower figure in the shape of the innocent Tom Pinch.

Presently Pecksniff's rich and frail cousin old Martin Chuzzlewit puts up at the local inn, the Blue Dragon. Greedy Chuzzlewit relatives gather, vultures circling above a stricken wayfarer. Yet all Dickens can extract in on-stage dramatics is wordy speeches by Pecksniff and, in off-stage developments, old Martin's sudden departure while the relatives bicker *chez* Pecksniff.

Cue young Martin Chuzzlewit, old Martin's grandson. Young Martin loves, and is loved by, one Mary Graham, old Martin's young lady companion. She is well paid by old Martin for now but will have no security once he dies, or so he tells her. (She is also, we later discover, loved by Tom Pinch, but unrequitedly.)

Old Martin thinks his grandson has undermined Mary's loyalty to himself by getting involved with her. The two Martins thus quarrel. Young Martin has answered an advertisement of Pecksniff's for a resident architect's pupil, chiefly to irritate his grandfather, and is accepted. By his earliest dealings with Tom Pinch he shows himself a self-centred cub.

Such a cast of characters looks promising. But *Chuzzlewit* suffers from flaccidity. A major problem is its 'villains'. Many of the unpleasant characters in *Martin Chuzzlewit* don't really qualify – though God knows there *are* many, itself off-putting to readers. Pecksniff is a hypocrite, and not just in proclaiming high-minded sentiments which no one could live up to. He is also a secret drinker, at Mrs Todgers's spilling over into an open one. Old Martin is grumpy, manipulative, narrow-minded. Young Martin's shortcomings we have mentioned already.

But faults like these are only ones of character, moral slippage, minor sins. They do not render their possessors wicked, as Fagin, Bill Sikes, Ralph Nickleby, Wackford Squeers, the Brass siblings and Quilp are wicked. Moreover, hypocrisy contrasts what a man says with what he does. This inevitably makes a hypocrite gabby. It can work on stage, as Molière's *Tartuffe* does. In print, bereft of dramatic action, it risks becoming tedious. Pecksniff's endless moralising slows the pace.

Dickens gives us two successes in the villain class. They include Tigg Montague, a nicely pencilled sketch of a glib, *faux bonhomme* and fraudulent company promoter. And there is Jonas Chuzzlewit (though his favourite ejaculation 'Ecod' [Ah, God] was an archaism even then). Jonas is a nasty piece of work in a way that, being for most of the book understated, is more modern, therefore believable, than the Jonsonian staginess of such as Quilp and Fagin. He is vindictive, duplicitous, mean-spirited, avaricious, underhand, vengeful but cowardly and pawkily lustful rather than gloriously priapic. He is also parricidally inclined. His being revealed as a murderer therefore comes as a near anticlimax, not least because it is heralded in the most glaring way. Dickens could seldom resist this with major plot twists.

Where Dickens is particularly good is in depicting Jonas's naïveté, despite his business experience. Tigg Montague exploits this by hinting to Jonas that Jonas and the Anglo-Bengalee's directors are all rogues together. One only wishes Dickens would describe Tigg Montague's swindling of a fellow crook in more detail. Bertholt Brecht in *A Threepenny Novel* succeeded. Dickens lacked the knowledge of finance.

After welcoming young Martin to his Wiltshire house, Pecksniff and his daughters travel to London. There Pecksniff sees old Martin; the latter expresses his intention of making his home with Pecksniff. Pecksniff, taking this to mean he will be old Martin's heir, agrees. On returning to Wiltshire he therefore ignores young Martin, who so resents the insult as to threaten Pecksniff. Pecksniff steps back, trips and falls to the floor. Young Martin storms out. He decides to seek his fortune in America.

Back in London, Anthony Chuzzlewit has a stroke and dies. His son Jonas feigns filial devotion lest gossip assume he facilitated the death, which it later turns out he had intended doing but never actually pulled off.

Jonas hitherto has appeared keen on Charity Pecksniff. He negotiates with Pecksniff a dowry of £4,000 for her hand in marriage (say £500,000 today). He accompanies Pecksniff to Wiltshire to continue negotiations. Presently he declares he was all along after Mercy instead. She rejects him, archly calling him 'Griffin' in reference to his uncouth malevolence. Jonas imperturbably maintains his suit for her but ups the ante, requesting of Pecksniff a £5,000 dowry (say £625,000 today), equivalent to a 25 per cent surcharge.

Pecksniff learns from Tom Pinch that old Martin and Mary are about to arrive. An awkward confrontation takes place involving Charity, Jonas, old Martin, Mary, Mercy, Tom and Pecksniff, each wary of or secretly detesting one or more of the others. Old Martin announces that he is putting up at the Blue Dragon.

He asks Tom to accompany him and Mary there. Tom (who at this stage still genuinely admires Pecksniff) praises Pecksniff to old Martin. The latter, knowing Pecksniff better, for the time being writes Tom off as just another designing rogue. Later he comes to appreciate Tom's solid worth. On returning home Tom is waylaid by Jonas, jealous of Tom's apparent favour with old Martin. Jonas and Tom struggle. Tom strikes Jonas, drawing blood.

Old Martin catechises Mercy, by now Jonas's fiancée, as to whether she genuinely wishes to marry Jonas. She airily proclaims that she does, asserting that she can control him even when once his wife. Jonas knows better, and after further teasing by Mercy resolves to make her married life hell. (The law then granted husbands vast powers over wives, including ownership of their property; see *Nicholas Nickleby*.) Dickens subsequently implies that once they are man and wife Jonas beats her.

Pecksniff allows Charity, still seething from her rejection by Jonas, to stay at Mrs Todgers's in London. Old Martin appears to fall in with Pecksniff's ascendancy over him. Pecksniff makes advances to Mary, is rebuffed but persuades her to hush things up by warning her that if she complains to old Martin she might further damage the prospects of young Martin.

Charity Pecksniff is consoled over losing Jonas when Moddle, a boarder at Mrs Todgers's, proposes to her. Meanwhile young Martin nearly dies of fever in the American backwoods, conveniently sheds his self-centredness in recuperating, as if it were a poultice drawing off some noxious pus, and with Mark Tapley returns to England.

Mrs Gamp, by Kyd.

Tigg Montague blackmails Jonas into getting more deeply involved with his insurance swindle, also into helping him, Montague, ensnare Pecksniff as an investor. Jonas resolves to murder Montague, supposing his own guilty secret will be buried at the same time. Young Martin tries to effect a reconciliation in an interview with his grandfather, now firmly ensconced with Pecksniff. The latter, in a wonderfully funny scene, delivers a sort of Greek Tragedy chorus commentary on Martin's speech, Dickens pointing to the resemblance himself.

Jonas murders Montague, is exposed as having planned the death of his father with drugs he obtained from Lewsome and through Nadgett's watchfulness is arrested for the murder. He tries to bribe with a purse containing £100 (say £12,500 today) his cousin, the police officer Chevy Slyme, so as to buy five minutes alone, clearly in order to commit suicide. Slyme accepts, but when the time is up finds that Jonas has funked it. Slyme thrusts the purse back at Jonas. The police bundle him into a carriage and drive off.

As they pass a fruiterer's one of them remarks on the strong whiff of peaches. It is in fact cyanide. Jonas has killed himself after all. By this marvellous denouement Dickens, as so often with him, redeems his earlier corniness in over-dramatising, over-writing and over-advertising its imminent arrival.

Old Martin arranges the humiliation of Pecksniff amidst a circle of his relatives and acquaintances. He brings young Martin and Mary Graham together, anointing their union with his patriarch's blessing. He becomes so incensed personally against Pecksniff as to address him as 'ye' rather than 'you'.

Sales of *Martin Chuzzlewit* in monthly magazine form never exceeded the low 20,000s. There had been a sharp downturn in the book trade generally in 1842, so *Chuzzlewit*'s disappointing performance may not entirely reflect the book's faults.

Dombey and Son

Monthly serial, 1846 to 1848
Book published 1848

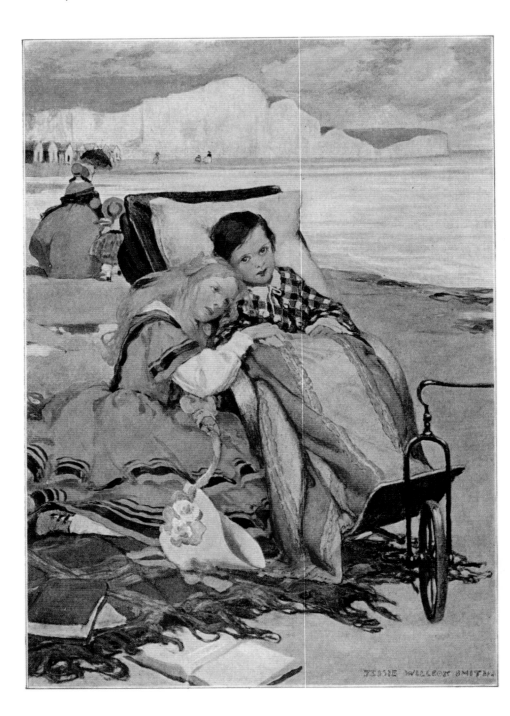

Paul Dombey, the shadow of early death upon him, tended by Florence on a beach near Brighton, an illustration by Jessie Willcox Smith.

Characters

Bagstock, Major Joe ('Old Joey'/'old Josh'/'Joseph')

Retired army officer; constantly (and with some justification) pats himself on the back as 'sly, devilish sly', for he first scrapes acquaintance with the hugely wealthy Mr Dombey then introduces him to the lovely and aristocratic Edith Granger, who becomes Dombey's second wife.

Berinthia ('Berry') Niece to Mrs Pipchin.

Bitherstone, Master Inmate of Mrs Pipchin's horrible boarding-house in Brighton; his father Bill Bitherstone has long ago asked his brother officer Major Bagstock to look the boy up (and was till now ignored); Bagstock does so once he learns of young Paul Dombey's being settled at Mrs Pipchin's as a means of getting to know Mr Dombey.

Major Joe Bagstock (above) and Dr Blimber (below).

Blimber, Cornelia The private school-proprietor Dr Blimber's daughter.

Blimber, Dr Crams the 10 pupils at his school in Brighton with too much learning and too little understanding.

Blimber, Mrs Dr B's wife.

Blockitt, Mrs Midwife in attendance on the first Mrs Dombey.

Briggs Shares a dormitory at Blimber's with Paul Dombey.

Brogley Creditor of Solomon Gills to the tune of some £370 (rather over £36,000 today).

Brown, 'Good' Mrs; alias Marwood

Crone who abducts Florence Dombey, Mr Dombey's daughter, when latter taken by the nursemaids Susan Nipper and 'Richards'/Polly Toodle on clandestine visit to Toodle children in Camden Town; Mr Dombey finds out and sacks 'Richards'/Polly Toodle; in the course of the adventure Florence meets for the first time her future husband Walter Gay; Dickens resurrects 'Good' Mrs Brown some 120,000 words later as mother to Alice Marwood.

Bunsby, John ('Jack') Seafarer friend of Captain Cuttle; eventually 'caught' as husband by Cuttle's ex-landlady, Mrs MacStinger.

Carker, Harriet Sister to James and John below; eventually marries the Dombey and Son third-in-command, Morfin.

Carker, James

Head clerk to Mr Dombey and his right-hand man in business; has good but shark-like teeth and a florid complexion; the novel's villain.

Carker, John Elder brother of the above by two or three years but much less senior at Dombey and Son since he many years before, when old Mr Dombey, father of its present head, was in charge, stole money from the firm; is sacked by Dombey after his brother James elopes with Edith, since, as Dombey tells him, the very name Carker has become 'painful'.

Chick, Louisa, *neé* Dombey Mr Dombey's sister; is prepared to have her brother come and live with her after he is ruined; known as 'Loo' to her husband.

Chick, John Louisa's husband.

'Chicken, The Game' Professional boxer who young Paul Dombey's ex-schoolfellow Mr Toots employs as a kind of bodyguard-cum-sponsored-sportsman, the sort of thing which Regency bucks had done a generation early but which by now, the late 1840s, was out of fashion; the Chicken's parting conversation with Toots (indeed their only recorded conversation in the entire book) is pure Wodehouse in idiom, more evidence of Dickens's influence in that quarter.

'The Game Chicken'.

Cuttle, Captain Edward ('Ned')

Former seafaring man, as pilot, skipper or privateersman (Dickens himself is vague as to which; commanding a privateer involved more or less licensed piracy, so seems unlikely given Cuttle's kindly nature, let alone his ignorance of precious metal values – witness mention of his trinkets below – while his glazed hat, at that period the headgear of an ordinary seaman, would have sat oddly on the skipper of any vessel); lives in Brig Place (a Brig Mews hard by the Thames in Deptford, London SE8, survives today), but departs secretly to avoid encountering his landlady Mrs MacStinger, his main purpose being to house-sit for Sol Gills in the latter's shop after the latter vanishes; he thus never gets the letters Sol in his search for Walter Gay sends him from Barbados, Jamaica and Demerara; Cuttle thinks himself hugely sagacious and twice tries to help his friends Walter Gay and Sol Gills with Mr Dombey; on the first occasion he annoys Mr Dombey; on the second, he fails to establish human contact with Dombey altogether; later still Cuttle confides his aspirations for Walter Gay to the scheming James Carker, who he thinks an admirable fellow; Cuttle is too much of a throwback to Dickens's early-period grotesques for even this much self-delusion to touch us nowadays; the one exception is when down in Brighton he tumbles the silver trinkets on the table in front of Mr Dombey in the belief that they constitute significant collateral for Mr Dombey's assuming Sol's debt; this is moving due to the inadequacy of the horde not Cuttle's misjudging the situation; he does, however, eventually see through Carker, and his speech then, though larded with his usual tiresome nautical metaphors, is a fine one in its honest but telling excoriation.

Captain Cuttle.

Dombey, Fanny Mr Dombey's first wife and mother of Florence and Paul; dies an hour or so after giving birth to Paul.

Dombey, Florence

Mr Dombey's daughter, 'about' six years older than Paul, so 'about' 14 when he dies and wholly pubescent by the time the action of the second half of the novel gets into its stride; by the time of the crisis is 'almost seventeen'. Played by Lysette Anthony in the 1983 BBC TV adaptation.

Dombey, Mr

Usually known thus, though his forename is Paul, his father's, son's and grandson's too; leading City of London merchant dealing with goods 'wholesale, retail and for exportation', as the original title page puts it; aged 48 when the story opens, therefore 60–61 at the crisis; his domestic residence lies 'between Portland-place and Bryanstone-square [*sic*]' in the Marylebone area north of Oxford Street, a perfectly adequate address then but not quite as good as the wholly aristocratic enclave of Mayfair, south of Oxford Street, where (in Brook Street, to be precise) his eventual mother-in-law Mrs Skewton borrows from one of her grand relations a house for her daughter Edith's wedding to Dombey; his business premises are 'just round the corner' from East India House (headquarters of the East India Company, which at this date controlled the entire sub-continent of India) in Leadenhall Street, in the City of London; this suggests it was in either Billiter Street or Lime Street; at first sight Dombey is the standard 19th-century tycoon: single-minded, industrious, commercially astute, joyless, unimaginative; soon,

Florence Dombey, by Harold Copping.

then with gathering momentum, it becomes clear he is easily imposed upon, first by the fashionable doctor, Peps, then by his son's nursemaids Susan Nipper and 'Richards'/Polly Toodle, then by the people he pays to rear his son (the humbugs Mrs Pipchin and Dr Blimber), then by Joe Bagstock, then by his second wife (who does not love him), then by James Carker; he is, in short, a hollow man from the start; he is wholly friendless before Bagstock intrudes on his life and Bagstock only does so because of Dombey's wealth; he has not even built up the business himself, merely inherited it and run it satisfactorily till Carker overextends its operations, whereupon his fatuous pride prevents him retrenching so that the business fails, though he insists on paying all his debtors everything he can, leaving himself destitute – a noble pride of sorts; his ultimate salvation as a human being is not quite the transformation from marmoreal insensitivity to grandfatherly lovingness that Dickens would have us believe, for there was early on that propensity to bite his lip and give way to tears; he was in short a sensitive fellow beneath his slightly bogus 'titan-of-commerce' shell; it is an artful portrait. Played by John Carson in the 1969 televisation; Julian Glover in the 1983 BBC one.

Mr Dombey and Paul, by Harold Copping.

Dombey, Paul

Dombey's son; new-born when the story opens, therefore 48 years younger than his father, an age difference that would be wide even today; perhaps the mercantile class differed from most people then in procreating late, for Jonas and Anthony Chuzzlewit seem to have been similarly placed; unsociable with other children, Paul is wrapped up in his sister, who he calls 'Floy'; grows into a sickly boy, often complaining of fatigue, and given to asking awkward questions of grown-ups like a little Socrates; his sickliness marks him out for early culling by Dickens (his awkward questions too? – they were what got Socrates put to death, after all).

Feenix, Lord ('Cousin')

Cousin of Edith Granger (subsequently Dombey) and nephew of Mrs Skewton, though not much (if at all) younger than her, having been 'a man about town … forty years ago'; an MP before succeeding to the peerage; his motor functions not what they once were, since he has a tendency to veer off to one side when purposing to walk straight; muddle-headed too, since after his cousin's wedding he signs the church registry in the births section; good-natured, however.

Gay, Walter Nephew of Gills; sighs after Florence and eventually marries her.

Gills, Solomon ('Old Sol')

Ships' instrument-maker, as which he keeps in the City of London a shop with no customers; uncle of Walter Gay, for whom he has got a job as 'office junior' with Dombey and Son on the strength of an old business connexion; like Nell's grandfather in *The Old Curiosity Shop*, stealthily decamps from the premises after his business difficulties overwhelm him; or so it seems at the time; later it turns out he has gone overseas to look for Walter; his investments do well towards the end of the tale, from which we can infer that Walter will inherit a fair sum, since Sol has no other known kin.

Granger, Mrs (Edith)

Dombey's second wife; widow of a Col Granger, of the same regiment as Maj Bagstock's, having aged 18 married Granger, who was then 41, and lost him within two years, together with a son by Granger who was drowned two or three years later; this bereavement, so like Dombey's own, adds to her physical attractions in Dombey's eyes; although an improvement on Dickens's earlier, insipid beauties, she is nonetheless given too much to the same high-flown sort of speech as Kate Nickleby's, indeed in the splendidly horrible eve-of-their-second-wedding-anniversary scene she tears into Mr Dombey just before demanding a separation by using exactly the anaphora rhetorical device Kate did ('it is not enough ... ; it is not enough ... ; it is not enough ... '); her 'womanly' status (as opposed to young girl's, that is, someone 10 years her junior) is conveyed by the frequency with which her bosom heaves, a convention in Victorian melodrama for comely females of slightly riper years than an *ingénue*'s; her intense pride intended by Dickens as foil to that of her second husband, a case of the irresistible force colliding with the immoveable object; after her desertion of Dombey she retires, chaperoned by 'Cousin' Feenix, to southern Italy – oddly enough the same part of the world Carker had talked of settling with her in.

Jemima Polly Toodle's unmarried sister; lives with Toodle family, rather as Dicken's wife's sisters successively did with his.

MacStinger, Mrs Captain Cuttle's landlady.

Marwood, Alice

'Good' Mrs Brown's bastard daughter by Edith Dombey's paternal uncle and roughly Edith's age; known as 'Ally' to her mother; was long ago seduced by James Carker and got involved in a robbery, for which she was transported; returns to England after 'ten or a dozen' years (Dickens by now frequently resorts to such vague time scales to avoid the chronological mess he got himself into in *Pickwick Papers*); encounters Harriet Carker, who later tends her in her last illness, for like Martha in *David Copperfield* Alice has squandered her 'purity' hence must pay; Alice is so obviously an underclass equivalent of Edith Dombey, not least in her testy relationship with her mother and intense pride, that the revelation of their kinship is a bit of an anti-climax.

Morfin Number three in the hierarchy of Dombey and Son; lives in Islington; amateur cellist.

Nipper, Susan

Nanny then maid to Florence; many years later tries to tell Mr Dombey what a devoted daughter he has and gets sacked for her pains; marries Mr Toots and bears him three daughters.

Peps, Dr Parker Obstetrician attending on Fanny Dombey at Paul's birth; accidentally-on-purpose confuses Mrs Dombey's name with that of titled ladies so as to remind Dombey of his practice among the aristocracy; Dickens in this way announces Dombey's fatal weakness: susceptibility to flattery arising from his pride in the family business; for once Dickens's habit of heralding a later plot development works well.

Perch Head porter at Dombey and Son; when Edith runs away with Carker is pestered by the papers, especially one of the Sundays, an interesting revelation of how the press fed the public appetite for salacious gossip about the very rich even in those days.

Pilkins Family 'surgeon' practitioner to the Dombeys; as a surgeon much lower in professional and social prestige than Peps.

Pipchin, Mrs Proprietress of a Brighton boarding house where the six-year-old Paul is sent for sea air, something that in those days was thought good for weak constitutions.

Mrs Pipchin, by Harold Copping.

Richards Name Mr Dombey bestows on Polly Toodle as less vulgar than Toodle.

Skettles, Sir Barnet MP and prospective parent at Blimber's school.

Skewton, Hon Mrs

Mother of Edith Dombey; old friend of Maj Bagstock; said by Dickens to be about 70, in which case she must have given birth to Edith aged 41.

Toodle, Rob(in) ('Biler')

Eldest Toodle son, so called 'in remembrance of the steam-engine [boiler]'; nominated by Mr Dombey to a vacancy in a school called The Charitable Grinders, whose pupils wear an antiquated uniform rather like that of Christ's Hospital pupils in West Sussex, a circumstance which causes 'Biler' to be set upon by other boys; 'Biler' later goes to the bad and is taken up by James Carker, who places him as assistant with Sol Gills to spy on the latter, especially when Florence visits; Rob, as he is by now known, later directly employed by Carker; later still by Miss Tox, under whom it is safe to say he turns over a new leaf.

Toodle, Mr Stoker then engine-driver on the railways (or 'railroads', as he calls them, for though nowadays an Americanism, 'railroad' is as much British English in origin); Toodle's involvement in railways is the first mention by Dickens in fiction of this new form of transport in a British setting; the district surrounding Toodle's home in Camden Town is uprooted by the new 'railroad' passing through it.

Toodle, Mrs (Polly)

Paul's wet nurse and foster mother; Dombey's renaming her 'Richards' symbolic of his economic tyranny over her, though she has the nous at that point to request a wage-rise in compensation; many years later is taken on to tend the shattered Mr Dombey following his business failure.

Toots

Head boy at Dr Blimber's academy; crammed silly by excessive study under Blimber; a would-be dandy, he is much puzzled immediately before Dr Blimber's party whether to leave undone his bottom waistcoat button; this fashion, and concomitant disapproval as 'common' of those who don't, is often said to derive from Edward VII ('Tum-Tum' to his intimates), whose girth made any full buttoning impracticable; Toots's pioneering confusion on the point *c.* 1848, when 'Tum-Tum' was a mere child, demolishes the theory; further, Toots is unsure whether to do up or leave undone his top waistcoat button, so the waistcoat question was probably one of those arbitrary dress taboos that bother the fashion-conscious in every generation and don't depend on royalty at all; Toots falls in love with Florence.

Toots, by Kyd.

Towlinson, Tom Servant in Dombey's employ; from his being referred to by Dickens as 'Mr' we can infer he is Dombey's butler, for Dickens knew all about below-stairs forms of address and etiquette, being the grandson of a butler.

Tox, Miss Lucretia Friend of Louisa Chick till the latter tells her Mr Dombey is going to marry again, whereupon Miss Tox faints from disappointment and Louisa Chick, realising Miss Tox has had hopes in that direction herself, breaks with her.

Tozer Shares a dormitory at Blimber's with young Paul Dombey.

Wickam, Mrs Succeeds 'Richards'/Polly Toodle as young Paul's nurse.

Withers Mrs Skewton's page boy.

Dombey and Son

Story Commentary

With *Dombey and Son*, Dickens enters on the maturity of his later novels. They are the ones that win most respect from modern critics, not least for their 'seriousness'. A deplorable attitude in some ways. Novels are not tracts, least of all with a self-proclaimed popular entertainer like Dickens. Nonetheless, in their slightly crass way such critics have a point.

The 'Dombey and Son' refers to a leading business in the City of London owned by Mr Dombey. Dickens typically doesn't tell us what it trades in, but given the Barbados outpost (discussed further below in relation to Walter Gay), its wares probably include tropical produce. Yet if the Barbados outpost is unimportant, as Dombey states, why retain it? Perhaps from inertia, it having once been important, most obviously before the abolition of the slave trade in 1807, back when Dombey's father was running the show, then abolition of slavery in most British possessions in 1833, by which time the current Dombey would have taken over. So the house of Dombey and Son (like Pickwick?) may well have sucked its earlier profits from human bondage. It would explain why our Dombey is so bad at accepting people as equals and looks on his wife Edith as a chattel.

Having in addition an almost superstitious reverence for the 'and Son' bit, Mr Dombey concentrates all his considerable family and corporate pride on his delicate son Paul, neglecting his daughter Florence. But even Paul is only a projected ornament to the business. Corporate prestige, the 'brand name' as we might say now, is the true focus of Dombey's existence. This was the more vital then since by the unlimited liability system merchants could lose all personal property on their firm's failing.

Dickens for the first time examines the minds of several of his characters in searching detail and with due regard to what is emotionally plausible. There is Dombey's attitude towards Florence, now distaste, now icy indifference. Or Dombey and his highly uncharacteristic bailing out of the debt-stricken Solomon Gills, Dombey asking his infant son Paul what he would do in the circumstances. Paul says in effect, 'give him the money'. Dombey does so. For such a dyed-in-the-wool commercial type, this would normally represent largesse of a fantastic, fairy-tale nature. But because Dombey is besotted with his vision of Paul as future business partner, it rings true.

Then there is Walter Gay, who when petitioning Dombey on behalf of his uncle Sol on the occasion just mentioned is aged about 19. Hitherto he has taken a blithe make-believe attitude towards Florence, Dombey's daughter, assuming that like Dick Whittington and other heroes of legend he will somehow make his fortune and win her hand. He now apprehends how huge a gulf exists between her and himself, a very junior employee of Dombey and Son. Nicholas Nickleby or young Martin Chuzzlewit would never have been so self-aware.

Dickens reverts to his old bad habits in advertising Paul's death several chapters in advance. But he ups the poignancy rating. At the end of Chapter XIV, when Paul's mortal illness dominates every paragraph, Mr Dombey, usually the most self-controlled of men, gives way to tears. This is heart-rendingly effective, all the more since it follows Dombey's cynicism in sending Walter Gay out to Barbados. Privately Dombey must know that the posting is not just of no great importance, but that there is a danger of yellow fever, then usually fatal, something that implicitly Walter is aware of too.

Dickens's plucking at our heart-strings is now more subtle also at the post mortem stage. Gone his keening for page after page over Little Nell. He has learnt to handle death more tautly. The gloom Paul's funeral throws on a street juggler's wife with her young child; the slight change in Mr Dombey's appearance (nothing drastic, just sunken, rigid and pale, but this in an impassive countenance is enough); the new sense of freedom in Mr Carker's mien at the office, as if an obstacle is removed from his path; the lugubrious moralising (over a vast intake of food and wine) by the servants' hall at Dombey's; and, best of all, Dombey's instructing a stonemason to erect a plaque to Paul calling him 'beloved and only child', whereupon the stonemason timidly suggests it should read 'son', Dombey acknowledging the error. This is superb. With *Dombey* Dickens graduates from tale-spinner in the English provincial-sensationalist-comic tradition to novel-writing in the grand European one.

Major Bagstock (artist unknown).

Even James Carker, despite some stage villain left-overs (his adopting an 'ugly sneer' towards his boss Dombey the moment the latter's gaze is averted), is a greatly improved embodiment of turpitude, as far in realism beyond even Jonas Chuzzlewit as Jonas was beyond Quilp, Sikes or Fagin. And Edith Granger, offered up to Dombey as sacrifice in Mammon's temple by her simpering harridan of a mother, can be gratifyingly earthy, not just blue-bloodedly cool. When the excursion to Warwick Castle is proposed which, as she, her mother and Joe Bagstock all know, will conjure forth a marriage proposal from Dombey (technically the proposal comes next day, but no matter), she turns 'very red'. Not 'blushed'. Not 'coloured'. To write of a beautiful female character as turning 'very red' in Dickens's day was akin to having her exude 'sweat' rather than 'perspiration'. Dickens, abandoning genteelisms, has become bold.

When Dombey is at last brought to notice Florence's existence he bends a stealthy but unwavering gaze on her from under a handkerchief he has draped over his face while affecting to take an after dinner nap in a drawing room armchair. He is just about to say 'Florence, come here!' when his new

Captain Cuttle, by Kyd.

wife enters, relaxed, kindly, affectionate, her hair loose, dressed in a flowing robe, and lovingly chats – almost coos – to Florence. Both females suppose Dombey asleep. Dombey's wife has bestowed intimacy on his daughter, not him. The revelation mortifies him. The two females leave the room together. Dombey sits on till three o'clock in the morning. His sense of exclusion could hardly be more lacerating if he had caught them in bed making love to each other. It is a critical moment, magnificently handled.

Presently Dombey reproves Edith for her extravagance and lack of submission to his will. Dickens here leans too much on high-flown dialogue. Verdict: five out of ten. Edith's mother Mrs Skewton has a stroke and slides with increasing imbecility towards the grave. Dickens recounts this superbly (nine out of ten). Conversely, Dickens's increasing skill with major characters and themes central to his purpose shows up the antiquated nature of the 'low' comic interludes involving Captain Cuttle and Mrs MacStinger. Verdict (as regards them): two out of ten. Likewise, his contriving an encounter on the Brighton Downs between on the one hand the decrepit Mrs Skewton with proud Edith and on the other the fawning 'Good' Mrs Brown with equally proud Alice Marwood. Verdict: unalloyed melodramatic hokum; two out of ten.

The crisis approaches. Dombey charges Carker with conveying to Edith his displeasure at her various displays of independence. She is not to be permitted any reply, let alone remonstration. Eventually she cannot bear any more and leaves him, meeting Carker at the house in Brook Street her mother had borrowed for the wedding two years before. Dombey, who in his slightly earlier hubris has laughed at her aspirations to carve out some kind of independence of him (the only time he ever gives way to mirth), is driven to a frenzy of stung pride by her desertion, especially since it involves Carker, and lashes out at Florence, believing her in league with Edith. Florence in anguish rushes from the house. She takes refuge at Old Sol's instrument shop with Captain Cuttle.

Till now Cuttle has been for the most part a buffoon. But in his picking at the scab on Florence's mind of Walter Gay's supposed drowning, coming back to it every other sentence like a dog to its vomit, there is something almost sadistic. Yet Dickens makes it clear that in his view Cuttle has the best of hearts. It is an interesting glimpse of a creepy side to Dickens (one that occurs again with David Copperfield concealing from Aunt Trotwood and his friend Traddles his early return from his three-year tour of the Continent so that he 'might have the pleasure of taking them by surprise').

Things turn out well, however, for Walter soon reappears. He was never drowned, just shipwrecked. Cuttle's ghoulish reiteration of 'Poor Wal'r! Drownded, an't he?' was his oafish way of winding up Florence so that her ultimate joy should be all the greater. Walter and Florence get engaged and voyage to China, Walter having been offered a sea-going post as super-cargo (Merchant Navy officer in charge of goods being shipped).

Dombey has made no effort to find Florence. But he has got word of Edith and Carker's whereabouts. The source? 'Good' Mrs Brown. He visits her, she hides him in the next room and he overhears Rob the Grinder blabbing as to Carker's and Edith's planned rendezvous at Dijon, in Burgundy, for they are travelling there by different routes, the better to baffle any pursuers.

Next scene Dijon. Carker and Edith meet. He believes she will become his mistress, her submitting to an earlier embrace or two by him giving him, as he thinks, good grounds. But she spurns him, and sweeps from the apartment. It is besieged by Dombey, who batters on its main door. Carker panics, rushes back to England and goes to ground deep in the country, away from London. He stays at an inn beside a railway, becoming mesmerised by the rush and noise of the iron beasts as they pass his window. He leaves the inn but on turning back sees Dombey emerging from its door. He stumbles in alarm onto a railway track and is mown down by a train.

Hitherto the ultimate manipulator, involving Dombey and Son in vast financial commitments (much as destroyed Baring's Bank in 1995), and so astute a psychologist that he has half-bent Edith to his will by glances and insinuating speeches alone, Carker is unconvincing in his nervous collapse and misreading of his female prey's sexual availability (though what man is ever infallible there?). But Dickens had to get rid of him somehow. And he lacked the technical knowledge to do it professionally through business, while Victorian convention forbade him destroying Carker through sex (syphilis, say, or social ruin through his pornographic collection being exposed), though either would have been more artistically fitting and a combination of the two better still.

Harriet and John Carker inherit their brother's substantial wealth and they, especially Harriet, secretly divert much of it to shore up Mr Dombey's finances. Eventually Dombey learns to love Florence and he settles with her, Walter and his grandchildren somewhere by the sea – Dickens hints in Kent.

Dombey and Son sold moderately well in its periodical form, at an average of 35,000 copies of each monthly number of the serial. But the heady days of Little Nell, fetching 70,000–100,000 each month, had gone.

David Copperfield

Monthly serial, 1849 to 1850
Book published 1850

David's calf love for Em'ly; she dreams already of becoming a 'lady'; her fate is fallen woman, an illustration by Jessie Willcox Smith.

Characters

Barkis, C P Dickens doesn't say what the initials stand for. Carrier across East Anglia; marries David's old nurse Peggotty, carrying out his wooing via David with his catch-phrase refrain 'say that Barkis is willin''. Played by Freddie Jones in the 2000 made-for-TV film.

Chillip Blunderstone doctor attending on David's mother at time of his birth.

Copperfield, Clara

David's widowed mother; soon marries Mr Murdstone but dies shortly after bearing his son, who survives her by only a day. Played by Emilia Fox in the 1999 BBC televisation.

Copperfield, David

Hero; based very much on Dickens himself as regards menial labour in childhood, an inadequate wife married by him when too young to know better and literary career; born at Blunderstone, Suffolk (based on Blundeston, a village Dickens visited the year before starting *David Copperfield*; its rectory inspired, and suggested the name of, David's mother's house 'The Rookery'). Played by Freddie Bartholomew as the young DC in the George Cukor 1935 film; Julian Lennon (son of John) as the voice of a cat DC in a 1993 cartoon musical; Daniel Radcliffe, again as the young DC, in the 1999 televisation.

David Copperfield, by Arthur Dixon.

Creakle Headmaster/proprietor of Salem House, in Blackheath, southeast London; later becomes a magistrate and prison-overseer. Played by Laurence Olivier in the 1969 film; Ian McKellen in the 1999 televisation.

Crewler, Sophy Daughter of a Devon cleric, the Rev Horace Crewler; marries Traddles.

Crupp, Mrs David's landlady at his chambers in Buckingham Street off the Strand in the West Central district of London (the street exists still) when he is articled to the proctors' (effectively solicitors') partnership of Spenlow & Jorkins, of Doctors' Commons (association of lawyers handling among other things marriage and (more rarely) divorce, since everyone in Dickens's day got married in a place of worship; Doctors' Commons was done away with not long after *David Copperfield* was published). Played by Dawn French in the 1999 televisation.

Dartle, Rosa Companion to Mrs Steerforth; dotes on James Steerforth.

Dick, Mr (real name Richard Babley)

Mildly lunatic inmate of David's great-aunt Betsey Trotwood's Dover cottage; spends time composing a memorial into which he cannot prevent his *idée fixe* of King Charles I entering, hence the expression 'A King Charles's head'. Played by Emlyn Willliams in the 1969 film; Timothy Bateson in a little-known 1974 screen version.

Em'ly

Niece of Clara and Dan Peggotty; gets engaged to her cousin Ham but runs away before her wedding day, hoping an as yet unnamed 'he' (Steerforth, it turns out), her new 'protector' (Victorian term for male keeping an unmarried female), will bring her back to Yarmouth as a 'lady'; lives with Steerforth in France, Switzerland and Italy, in which last country, near Naples, Steerforth abandons her; she returns to London and teeters on the verge of prostitution till found by her uncle Dan. Played by Sinéad Cusack in the 1969 film.

Endell, Martha Ex-schoolfellow of Em'ly; local bad girl in Yarmouth, which she leaves for London, where (one infers) she prostitutes herself to a more up-market clientele; emigrates with the Peggottys to Australia, where she marries a farm labourer.

Gulpidge Guest at dinner party where David encounters Tommy Traddles again.

Gummidge, Mrs Widow of Dan Peggotty's dead partner.

Heep, Uriah

Pallid, red-haired, eyelash-less, obsequious assistant to Mr Wickfield, with a clammy handshake to boot; studies law in his spare time; constantly describes himself as ''umble'; succeeds Murdstone as the novel's chief villain, defrauding Wickfield and indirectly David's Aunt Trotwood; is unmasked by David, Mr Micawber and Traddles and forced to disgorge the proceeds; ends in Creakle's prison. Played by Ron Moody in the 1969 film; Nicholas Lyndhurst in the 1999 televisation.

Uriah Heep.

Jip

Dora's pet; first dog in English fiction to forward a novel's plot (Pug in *Mansfield Park* not counting, since no more than emblematic of Lady Bertram's indolence); Jip's role is to grab in his mouth a love letter of David's to Dora, such plaything, as it initially seems, being discovered by Miss Murdstone, who notifies Spenlow of the illicit correspondence, whereupon Spenlow reproves David; Jip becomes enfeebled and dies more or less simultaneously with Dora.

Joram, Dick Coffin-maker.

Littimer

Steerforth's manservant; prototype of Wodehouse's Jeeves to Bertie Wooster in his Olympian handling of David Copperfield, his superior socially but inferior as to worldly knowledge; procures Em'ly for his master; is dismissed from Steerforth's employ; ends in Creakle's prison following his theft of £250 (well over £30,000 today) from another employer when trying to flee to America in a 'flaxen wig and whiskers'.

Maldon, Jack Cousin of Annie Strong; as 'kissin' kin' a threat to Dr Strong's marriage.

Markleham, Mrs Annie Strong's mother.

Mell Assistant master at Salem House; dismissed by Creakle once he learns Mell's mother is an object of charity.

Wilkins Micawber.

Micawber, Emma

Wife of Mr Micawber; tries keeping a young ladies' seminary at their house, rather as Dickens's mother had done in real life; her catchphrase 'I never will desert Mr Micawber' has entered the language. Played by Wendy Hiller in the 1969 film; Imelda Staunton in the 1999 televisation.

Micawber, Wilkins

Travelling salesman (for Murdstone & Grinby and other businesses, including ones dealing in coal and corn) with whom David lodges in London, specifically at Windsor Terrace, City Road; a street by that name exists today between Finsbury and Shoreditch in the N1 postal district; a Micawber Court apartment block in the Terrace itself and a Micawber Street bisecting it at its top commemorate the connexion; Micawber later puts up at lodgings in Pentonville, then in Camden Town, where he imposes on Traddles, now his upstairs neighbour; Dickens based Micawber's improvidence and jaunty optimism on his father John (Micawber's high-flown declamation too, the gift of words being passed by John to his son); Micawber's catchphrases 'if anything turns up' and 'Annual income twenty pounds, annual expenditure nineteen nineteen six [£19.98 in today's currency], result happiness. Annual income twenty pounds, annual expenditure twenty pounds ought and six [£20.02 in today's currency], result misery' have entered the language (see also under Russia in 'Dickens Abroad'). Played by W C Fields in the 1935 film; Ralph Richardson in the 1969 one; Bob Hoskins in the 1999 televisation.

Mills, Julia Friend of Dora Spenlow; rather sweetly brings Dora and David together at the picnic for Dora's birthday and again at her father's when Dora comes to stay; a romantic, given in her journal to *pensées* like 'Are tears the dewdrops of the heart?', as such the inspiration for P G Wodehouse's Madeline Bassett ('the stars are God's daisy chain').

Mowcher, Miss

Dwarf beautician, manicurist, trichologist and chiropodist; old acquaintance of Steerforth; from her a) interest in Em'ly while attending on Steerforth at Yarmouth, b) Steerforth's saying of Miss Mowcher that she had 'made herself useful to a variety of people in a variety of ways', c) her dropping the names of some very grand aristocrats and d) the imminence of Em'ly's seduction by Steerforth, not to mention e) Em'ly's being closeted that very night with Martha Endell, we are tempted to infer (as it seems David also does) that one way Miss Mowcher makes herself useful is as a procuress; even if so, it is not wholly in the matter of Em'ly (though Miss Mowcher does give Em'ly a letter from Steerforth), for on Em'ly's running away with Steerforth Miss Mowcher tells David a few home truths about his gullibility both in being duped by Steerforth and in David's mistrusting herself, Miss Mowcher, on the grounds of her dwarfish frame; Dickens intended to make Miss Mowcher the main agent of Em'ly's fall, but was threatened with a libel suit by one Mrs Hill, who as both a neighbour of his and a dwarf chiripodist-manicurist had a pretty strong case; so Dickens marked Littimer as chief culprit, a reminder of how serial publication enabled Dickens to get himself out of hot water in episode Y if in episode X he had offended someone; Miss Mowcher later helps get Littimer arrested by rolling between his legs and tripping him up to stop his getting away, she as a beautician having spotted the falseness of his wig and whiskers.

Murdstone, Edward

David's stepfather; wine merchant, or in some way David is vague about connected with a wine merchant; wormwood, not wine, is what he dishes out to David at home; Murdstone later marries a sprightly young woman who he and his sister by their 'firmness' reduce

Mr Murdstone and David by Harold Copping.

to imbecility. Played by Basil Rathbone in the 1935 film; Trevor Eve in the 1999 televisation; Anthony Andrews in the 2000 made-for-TV film.

Murdstone, Jane

Mr Murdstone's grim sister; later turns up as Dora Spenlow's duenna. Played by Anna Massey in the 1969 film; Zoë Wanamaker in the 1999 televisation; Eileen Atkins in the 2000 made-for-TV film.

Omer Undertaker; later tailor/haberdasher, employing Em'ly as dress-maker.

Omer, Minnie His daughter; marries Joram.

Peggotty, Clara

The Copperfields' family retainer. Played by Judy Cornwell in the 2000 made-for-TV film.

Peggotty, Dan

Clara P's brother and Ham and Em'ly's uncle; lives in a beached boat on Yarmouth sands; after his niece Em'ly runs away looks for her all over London, also in France, Switzerland and Italy. Played by Lionel Barrymore in the 1935 film; Michael Redgrave in the 1969 one; Nigel Davenport in the 2000 made-for-TV one.

Dan Peggotty.

Peggotty, Ham

Clara and Dan P's nephew via their dead brother Joe; drowns trying to rescue a stranger from a boat about to be shipwrecked, said stranger turning out to be Steerforth, who also drowns.

Quinion Manager of Murdstone & Grinby (chiefly suppliers of wines and spirits to ships), in which he employs the 10-year-old David as bottle-washer, labeller or cork-inserter at 6 or 7 shillings a week (just over £4,500 a year today).

Sharp First assistant master at Salem House.

Spenlow, Clarissa Younger of Francis Spenlow's two sisters; they take Dora in after Francis's death.

Spenlow, Dora

Daughter of Francis Spenlow; marries David. Played by Maureen O'Sullivan in the 1935 film; Pamela Franklin in the 1969 one.

Spenlow, Francis

Partner in the Proctors' firm of Spenlow & Jorkins, to which David is articled; pretends to David that he (Spenlow) is very comfortably off and that Dora will under terms of his will be an heiress; on his death it turns out his debts so engulf his assets as to leave but £1,000 (say £125,000 today).

Spenlow, Lavinia Elder of Francis Spenlow's unmarried sisters.

Spiker, Henry Guest at the Waterbrooks' dinner party.

Steerforth, James

Leading 'blood' at Salem House; at least half a dozen years older than David; treats Mr Mell shabbily, a sure sign with Dickens that beneath a paragon exterior he is flawed; sure enough, he seduces Em'ly then gets himself drowned; in his charm, dash, quick sympathy with others, love of boating on moonlit nights, tendency to now gloomy now irascible self-deprecation and appetite for sleeping with the more comely of the lower orders, Steerforth is a throwback to the Byronic type that Dickens gave us another side of with Jingle in *Pickwick Papers*, though Steerforth's watery end is more Shelley's than Byron's. Played by Corin Redgrave in the 1969 film.

Tommy Traddles.

Steerforth, Mrs

James's mother; confronted by Dan Peggotty when James Steerforth has lured Em'ly into running away with him, she insists that her son James would blast his prospects by marrying so far beneath him, therefore it is better that James should cast Em'ly aside once he has had his way with her. Played by Cherie Lunghi in the 1999 televisation.

Strong, Annie Very pretty and much younger wife of Dr Strong; apparently in love with her cousin Jack, but she later denies it to the Doctor.

Strong, Dr Headmaster of David's school at Canterbury; later employs David to help him compile a dictionary.

Traddles, Tommy

Schoolfellow with David at Salem House; later lives in same lodging house as Micawbers, being foolish enough to stand surety for Mr Micawber; becomes a barrister.

Trotwood, Betsey

David's paternal great-aunt, Trotwood being her maiden name, to which she reverted years ago on separating from her violent but handsome and younger husband, he having died (we are falsely told) by the start of the book; in fact he survives to touch her for small sums till much later; Aunt Trotwood adopts David but in proprietary fashion confers her name on him, calling him 'Trot' or 'Trotwood' Copperfield; David's seems to be the kind of personality that invites such behaviour, for when first sent to school he is booked on a coach under the name of Murdstone, as if he were his stepfather's property, and Steerforth on renewing their friendship calls him 'Daisy', as being fresh (i.e. green, or naïve); Miss Trotwood subsequently tells David she has lost all her money in foreign investments, but it subsequently turns out she thought Wickfield had been responsible and is too fond of him to hold him to account; her capital of £8,000 (say £1,000,000 today), less the £2,000 (say £250,000 today) she has put aside for a rainy day and the irrecoverable £1,000 Doctors' Commons premium for David, are restored to her by Uriah Heep's being made to disgorge his misappropriated moneys. Played by Edna May Oliver (see also *A Tale of Two Cities*) in the 1935 film; Edith Evans in the 1969 one; Maggie Smith in the 1999 televisation; Sally Field in the 2000 made-for-TV film.

Frontispiece to David Copperfield, *with illustrations by Phiz.*

Tiffey, 'Old' Clerk to Spenlow & Jorkins.

Tungay Man-of-all-work at Salem House. Played by Richard Attenborough in the 1969 film.

Waterbrook London lawyer connexion of Wickfield.

Wickfield

Lawyer and land agent in Canterbury with whom David lodges while attending school there; fond of his glass, hence messes up his estate accounts and law practice and has to take Uriah Heep into partnership. Played by Lewis Stone in the 1935 film.

Wickfield, Agnes

Daughter of above; about same age as David, who is 10 when they meet so that Agnes keeps house for her father when a child, an implausibility; starts as 'sister' to David but he eventually falls in love with her, and since she has always loved him they marry; is loved in vain by Uriah Heep. Played by Susan Hampshire in the 1969 film.

David Copperfield

Story Commentary

A perennial favourite with Dickens-lovers (and considered by Dickens his best novel), *David Copperfield* starts splendidly, with the author in complete command of his material. Gone at this point are the longueurs of previous books. Murdstone, the serpent intruder into David's Eden, makes his entrance quickly and economically. The child David is soon ejected from his cosy relationship with his mother, whose sexual absorption in Murdstone Dickens stresses frequently yet without overdoing it.

The little-touches Dickens deployed in *Dombey and Son* are more numerous and even more effective. Take the way Peggotty puts off telling David about his mother's new husband till they've arrived back at The Rookery from their visit to Yarmouth, and how in consequence David's child sense of bewilderment and dread is all the more oppressive. Take Murdstone's winking at his sister Jane when he takes up the cane with which to lash David for having got his saying lesson wrong. The Dickens even of two years before would not have left it at that. This Dickens knows he can afford to.

And take Murdstone to Peggotty, polite but menacing, 'I thought I heard you, as I came upstairs, address her [David's mother] by a name that is not hers. She has taken mine, you know. Will you remember that?' Never was a tyrant's iron hand gloved so deeply, so occludedly, in velvet. And the giving by the powerful of their own choice of names to the less powerful persists as a theme throughout the book (see also 'Characters'). The re-naming of one character by another, of whatever relative status, eventually breaks out nearly everywhere. Dora calls David 'Doady' and asks him to refer to her as 'Child-wife'. The Peggottys call him 'Davy' or 'Mas'r Davy'. Mr Micawber calls Mr Dick 'Dixon'. Aunt Trotwood calls Dora 'Little Blossom', as if she were a geisha (which in some ways she resembles).

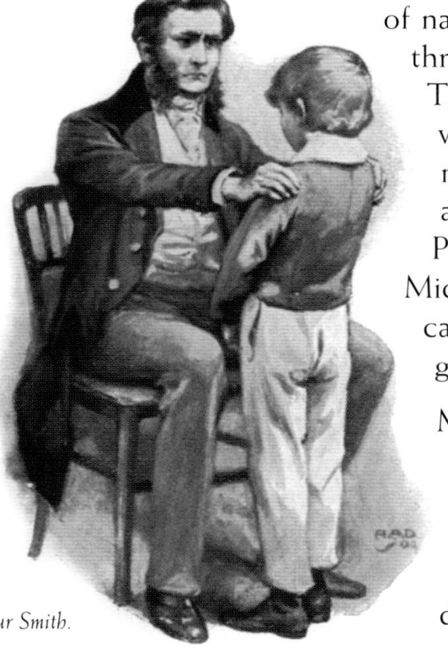

Mr Murdstone and David, by Arthur Smith.

Murdstone is tyrannical in other ways too. But he is joyless with it. When he beats David (as did the boys in their charge thousands of other stepfathers then – real fathers too), he does so from a quasi-evangelical sense of duty. This is quite different from Wackford

David Copperfield and Clara Peggotty beside the parlour fire, by Jessie Willcox Smith.

Squeers's uninhibited flogging sessions, Squeers revelling in them like a Bacchanal at an orgy. It is the contrast between the high Regency attitude – brutal, yes, but full-blooded, uninhibited – and the more costive one which had already started in the Regency period and which by mid-century had supplanted it.

Mr Peggotty and Em'ly, by Harold Copping (right).

Mr Peggotty, by Kyd (below).

The era in which *David Copperfield* is set more or less coincides with the first half of Dickens's own life span. A reference to 'His Majest's High Court' in a writ towards the end of the book, and coaches as the only form of long-distance transport, even when David has been a grown man for some years, mean the era in question can't extend later than 1837. So David as a child being tormented by Murdstone then thrust into the bottling warehouse would have taken place roughly between 1819 and 1822. The films and TV adaptations which depict child David in 1830s–40s 'Quality Street' get-up of bum-freezer jacket and cap with tassle are 20 years out of date.

Dickens the novelist is not at all out of date. He has matured, is on top form. He can now show an unpleasant man as possessing some estimable qualities. Murdstone weeps on losing his young wife Clara and infant baby son by her. He picks up a book but cannot read it. No hate figure in any previous Dickens novel would have evinced such sensitivity. But a brute is no less detestable for having tear ducts or literary leanings. David's hell at Murdstone's hands is the hell of every little fellow up against a much weightier opponent in terms of size, strength, command of resources and civil status.

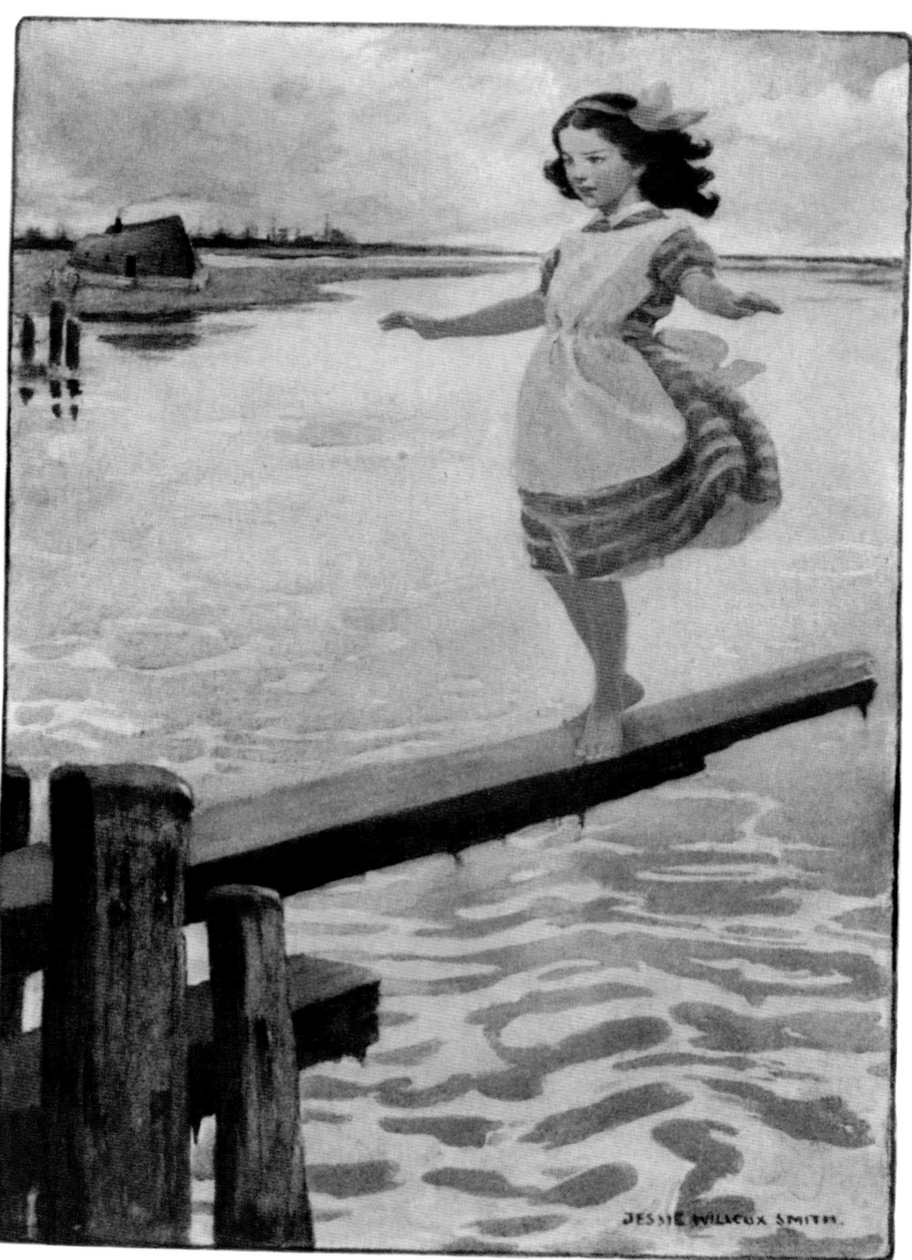

A painting of Em'ly by Jessie Willcox Smith.

The Murdstones brother and sister take David away from Salem House and Mr Murdstone sends him to London to slave for a pittance in his bottle recycling 'plant', in sordid actuality a tumbledown warehouse on the Thames in the Strand. David's chief complaint, repeated several times, is how 'common' his workmates are. This is a near-hysteria felt often by your petty bourgeois, terrified of sliding back into the working class from which his parents or grandparents have hauled themselves. David/Dickens (they are identical at this point) does not mention any true victimisation of himself. David Copperfield is clearly not treated as badly as a little toff down on his luck might be today. At all events, he eventually runs away to Dover and gets taken in by his great-aunt Betsey Trotwood.

Miss Trotwood sends him to a decent school, though he seems to have learnt a good deal of Latin already at the wretchedly conducted Salem House. Soon David, by now 17, goes to London, where he encounters Steerforth again. Steerforth encourages him in his notion of becoming a Proctor in Doctors' Commons. Aunt Trotwood pays the very stiff premium and David is articled to Spenlow & Jorkins there. She also installs him in snug chambers, paying the rent and what sound like service charges and giving him an allowance of £90 a year (over £9,000 a year today).

David's account of his callowness, naivety and lack of financial sagacity at this point in his life is marvellously done. One wonders if Dickens himself, beneath his pugnacious self-assertion, was as diffident at that age. The description by David of hosting his first bachelor dinner party includes

the best account in all fiction of what it is like to get hog-whimperingly drunk.

David gets taken up socially by his principal Spenlow and falls for Spenlow's almost ridiculously feminine, ditzy and cosseted daughter. After various ups-and-downs, the couple marry. Dora as housewife cannot cope. They get cheated left and right, by servants and tradespeople. They cannot entertain guests at the simplest level without the food being undercooked or having cost too much or the dining room proving too cramped.

David gloomily takes to heart a maxim of Annie Strong's when assuring her husband the Doctor that she has not encouraged her cousin Jack Maldon's advances: 'there can be no disparity in marriage like unsuitability of mind and purpose.' David recognises that it applies to Dora and him. Dora has previously shown a turn for maxims too: 'I didn't marry to be reasoned with' (on David's reproving her for her disorganised ways).

David Copperfield, by Harold Copping (right).

Mr Micawber, by Kyd (below).

In middle age Dora would have been as ridiculous as Flora Finching in *Little Dorrit*. Yet it would have defeated Dickens's artistic purpose for David, chief player in a *bildungsroman*, or story of a romantic hero's maturing, to experience any squalid domestic kitchen sink drama of disappointed hopes, such as a fat, blowsy, 45-year old Dora with her scatty ways making David's married life a misery of half-cooked roasts and undarned socks and insubordinate servants. So Dickens kills Dora with one of those conveniently debilitating illnesses Victorian novelists wielded so ruthlessly. After three years residence abroad, soothing his bruised heart and consolidating his literary reputation, David returns, marries Agnes Wickfield and has at least three children by her.

David Copperfield's long-term popularity could not have been immediately guessed from its initial sales. These

David Copperfield and the waiter, by Harold Copping.

(in the usual monthly magazine serial format) jogged along at 20,000, down over 42 per cent on *Dombey and Son*, itself by no means Dickens's top money-spinner. Was Dickens losing his touch? No, not artistically. Contemporary critics didn't think so either and gave *Copperfield* a good reception. But it may momentarily have saddened Dickens to reflect that as his novels got better their profitability declined, that it was his earlier 'penny dreadful' or slapstick stuff that had brought home the biggest flitch of bacon. The back number sales of *David Copperfield* picked up, however.

Bleak House

Monthly serial, 1852 to 1853
Book published 1853

'Jo moves on ... to Blackfriars Bridge, where he finds a baking stony corner ...' (Ch XIX).

Characters

Badger, Bayham Doctor; takes Rick Carstone as medical student.

Badger, Mrs His wife.

Bagnet, Joseph/Mat(thew) Former companion in arms of the ex-trooper Mr George.

Bagnet, Mrs ('old girl' to her husband) His wife.

Barbary Miss Represents herself to Esther Summerson as her godmother but in fact sister of Esther's mother, the current Lady Dedlock, hence Esther's aunt; mortified by the shame of Esther's bastardy, takes a false name and makes grim Esther's childhood.

Blinder, Mrs Landlady of Necketts children.

Boythorn, Lawrence

Extrovert friend and old schoolfellow of John Jarndyce (though 10 years older than him); Lincolnshire neighbour of the Dedlocks; said to have been modelled on the writer Walter Savage Landor, whose *Imaginary Conversations* involved colloquies between historic figures from widely different eras, a device self-consciously revived by Peter Ackroyd in his 1990 Dickens biography.

Bagnet (above) and Inspector Bucket (below).

Bucket

Detective Inspector; fiction's first policeman sleuth (Poe's Auguste Dupin in *The Murders in the Rue Morgue* of 11 years earlier being the first armchair one); bizarrely addresses Sir Leicester orally as 'Sir Leicester Dedlock, Baronet' but otherwise a beautifully observed blend of professional sagacity and homely figures of speech; solves Tulkinghorn's murder and tracks down the errant Lady Dedlock.

Carstone, Richard/Rick

Distant cousin of Lady Dedlock (hence of course Esther Summerson), John Jarndyce and Ada Clare, with whom he falls in love, she returning his love; cannot decide what profession to follow; gets so obsessed with *Jarndyce and Jarndyce* that he becomes estranged from John Jarndyce and dies young, his physical and mental health ruined. Played by Philip Franks in the 1985 televisation.

Chadband.

Chadband Unctuous evangelical.

Chancellor, Lord Hears *Jarndyce and Jarndyce*; at the time *Bleak House* was written (March 1852–September 1853) the Chancellors were Lords St Leonards, reckoned pretty competent, and Cranworth (28 Dec 1852 onwards), considered better at legal minutiae than the law's foremost principles but perfectly satisfactory; if you accept the legal historian Sir William Holdsworth's theory that Dickens set *Bleak House* before or in 1842 because he mentions the Six Clerks Office, which was abolished that year (the passage in question (Ch I, para. 10) is equivocal, however), the then Lord Chancellor would have been Lord Lyndhurst, who made no claims to being an equity expert; support for Holdsworth's 1840s dating comes from Dickens's statement in *Bleak House* that railways are absent from Lincolnshire, for the Great Northern Railway had run lines through that county as early as 1848. Played by Ian Richardson in the 2005 BBC TV adaptation.

Clare, Ada

Secretly marries Rick and bears him a posthumous son.

Dedlock, Lady

Forename Honoria; wife of Sir Leicester and 20 years his junior, hence 48 when the story opens, though still very good-looking; she is of obscure family background but her personal qualities have placed her at the head of the fashionable world, then comprising the leading aristocratic families; Esther Summerson's mother via 'Nemo', a fact betrayed by surviving love letters to Nemo signed 'Honoria'. Played by Sybil Thorndike (who as a child had lived under her clergyman father's roof at Minor Canon Row in Rochester, featured by Dickens in *Edwin Drood*) in a 1922 silent film; Diana Rigg in the 1985 televisation; Gillian Anderson in the 2005 one.

Dedlock, Sir Leicester

So devastated by Bucket's revelation of his wife's past and her all-too-near involvement in Tulkinghorn's murder that he has a stroke, yet still loves her and forgives the youthful lapse with Hawdon, the more understandably since, being 68 when the story opens, he would have been of the generation that came of age under the Regency, when the narrower outlook of mid-century had yet to prevail. Played by Timothy West in the 2005 televisation.

Dedlock, Volumnia Poor relation of Sir Leicester's.

Donny Maiden lady at whose Reading girls' school Esther Summerson is educated.

Flite, Miss

Dotty elderly maiden lady, another victim of *Jarndyce and Jarndyce* and a former ward of court too; as often with the dotty, can be uncomfortably penetrating, calling Esther 'Fitz-Jarndyce', i.e. bastard offspring of someone with an interest in *Jarndyce and Jarndyce*, and seeing before anyone else the ruin in store for Rick Carstone.

William Guppy.

George, Mr

Ex-trooper, as which he once served under Capt Hawdon (see Nemo); debtor to Grandfather Smallweed; turns out to be Mrs Rouncewell's younger son; arrested for Tulkinghorn's murder but soon released; becomes valet to Sir Leicester Dedlock.

Gridley

Farmer's son and 'man from Shropshire' perennially trying to catch the Lord Chancellor's attention regarding a pathetic little case of his own; neighbour of the Neckett children. Played by Frank Windsor in the 1985 televisation.

Guppy, William

Clerk with law firm of Kenge & Carboy; falls in love with Esther, hence investigates her origins, having already detected a likeness between her and a portrait of Lady Dedlock he has seen at Chesney Wold; doesn't realise that Esther is Lady Dedlock's daughter, but greatly discomposes Lady Dedlock by telling her what he has discovered, the piquancy being that his motive is simply to find out if Esther has grand connexions, or, better still, testamentary expectations, so that he can rise in her estimation and win her hand; loses interest in Esther after her disfigurement by smallpox but renews his suit late in the novel, by which time Esther is spoken for by Allan Woodcourt. Played by Timothy Bateson in the 1959 televisation.

Guster (apparently short for 'Augusta') Snagsby's epileptic maid.

Hortense

Lady Dedlock's earlier maid, dismissed in favour of Rosa, hence hates Lady D; importunes Tulkinghorn after he pays her only two guineas (about £260 today) for masquerading in Lady D's clothes before the crossing-sweeper Jo so that Tulkinghorn can determine if the lady who approached Jo about Nemo was indeed Lady D; Tulkinghorn threatens to get her imprisoned if she bothers him further; she shoots him dead.

Jarndyce, John

Esther Summerson's guardian (in response to her aunt Barbary's request, he having known Barbary earlier in life), also Rick Carstone's and Ada Clare's by a Chancery ruling; lives at Bleak House, in Hertfordshire, in one of whose rooms, the 'Growlery', he vents his dissatisfaction with life's unpleasantnesses by blaming the wind, particularly the east wind; good-natured but susceptible to charlatans, notably Skimpole. Played by Andrew Cruickshank in the 1959 BBC televisation; Denholm Elliott in the 1985 one.

Jellyby, Caddy (i.e. Caroline)

Daughter of Mrs J below; becomes friend of Esther.

Jellyby, Mrs

Philanthropist too absorbed in a remote area of Africa to undertake housekeeping and family management at home, hence anathema to Dickens, as also her untidiness, for Dickens was fanatically neat himself and almost always uses 'neat' to praise his female characters.

Jenny Wife of brickmaker working near Bleak House.

Jo

Boy crossing-sweeper (i.e. one who, so that more moneyed pedestrians can traverse streets in comfort, clears a passage across them of all the muck, not excluding excrement, that the horse-drawn traffic and inadequate sewage of 1850s London would have dumped there); is ordered by Lady Dedlock, gliding about London incognito, to show her where Nemo lived and died; Jo eventually dies from what is probably general debility following smallpox, having via Charley infected Esther Summerson with the smallpox.

Jobling, Tony Friend of Young Smallweed and Guppy; Krook's lodger under pseudonym Weevle.

Kenge, 'Conversation' John Jarndyce's lawyer, partner in Kenge & Carboy; called 'Conversation' from his mellifluous and over-deployed voice.

Krook

Illiterate junk-dealer; 'Nemo' and Miss Flite lodge in his house, which is hard by Lincoln's Inn (one of the Inns of Court, or barristers' colonies); tipples neat gin, hence spontaneously combusts; Dickens gets defensive over this, assuring readers that genuine reports of the phenomenon exist; but his date from the early 18th century, so may not be reliable; accounts since Dickens seem to constitute anecdotal evidence at best.

Liz Friend of Jenny's.

Neckett Dun, or bailiff, representing a spunging house (where debtors are temporarily detained, less official than a debtor's prison) which is called Coavins, hence Skimpole calling Neckett Coavins.

Neckett, Charley (Charlotte) Elder daughter of above, though little more than 13; heads family on his death, earning pittance as washer-girl then maid to Smallweeds; becomes Esther Summerson's maid.

Neckett, Emma Charley's infant sister.

Neckett, Tom Charley's brother.

Nemo, aka Capt Hawdon Ex-army officer, now a copyist (an essential service in pre-photocopier days, especially in law, where up to a dozen copies of a document might be needed); dies of a drug overdose. 'Nemo' is Latin for 'Nobody'; also early *nom de plume* of Hablot ('Phiz') Browne, Dickens's chief illustrator.

Pardiggle, Mrs Self-appointed district visitor in the St Albans area, bossing the poor about and making herself unpopular with them.

Rachael, Mrs Barbary's sole servant; not fond of Esther; later marries Chadband.

Rosa Lady Dedlock's pet maid.

Rouncewell, Mrs

Housekeeper to the Dedlocks at Chesney Wold, in Lincolnshire (based on Rockingham Castle in Northamptonshire, owned by the Hon Richard Watson, youngest son of the 2nd Lord [Baron] Sondes and a former Whig MP of liberal tendencies with whom, and still more his wife Lavinia, Dickens had struck up a friendship while living at Lausanne in the second half of 1846, often visiting Rockingham on his return to England and dedicating *David Copperfield* to them).

Rouncewell, Robert

Elder son of above; self-made industrialist; disconcerts the Dedlock circle by his independence both of mind and material resources, his courteous but insufficiently deferential attitude and his coolness towards his son Watt's desire to marry Rosa; hints that he thinks Rosa not an especially good catch despite her being in favour with Lady Dedlock, which to the Dedlocks suggests Jacobinism.

Rouncewell, Watt Son of above; marries Rosa.

Skimpole, Arethusa Eldest daughter of Harold S below.

Skimpole, Harold

Leech to Jarndyce; allegedly inspired by Leigh Hunt, the literary sponger on Byron and Shelley; only when he is revealed to have sold Jo's whereabouts on the night of Jo's disappearance from the Bleak House stable loft to Inspector Bucket for £5 (say £625 today)

Harold Skimpole.

does Jarndyce realise his worthlessness; Skimpole's elaborate casuistry as to his innocence in money matters parodies the more glib legal pleadings Dickens had in mind when attacking the Court of Chancery.

Skimpole, Kitty Youngest daughter of Harold S.

Skimpole, Laura Second daughter of Harold S.

Smallweed, Bart(holomew), also 'Young' or 'Chick' Friend of Guppy.

Smallweed, Grandfather

Bart's and Judith/Judy's usurer grandfather; bullies his senile wife (their grandmother and Krook's sister, so that on Krook's spontaneously combusting all his property, including his document collection, are inherited by Mrs Smallweed and Grandfather Smallweed). Played by Charlie Drake in the 1985 televisation.

Smallweed, Judith/Judy Bart's twin sister; makes artifical flowers.

Snagsby

Law stationer in Cook's Court, Cursitor Street, near Lincoln's Inn.

Snagsby, Mrs Wife of above; suspects him of infidelity and paternity of Jo; the sole case of festering marital jealousy in all Dickens's novels.

Squod, Phil Mr George's shooting gallery second-in-command.

Mr Turveydrop.

Stables, Hon Bob Fashionable sprig of nobility; admires (but no more than that) Lady Dedlock.

Summerson, Esther

One of two narrators (the other being the standard third person, though in the present tense); 14 at her aunt Barbary's death, following which she is taken away from Windsor, where Barbary had lived, and educated for six years at her guardian John Jarndyce's expense; often strikes others, notably Jo, as bearing strong resemblance to Lady Dedlock, her true mother; the resemblance diminishes with her disfigurement.

Tangle Counsel in *Jarndyce and Jarndyce*.

'Friendly behaviour of Mr Bucket', from an illustration by Phiz.

Tulkinghorn

Archetypal top person's lawyer, insinuating rather than frank, smooth to the point of feline, dissimulating rather than open, missing nothing, admitting nothing, tireless in what he conceives as his client Sir Leicester's interests; overreaches himself in investigating Lady Dedlock's dirty secret since this leads to her death and Sir Leicester's devastation. Played by Charles Dance in the 2005 televisation.

Turveydrop, Prince Dancing master, so christened by his superannuated buck of a father in commemoration of the Prince Regent; marries Caddy Jellyby.

Turveydrop, Mr Father of above.

Vholes

Lawyer; pays Skimpole commission to introduce him to Rick Carstone, who retains Vholes to help him with *Jarndyce and Jarndyce*.

Woodcourt, Allan Doctor; eventually marries Esther.

Woodcourt, Mrs Allan's mother.

Bleak House

Story Commentary

Frontispiece for the standard edition of Bleak House.

As with *The Old Curiosity Shop*, why *'Bleak House'* as title? Among the many bleak city habitations in the novel, the ramshackle Tom-all-Alone's jerry-built edifices would qualify soonest. As for country ones, Chesney Wold is clearly the inspiration, if not the avowed subject, of Phiz's frontispiece called 'Bleak House' in the standard editions of the book. As depicted elsewhere by Phiz, not to mention in descriptions by Dickens himself, Chesney is a bleak place mouldering in bleak weather with a bleak ghost's walk heralding bleak developments.

In contrast John Jarndyce's Hertfordshire house – called 'Bleak' only by the caprice of a past owner – is a downright misnomer. Under its (mostly) sunny-humoured owner it is predominantly cheerful, an airy, hill-top, compact gentleman's residence with well-appointed stables (ideal for accommodating stray crossing-sweepers) and a fine view of St Albans Cathedral. Further, the name 'Bleak House' is also bestowed by John Jarndyce on a dinky cottage he fits up for Esther and Allan Woodcourt as a married couple in Yorkshire. The name even got attached to a Broadstairs house which Dickens used as a summer residence during the 1840s. So the 'Bleak' of the book title should be seen as at most describing an institution (such as one's hopes of getting a settlement out of the Court of Chancery), not as specific to a dwelling.

The problem almost certainly arose from the same cause as with *The Old Curiosity Shop*. Dickens could modify plots under the magazine serial conditions determining his story development. He could not, once the pre-publication advertisements and the first number had come out, change the title of a novel.

Bleak House, Broadstairs, for a time a Dickens holiday residence, later a museum, now a hotel/events venue.

Never mind. Even if the title is a bit of a cheat, no other Dickens novel commences so powerfully. What with anyone else would be a backdrop, setting a scene and establishing a mood, the better to showcase the characters, here hogs the centre stage. Dickens dragoons fog, mud, gas, muck, a megalosaurus and the Law into his overture and clearly means them to be much of a piece with each other. Particularly the Law, as producing gas in prolix pleadings and judicial vapourings, throwing up fog and mud in its lack of clarity and muck in its disclosure of old scandals, while resembling a dinosaur in its failure to address the modern age. And within that Law, particularly the Court of Chancery.

In his Preface Dickens is at pains to point out that if anything he softens his case against Chancery. At the time of writing (August 1853), Dickens tells us there is a suit still before the Court, nearly 20 years in the maturing, having involved 30 to 40 counsel and run up costs of £70,000 (not far off £9 million today). He mentions another extant Chancery suit with its beginnings in the 18th century and costs to the moment of his writing of double the 20-year-old one, say nearly £18 million today.

There are dark doings in *Bleak House*, very dark ones. But there is no obvious villain. Or rather, there is no obvious human villain. Even Smallweed is merely unpleasant, while the murderess Hortense is but a stage southern European, all Mediterranean passion and broken English (though this Dickens does convincingly). However, a murky, far-reaching, destructive and powerful yet nebulous pall hovers over the story, ogre-like in its devouring of the substance of its victims. Some critics see this as the toxic miasmas seeping into the pages of *Bleak House* off unregulated cess-pools and night soil pits, or full-to-bursting burial grounds, culprits behind the early Victorian Age's atrocious public hygiene. Well, yes, as far as they go. But that is not the whole way.

For we are also dealing with a syndicate, a flesh-and-blood organisation. Slouch hangdog into the dock the Court of Chancery, aided and abetted by a gang of accomplices serving it under the arcane nomenclature of counsel, wrapped in gowns black as night as if to conceal their bodies, their heads disfigured Mohock-like by strange horsehair excrescences, badge of their ostensibly-clashing-but-in-practice-pally brotherhood, curled in the style of a past century as if to skew their countenances, the effect being to baffle honest folk; calling antiphonally across the courtroom in an outlandish argot which conceals their purpose from plain men; engaging in intricate procedural rituals the better, as it often seems, to throw dust in the eyes of lay onlookers; all obedient to a master-mind styled, in lofty fashion, 'Lord High Chancellor' (your ambitious underworld maestro ever dotes upon such aspirational titular adornments, redolent of a legitimacy he can but counterfeit), presiding over his minions' lightening of the purses of the innocent while cynically ensconced upon a woolsack, as if to underline his lamb-like disclaimer of culpability in the Chancery Mob's rampage of extortion … . One could continue a cod-Dickens indictment along these lines for paragraphs.

Yet when the Court of Chancery had first evolved in the 14th century, it had been intended as a forum dealing in equity, or fairness, a more flexible, generous and, as the cant term today has it, 'caring' system than the older Common Law. But it had undeniably got bogged down even by Elizabeth I's reign. Actually, as so often with Dickens, reforms had been introduced before he drafted his *Bleak House* prosecuting submission. A Vice-Chancellor had been instituted in 1813 (though he was only a deputy, passing more cases than ever up to his boss the Lord Chancellor to settle, and the latter, then Lord Eldon, was so anxious to be fair that he took ages to deliver decisions). Still, the Court of Chancery Act of 1842 had abolished the public legal office called the 'Six Clerks'. (Chancery clerks, taking fees not salaries, had had an interest in spinning out cases.) In 1851, the year before Dickens started *Bleak House*, the Court of Appeal in Chancery had been set up. Soon after his death the Supreme Court of Judicature Acts of 1873 and 1875 did away with Chancery as a separate court altogether, retaining it as the embodiment of equity but with the blander name 'Chancery Division' under a High Court of Justice umbrella. So Dickens had once again been beating on an open door.

Only, such was the vigour of his blows and the eloquence of his pleading that their echoes reverberate today. The very word 'Chancery' still conjures up to non-legal minds opacity little more penetrable than the Vehmgericht secret tribunals of late medieval Westphalia, and entangling tendencies more frustrating than the Slough of Despond in *Pilgrim's Progress*.

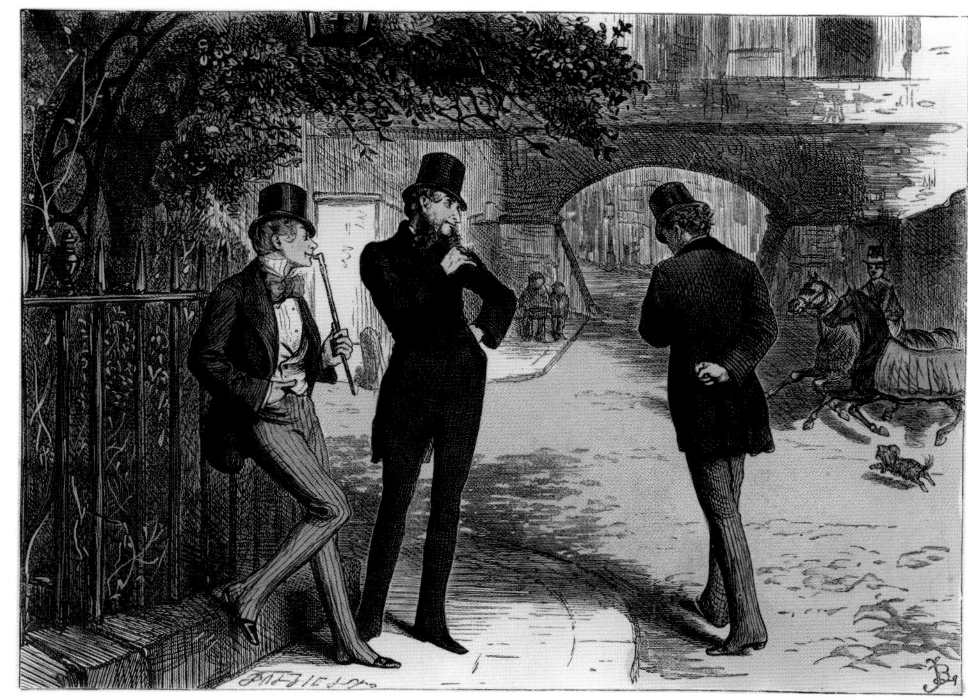

'Richard [Carstone] walks thoughtfully on and passes under the shadow of the Lincoln's Inn trees.' (Ch XXXIX).

Dickens in *Bleak House* comes up with what has since become a hackneyed device for gathering disparate types together and watching them interact. With lesser writers it is a house party that a murderer picks off one by one, or an aeroplane hijacked by terrorists. Dickens had the brainwave of letting the characters roam geographically but tying them together in the trammels of a law suit. And the beauty is, said suit means whatever you want. For Kenge it is the perfect case, 'a monument of Chancery practice ... every difficulty, every contingency, every masterly fiction, every form of procedure ... is [there] represented ... ' To Gridley it is the dismal past. To Rick Carstone a will-o'-the-wisp future. To Vholes, it is educating his daughters and providing for his father in the Vale of Taunton. For Lady Dedlock, a clew leading her into the labyrinth of past sexual indiscretion, with at its heart the Minotaur of revelation and a squalid death.

So it is apt that we start with 'My Lady Dedlock', 'bored to death'. Dickens naughtily tells us that she is childless, whereas a major item in the novel is the exact opposite, her bastard daughter Esther by 'Nemo'. Dickens has committed this sin before, the second of the two cardinal ones in a story-teller's catalogue of peccancies. Put simply, the novelist's code of honour says you can hint or imply things that turn out untrue in plot terms, or put in a character's mouth such hints or implications, but should never lie outright to your readers.

We are next introduced to Tulkinghorn, who quickly twigs that there is something fishy about Lady Dedlock's interest in the handwriting of a legal document, especially as she is usually so bored by life. Then to Sir Leicester, who thinks a Chancery suit quite an ornament to a gentleman's existence, and in any case his wife's interest in the property at stake constitutes her dowry, elevating a mere spat into an aristocratic appurtenage.

Lady Dedlock has agreed to Guppy's showing her some old letters in which he thinks she might be interested. They are her old love letters to Captain Hawdon. She knows that. Guppy does not fully realise it. (He suspects something, however.) He has now just told her that the person he was to have got them from (Krook) has 'come to a sudden end'. Lady Dedlock asks if the letters are destroyed too. Guppy says he believes so, but is not convinced himself. Nor does he convince Lady Dedlock. Then Tulkinghorn enters, the legal representative of the letters' new owner, Smallweed. Guppy slinks past him. Lady Dedlock suspects Tulkinghorn's inquisitive nature and powers of detection will uncover her secret. Illustration by Phiz to Ch XXXIII

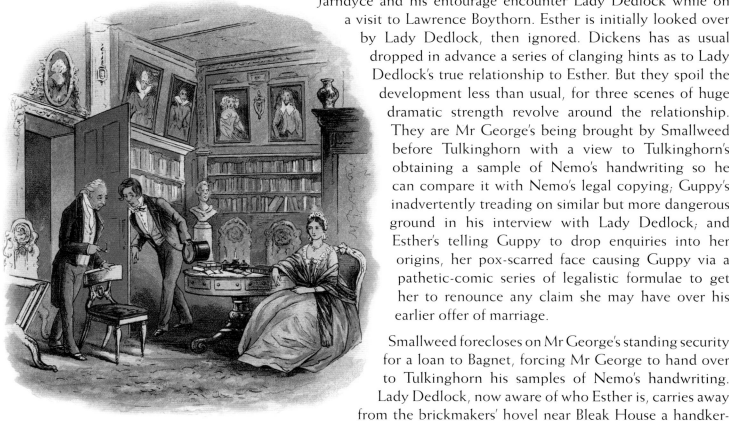

Jarndyce and his entourage encounter Lady Dedlock while on a visit to Lawrence Boythorn. Esther is initially looked over by Lady Dedlock, then ignored. Dickens has as usual dropped in advance a series of clanging hints as to Lady Dedlock's true relationship to Esther. But they spoil the development less than usual, for three scenes of huge dramatic strength revolve around the relationship. They are Mr George's being brought by Smallweed before Tulkinghorn with a view to Tulkinghorn's obtaining a sample of Nemo's handwriting so he can compare it with Nemo's legal copying; Guppy's inadvertently treading on similar but more dangerous ground in his interview with Lady Dedlock; and Esther's telling Guppy to drop enquiries into her origins, her pox-scarred face causing Guppy via a pathetic-comic series of legalistic formulae to get her to renounce any claim she may have over his earlier offer of marriage.

Smallweed forecloses on Mr George's standing security for a loan to Bagnet, forcing Mr George to hand over to Tulkinghorn his samples of Nemo's handwriting. Lady Dedlock, now aware of who Esther is, carries away from the brickmakers' hovel near Bleak House a handkerchief Esther has left there and on Esther's recuperating from her smallpox up in Lincolnshire seeks her out, tearfully embraces her and discloses her identity as mother.

A general election is called. The Dedlocks convene a large house party at Chesney to help canvass up and down the district. (Only now does Dickens reveal that Sir Leicester is an MP.) Industrialist Rouncewell has organised effective opposition to Sir Leicester's party in the manufacturing seats. Tulkinghorn arrives and imparts news of this. He also says that the Rouncewell people are likely to scotch Watt Rouncewell's courtship of Rosa, Lady Dedlock's pet maid, and on Sir Leicester protesting at such insolence tells in front of the entire company the tale of Lady Dedlock's long-ago fling with Hawdon and its consequence, Esther. Only he pretends it is about quite a different lot of people. His purpose – or alleged purpose – is to explain that the Rouncewells may well repudiate someone they would otherwise become connected with by marriage if scandal should taint that person, even though she be the protégée of the Rouncewells' social superiors.

We now embark on a fourth dramatic scene, and it is even richer than the other three. Lady Dedlock confronts Tulkinghorn later that evening in his room, aghast at his recent indiscretion. She declares she will depart Chesney that night. Tulkinghorn forbids her, on pain of raising an alarm and telling her story to everyone in the house. She shall remain by her husband's side as his beloved and honoured helpmeet or his happiness may suffer. Lady Dedlock asks if she must live for ever tormented by Tulkinghorn's knowing her secret, aware that he will reveal it if he thinks it in Sir Leicester's interest. Tulkinghorn effectively says yes, though with lawyer's wordiness taking several paragraphs to do so. All this amounts to one of the most masterly passages Dickens ever penned. A coda to it, in which Tulkinghorn revokes his pledge of limited silence since Lady Dedlock is sending Rosa away, is scarcely less so.

Tulkinghorn's murder fails to bury Lady Dedlock's secret. The Smallweeds, Chadband and Mrs Snagsby demand hush money from Sir Leicester over Lady Dedlock's love letters to Nemo. Mrs Rouncewell begs Lady Dedlock to intervene over Mr George's remand for Tulkinghorn's murder. And Guppy tells Lady Dedlock of the Smallweed contingent's meeting with Sir Leicester. Convinced that her secret is now known to many, or will be soon, Lady Dedlock flees from her husband's house after writing him a letter protesting her innocence of Tulkinghorn's murder.

Sir Leicester, though handicapped by his recent stroke, deputes Bucket to find her. Bucket searches Lady Dedlock's rooms, discovers Esther's handkerchief (with Esther's name on it) and takes Esther with him to search for her mother. He carries out his search both in an official capacity, enlisting the help of police officers, and as a private commission from Sir Leicester (to hush up whose involvement over Jo he has previously worked also, likewise in trying to buy off Smallweed's blackmailing party). Sir Leicester gives him £160 (£20,000 today) petty cash for expenses.

This suborning of a public office-holder for private ends is disgraceful. Much more so than the sinecure-hunting of idle sprigs like the Hon Bob Stables that Dickens has excoriated with such contempt earlier. Yet it is one which Dickens seems to find unexceptionable. A sign perhaps that his radicalism now had its limits, the corners smoothed off by his consorting on so many occasions with the Hon Richard Watson at his castle of Rockingham.

Lady Dedlock struggles on foot through snow up to St Albans to see her daughter, then back to London, and dies at the gates to the paupers' cemetery where her daughter's father is buried. Smallweed discovers among the papers he has inherited from Krook a will that will settle *Jarndyce and Jarndyce*. Accumulated costs in *Jarndyce and Jarndyce* swallow up its assets, however. Esther at her guardian John Jarndyce's prompting renounces him for Allan Woodcourt and settles with Allan in Yorkshire.

Bleak House appeared in monthly numbers between 1852 and 1853. The publishers, recalling *David Copperfield*'s sluggish performance, arranged the first month's print run of 25,000. It sold out in three days and two immediate reprints followed. Within four months 38,500 copies had been sold and subsequent monthly sales never dipped below 30,000. *Bleak House*'s success persuaded Dickens to strike the Harper's deal in America (see 'Dickens Abroad'). Takings from the first six numbers alone had brought him by spring 1853 £3,106–13s–6d (£3,106.66, or almost £110,000 in today's money). 'The Inimitable' was back on form as the most cerulean of blue-chip literary stocks.

Hard Times

Weekly serial, 1854
Book published 1854

Gradgrind tells his daughter of Bounderby's marriage proposal.

Characters

Bitzer

Pallid swot at the school in Coketown (based on Preston in Lancashire) where the novel opens; graduates to working at Bounderby's bank, for most of the story as a porter, but also as spy on other employees; desiring promotion, tries to arrest Tom Gradgrind junior for a robbery at the bank; justifies such rigid adherence to civic duty to Gradgrind senior on the utilitarian principles Gradgrind senior has dinned into him, but Sleary frustrates his efforts by sicking on him one of Sleary's trained dogs, who thus extends the doggy tendency to forwarding the plot that Dickens had introduced via Jip in *David Copperfield*.

Thomas Gradgrind.

Blackpool, Stephen

Power-loom weaver; aged 40 when story begins; long married to an alcoholic wife whom he can't afford to ditch, divorce then being a costly process dependant on intricate legal manoeuvres; tricked by Tom Gradgrind junior into lurking near Bounderby's bank when Tom robs it, hence attracts official suspicion; refuses to join a trade union so is blacked by fellow-workers as a scab, while also boycotted by employers as a malcontent; seeks work elsewhere till summoned back to Coketown to answer charges of bank-robbing, but en route falls down abandoned mine and dies, though not before a heart-rending farewell scene with Rachael.

Bounderby, Josiah

Balding Coketown banker, merchant and manufacturer; the archetypal coarse, self-made, bluff, plethoric, no-nonsense North Country plutocrat, constantly boasting of his impoverished origins and how his drunken mother abandoned him when an infant (implying how clever he has been to overcome such handicaps), while secretly admiring the grand connexions of his housekeeper Mrs Sparsit; later much discomfited when his mother announces to a crowd of Coketownites that she made huge sacrifices to push his prospects and, far from having long abandoned him, gets from him an annuity of £30 (£3,750 today) to stay away.

Childers, E W B Circus performer in a Wild West act.

Gradgrind, Thomas/Tom

Retired wholesale hardware merchant and a utilitarian even more doctrinaire than the un-reformed Scrooge inasmuch as he calls his two youngest children Adam Smith Gradgrind and Malthus Gradgrind after the economist and demographer respectively; dominates the novel's opening scene at the school in Coketown, though whether as a governor, self-constituted inspector or busybody casual visitor is not explained; obsessed with facts and detests fancy; as such blights the lives of his two older children, Louisa and Thomas junior; later becomes Coketown's MP; on his daughter Louisa's near-fall from grace, reforms and becomes quite human.

Gradgrind, Louisa

Gradgrind's elder daughter; takes over from Sissy Jupe the role in the novel of spokesman for the emotions, in Chapter XV, during the scene with her father when Bounderby's offer of marriage comes up, constantly worsting him in cross-examination like a 19th-century Cris(tina) Arguedas; marries Mr Bounderby, is miserable with him and eventually separates from him after very nearly allowing herself to be seduced by James Harthouse.

Gradgrind, Mrs

Gradgind's wife; broadly loyal to her husband's outlook but less than enthusiastic about its particulars, referring to his recommended fields of study as 'ologies' (a homespun-ism that surfaced again in the 1980s British Telecom TV ads involving Maureen Lipman).

Harthouse, James or 'Jem'

Fashionable swell from down South, hence with more polish than Coketown folk are used to; ingratiates himself with Tom Gradgrind junior and initially with Mrs Sparsit, but she divines his aim of seducing Louisa and eavesdrops on his attempt at it.

Jupe, Sissy

'Sissy' short for Cecilia, a less fanciful version that Gradgrind imposes on her; daughter of a circus clown-cum-bare-back-rider-cum-juggler-cum-tumbler who, after his performances deteriorate, steals shamefacedly away, accompanied by his performing dog Merrylegs; taken to live with Gradgrind's family as companion to his children and wife; represents human sympathy in opposition to the prevailing materialism, pointing out on one occasion, innocent casuist that she is, that the answer to M'Choakumchild's question of what percentage of sea-passengers are drowned or burned if only 500 perish in 100,000 man-voyages is 'nothing' – to their nearest and dearest; eventually marries (but whom, Dickens doesn't tell us) and has children.

Kidderminster Circus performer; plays Childers's infant son, since a jockey in stature though post-pubescent.

M'Choakumchild Schoolmaster at Coketown school where Sissy Jupe and Bitzer educated; the 'M' plus apostrophe form at the front of surnames was the common 19th-century version of 'Mac-' or 'Mc-'.

Rachael Mill girl; loves and is loved by Stephen Blackpool, but, he being married, they are too virtuous to live together.

Slackbridge Local trade unionist agitator.

Sleary

Lisping circus-proprietor.

Sleary, Josephine His daughter; bare-back rider who performs a Tyrolean flower act.

Sparsit, Mrs (*née* Scadgers)

Housekeeper to Bounderby; has grand connexions, her late husband having on his mother's side been of ancient family and her great-aunt being Lady Scadgers; as such is patronised by Bounderby, he being the sort of self-made man who draws extra relish from keeping some broken-down near-aristo in a state of dependence; she later officiously unearths Mrs Pegler, Bounderby's mother, whereupon Bounderby dismisses her.

A Spitalfields weaver at work, 1895.

Hard Times

Story Commentary

Hard Times is the shortest Dickens novel, roughly 120,000 words. Even that is about one-and-a-half times the length most publishers would accept from a novelist today. It is also reputed to exist in over 1,500 textual variants, testament to Dickens's erratic punctuation and spelling. Under today's neo-Gradgrind educational policies Dickens would be unlikely to get a good A level grade in a paper on one of his own works: his written presentation would not pass muster. 'Hard Times' are also our times, therefore.

We start in Coketown, in or near which all the action is set. It is a smoke-ridden, factory chimney-bound, ruddy-bricked dystopia. Its most choking aspect is the narrow minds of the clique that run it: provincial, statistics-ridden, mean-spirited, and ignorant of the work force on whom their profits depend. Their sole excursion into imagination is to fancy that the proles are after venison, turtle soup, gold spoons to eat them with and carriage rides to digest them during.

The circus folk from whom Sissy Jupe springs represent the very opposite, though Dickens is not so foolish as to paint their life all beer and skittles. Stiff knee joints spell your end as acrobat. Sleary, the circus proprietor, is as box-office minded and near as cautious over aiding and abetting criminal activity as any merchant banker.

Coalbrookdale by Night, 1801, by Philipp-Jakob Loutherbourg the Younger (right).

Industry at Work, by an unknown artist (opposite).

Louisa Gradgrind's dreary married life owes as much to the limited outlook of the locals as to her father's and her husband Bounderby's materialism. So too Stephen Blackpool and Rachael. Had those two dwelt somewhere less provincial they might have had the guts to defy convention and live with a person they loved rather than stay shackled to a spouse they didn't. One hesitates to say that only London would have been big enough. On the other hand Coketown clearly wasn't. The novel is thus as much about the restraint of life well away from the capital city as it is to do with the narrow-mindedness of individuals. No other novel by Dickens has so total a setting so far from London.

As a serial *Hard Times* raised the circulation of its parent magazine *Household Words* by over 100 per cent, to the upper 30,000s. Dickens's fee for the story was £1,000 and the public had bought 5,000 copies of the book version of *Hard Times* by the end of 1854, although its last magazine episode had come out as recently as mid-August. He had in less than a year made from it £1,500 in all (not far off £200,000 in today's money).

Little Dorrit

Monthly serial, 1855 to 1857
Book published 1857

Little Dorrit asks Bob the turnkey if fields are locked.

Characters

Bangham, Mrs Marshalsea charwoman/messenger at time of Amy Dorrit's birth there.

Barnacle Easy-going civil servant in Circumlocution Office (Dickens seems to have had in mind the Treasury since, when Sparkler is appointed to the Circumlocution Office he is termed a 'Lord' of it, and this could mean no other department of state).

Barnacle, Clarence Son of Tite Barnacle below; Circumlocution Office sinecurist; friend of Gowan.

Barnacle, Lord Decimus Tite Leading politician, also a peer, or so Dickens assures us, showing that he has learnt nothing about titles since his solecism of nearly 20 years earlier over Verisopht in *Nicholas Nickleby*; for if Barnacle is a peer the form 'Lord Decimus [forename] ... Barnacle [surname]' is incorrect, since it applies only to a marquess's or duke's younger son, yet if 'Barnacle' is the man's surname alone, he won't be a peer. Played by Robert Morley in the 1988 film, the fourth such, there having been 'silents' in 1913 and 1920 and a German 'talkie' in 1934.

Tite Barnacle (above) and Christopher Casby (below).

Barnacle, Ferdinand Another sinecurist.

Barnacle, Tite Yet another Circumlocution Office sinecurist.

Blandois/Lagnier/Rigaud

Belgium-born son of a Swiss father and England-born French mother; formerly married to a French inn-keeper's widow whom, we infer, he has murdered.

Bob Marshalsea turnkey during Amy Dorrit's childhood.

Casby, Christopher Urban landlord, benevolent-looking, in reality rapacious; father of Flora Finching. Played by Bill Fraser in the 1988 film; John Alderton in the 2008 BBC televisation.

Cavalletto, John Baptist/Gian Battista

Genoese petty smuggler; former cell-mate in Marseilles of Blandois/Lagnier/Rigaud; moves to London, where lives in Bleeding Heart Yard and is known as 'Mr Baptist'.

Chivery Marshalsea turnkey by time of Amy Dorrit's early adulthood.

Chivery, 'young' John

Son of above; loves Amy Dorrit; Amy turns him down; Chivery senior in consequence gets gruff with Mr Dorrit, who in turn almost, but not quite, asks Amy to accommodate John Chivery's advances since among other things young John regularly brings him gifts of cigars.

Chivery, Mrs John's mother.

Clennam, Arthur

Disillusioned 40-year-old China merchant; returns to England after 20 years out East, his father having died there; clearly fancies Amy Dorrit from first sight of her at his mother's, where she goes to do sewing, since he stalks her all the way back to the Marshalsea and pays £40 (£5,000 today) in getting her worthless brother Tip released from the Marshalsea so as to ingratiate himself with her; later nearly falls in love with 'Pet' Meagles; she prefers Gowan's specious charm; finally consoles himself with Amy Dorrit; a bit of an old stick, being solemn and rather disapproving, but someone Dickens came to identify with, suddenly referring to him in Chapter XII as 'Arthur' rather than, as previously, 'Clennam', then alternating in following chapters between 'Clennam' and 'Arthur', often within a few lines. Played by Derek Jacobi in the 1988 film; Matthew Macfadyen in the 2008 televisation.

Clennam, Mrs

Arthur's father's grim, wheelchair-bound, gloomily pious widow. Played by Joan Greenwood in the 1988 film; Judy Parfitt in the 2008 televisation.

Arthur Clennam calling on Little Dorrit and her father at the Marshalsea.

Dorrit, Amy ('Little')

William Dorrit's younger daughter, aged 22 when the story opens but looks about 13 (Dickens's favourite age in girls: Little Nell, 'The Marchioness' and Florence Dombey, even Dora Copperfield as regards emotional maturity); keeps Dorrit family together by unobtrusive responsibility; rather oddly refers to herself as 'Little Dorrit' (and at one point, also oddly, is addressed by Clennam in their first love scene as 'darling Little Dorrit'); for her part has fallen in love with Clennam by Chapter XXXII, a point at which his 'interest' in her is still that of a nymphet-fancier with charitable urges, and she anyway believes him keen on 'Pet' Meagles. Played by Claire Foy in the 2008 televisation.

Dorrit, Fanny

Amy's elder sister; dancer in a theatre; marries Sparkler ('almost an idiot' she calls him) out of revenge on his mother for her superciliousness.

Dorrit, Frederick Orchestra clarinettist in the theatre where his niece Fanny dances; younger brother of William. Played by Cyril Cusack in the 1988 film.

Dorrit, 'Tip' Christened Edward, next 'Ted' then 'Tip'; William's son; has had dozens of jobs and not stuck to one. Played by Daniel Chatto in the 1988 film.

Dorrit, William

'Father of the Marshalsea' (see further under 'Story Commentary'). Played by Alec Guinness in the 1988 film (see also *Great Expectations*); Tom Courtenay in the 2008 TV adaptation.

Doyce, Daniel Inventor, though of what Dickens characteristically fails to tell us; forms partnership with Arthur Clennam; the latter handles finance, Doyce technical matters.

Finching, Flora

Widow of a Mr Finching and old flame of Clennam's, towards whom she behaves roguishly; kind-hearted, especially to Amy Dorrit, who one otherwise might expect her to be jealous of. Played by Miriam Margolyes in the 1988 film.

F[inching]'s Aunt, Mr Flora's aunt-in-law; develops great aversion to Clennam.

Clennam (arm round Flora), wanting a private word with Affery (who here lights the party down the staircase), persuades Flora to ask to see round Mrs Clennam's quaint old house. Flintwinch (following) determines to prevent any Clennam-Affery confidences. Illustration by Phiz to Ch XXIII of Book 2.

Flintwinch, Affery Housekeeper to Mrs Clennam; Jeremiah F's wife, of whom, with Mrs Clennam, she is in awe as 'them two clever ones'. Played by Patricia Hayes in the 1988 film.

Flintwinch, Jeremiah

Mrs Clennam's right-hand man in the moribund family business. Played by Max Wall in the 1988 film; Alun Armstrong in the 2008 televisation.

General, Mrs

Lady companion-cum-chaperone hired to form the Dorrit girls' minds and manners on their Continental tour; advocates enunciating the words 'prunes' and 'prism' as forming the lips; may have inspired Oscar Wilde's governess Miss Prism in *The Importance of Being Earnest*.

Gowan, Henry

Upper-class, and successful, wooer of 'Pet' Meagles.

Gowan, Mrs Henry's mother; expresses her contempt for the Meagleses, whose daughter's money is to keep her son, by referring to them as 'Mickles' or 'Miggles'.

Haggage, Dr Marshalsea inmate who delivered Amy Dorrit.

Lion

Gowan's Newfoundland dog; forwards the plot by helping make his master agreeable to 'Pet' Meagles and becoming the focus of Mr Meagles's anguish over the incipient match; in Venice, Lion's savage kicking by Gowan underlines what a swine Gowan is beneath his veneer of sophisticated good-breeding; Lion's poisoning, almost certainly by Blandois, who is now a hanger-on of the Gowans, shows what extremes of malice Blandois will go to; significantly, Byron had a Newfoundland dog called Lyon (see also against Jingle in *Pickwick Papers*) and Dickens's catty reference to Gowan's 'perceptible limp, both in his devotion to art and his attainments' is a below-the-belt hit at Byron's literary reputation via his club foot, also stressing the gentleman-amateur nature of Gowan's involvement in the arts, one that Dickens implicitly held Byron had been guilty of as regards poetry.

Maggy Semi-moron friend-cum-dependant of Amy Dorrit, whom she addresses as 'Little Mother'; addicted to 'chicking', as she calls chicken (then a luxury).

Meagles

Retired banker, now given to sight-seeing and antiquity-collecting abroad, although terribly insular, refusing to acquire a single word of a foreign language, and a bit homespun (refers to/addresses his wife as 'Mother'); depressingly snobbish, relishing Clarence Barnacle's aristocratic connexions. Played by Bill Paterson in the 2008 TV adaptation.

Meagles, Mrs His wife.

Meagles, 'Pet' (real name Minnie)

Their daughter; 'spoilt', Dickens says, but 'pampered' more accurate, for though doted on by her parents she has a pleasant enough, if insipid, personality; Dickens shows signs towards her of confused nomenclature similar to his Arthur/Clennam see-sawing, now referring to her as 'Minnie', now as 'Pet'.

Merdle

Very dull but very rich, or thought to be; his wealth the fruit of theft and fraud, to escape detection of which he commits suicide.

Merdle, Mrs

His wife, widow of a Col Sparkler; voluptuous, affected, insincere, bored; condescends to Fanny Dorrit. Played by Eleanor Bron in the 1988 film; Amanda Redman in the 2008 televisation.

Nandy, John Edward ('Old') Mrs Plornish's father.

Pancks

Rent-collector for Christopher Casby; also investigates unclaimed estates, as which discovers that William Dorrit is beneficiary of a fortune; on being ordered by Casby to squeeze more rent from his tenants denounces him to the Bleeding Heart Yard residents and cuts his patriarchal locks off, thus exposing him as a humbug.

Plornish, Thomas Plasterer friend of Tip Dorrit; lives in Bleeding Heart Yard.

Plornish, Sally His wife.

Rugg Pancks's Pentonville landlord.

Sparkler, Edmund Mrs Merdle's son by her first husband; appointed to a plum post in the Circumlocution Office following a piece of jobbery between Lord Decimus Tite Barnacle and Mr Merdle; marries Fanny Dorrit.

Tattycoram

'Pet''s maid; rescued by Meagleses from Thomas Coram's Foundling Hospital in Bloomsbury (orphanage rather than health-restorative institution), the 'Coram' being tacked by the Meagleses onto a corrupted diminutive of her baptismal name Harriet, thus 'Hatty' then 'Tatty' then 'Tattycoram', a label its bearer understandably detests as condescending; seduced away from the Meagleses' rather too cosy hearth by the enigmatic, lesbian-inclined Miss Wade, but whatever their subsequent intimacies (if any) addresses her with the utmost formality as 'Miss Wade'; eventually returns to the Meagleses, bringing Clennam's great-uncle's missing will codicil which bestows 1,000 guineas (over £125,000 today) on Amy Dorrit, Rigaud having left it for safe-keeping with his former paymaster, Miss Wade.

Wade, Miss

Fellow hotel-guest at Marseilles with Meagleses and Clennam; Dickens specifically calls her 'repressed', so any lesbianism is latent; beneficiary of a modest fund of which Casby is trustee, drawing on it from time to time; once 'almost' (her word) fell in love with Gowan, but has since taken against him and his wife Pet, hiring Blandois to spy on them; a chip-on-shoulder neurotic who interprets the smallest kindness as an act of condescension.

Little Dorrit

Story Commentary

The time, Dickens says, is 30 years back, about 1826. He soon forgets this, having Mr Meagles refer to France's military government, which must mean Louis-Napoleon's Prince-President regime of 1851–52 or his Second Empire (1852–70). Apart from the Marshalsea every feature of *Little Dorrit* bespeaks the 1850s: useful inventions scorned by lethargic bureaucracy; aristocratic jobbery, once common, now coming under fire; new money swiftly admitted to the highest society instead of having to cool its heels till it becomes less new, or, better, semi-old; even fashions in clothes, notably the crinoline, as Phiz's illustrations depict.

But in 1826 the Marshalsea debtors' prison still stood (it was closed in 1842, hence Dickens's need to travel in a time machine, if a rickety one). Its location was Southwark, on the Surrey bank of the Thames, and it had in real life lately hosted John Dickens. Its current fictional prisoners in the 1826–56 time-warp include William Dorrit, of a once notable Dorset family. By residing in the Marshalsea nearly 23 years he has become its 'Father'. His wife has died after a piffling eight years there.

As Marshalsea 'Father', he receives newcomers. A custom has grown up of inmates giving him tips when set free. (Possibly the origin of his son's nickname, for Dickens, though claiming 'Tip' a variant of Ted, is slyly given to that sort of wordplay.) William Dorrit's euphemism for them is 'Testimonials'.

On one occasion, a plasterer has the effrontery to offer him a Testimonial of a few pence in coppers (£2 or £3 today) rather than the more usual half-crowns or crowns in silver (12p or 25p equivalent then, say £15 or £30 today). 'The Father' exclaims 'how dare you!' and bursts into tears. Yet he is not too delicate to ask for the money back.

The Marshalsea is called by Dickens a college and its inmates collegians, meaning at first a literal 'collection' of human beings. But it also proves a college in the educational sense. Lenin's epigram ('prison ... the revolutionary's university') doesn't stop its being the bourgeoisie's polytechnic. Thus a dancing master debtor inmate while waiting for his release instructs Fanny Dorrit in tripping a court minuet. A seamstress debtor inmate teaches Amy how to ply her needle.

Presently William Dorrit comes into an immense fortune. Dickens is maddeningly vague as to details. One might as well be talking about a dragon's hoard of faërie gold. But he atones for it with a splendid slice of drama showing all William Dorrit's contradictions of personality. For

William rather than Clennam is the book's true male lead, being not only less-buttoned up but more 'complete'.

So on becoming suddenly prosperous he is at first genially seigneurial, anxious to repay not just all his own debts but all his son Tip's, anxious to show his gratitude to the Chivery family of warders, anxious to compensate Pancks for his labour and capital outlay (some £1,000, or £125,000 today). Then he reverts to the newly released prisoner of tradition, sobbing out tears of relief and gratitude for his delivery. Next he turns to family matters, giving precise instructions for improving Fanny's and Frederick's lives.

There is more. The question arises of how soon he can complete formalities for evacuating the Marshalsea. Clennam tells him it will be but a few hours. The pustule of a quarter-century's imprisonment bursts. William Dorrit turns on Clennam, the bringer of good news, with one of the most poignant reproaches in all literature, 'You talk very easily of hours, sir! How long do you suppose, sir, that an hour is to a man who is choking for want of air?' He weeps a bit more then falls asleep. This is art of the front rank.

Little Dorrit and her father hear some good news; an illustration by Harold Copping.

And the effect on Little Dorrit? She seems troubled, despite the wonderful news. Clennam asks why. She inquires if her father will repay all his debts. Yes, says Clennam. All the ones he was imprisoned for in the first place, as well as those he has run up while in prison? – she in effect asks further. Yes, says Clennam. It seems hard that her father should lose so many years and suffer so much and at last pay all the debts as well, says Little Dorrit. A reasonable point.

The Dorrits, now rolling in money, travel to Italy. William, his son and elder daughter display all the arrogance, abrasiveness and insensitivity-yet-insecurity of the new rich. But they are not standard new rich. Their past poverty followed

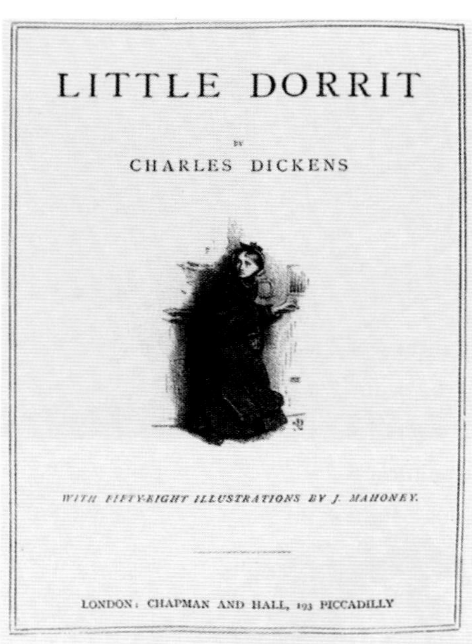

The title page of Little Dorrit (Chapman and Hall).

on earlier 'comfortable circumstances'. The true sequence is 'old well-off', 'new poor' shading over time into 'long-term poor' to 'new super rich', a much subtler process, especially since the 'long-term poor' bit has its extra-shameful debtor's prison side. William Dorrit is touchy as a raw wound to every innocent reference even by chance strangers to involuntary confinement. Fanny flounces. Edward, rejecting 'Tip', otherwise remains vacuous.

Even the 'nice' Dorrits are changed. Amy, though still Miss Mouse, hankers after the old days, when her adored father was more approachable. Uncle Frederick, usually maundering in near-senility just as before, is yet capable of tigerish springs at any attendant who neglects Amy. The power of riches to imprison you no less effectively than do bars and cells and locks and high walls is neatly pointed.

En route the Dorrits encounter Mrs Merdle and her son Edmund Sparkler. The latter renews his wooing of Fanny. The Dorrits stay a month or two in Venice then move on to Rome. Here Fanny and Sparkler become engaged. Dickens tips us off to William Dorrit's impending breakdown via the rage with which he reacts, on a brief trip to London, to John Chivery's bringing him the traditional present of cigars. John's secret motive is to ask after Amy. William Dorrit's reaction, equally secret, is being reminded of his imprisoned debtor days.

William, quickly ashamed of his rage, makes amends by scribbling a cheque for £100 (£12,500 today) to share among the Marshalsea's present occupants. But signs of his mortality intrude. The writing on the cheque is a scrawl, executed in a trembling hand. Back in Rome, he gropes at his head as if searching for the old black cap of his Marshalsea days. He frequently drops off into a doze. Then the catastrophe.

At a big farewell dinner party given by Mrs Merdle just before her departure for England, he gets to his feet and calls down the crowded table to Amy to see if Bob, the Marshalsea turnkey of years ago, is 'on the lock', then adds 'send for Bob – best of all the turnkeys ... ', employing the broken, craven, prostrated language of his time as a new inmate of the Marshalsea a generation earlier. He pulls himself together a bit, but only so far as to address the company patronisingly, as if he were still the Father of the Marshalsea and his audience a rabble of lesser debtors. Consternation overwhelms the other guests. He lingers a day or two, then dies. His brother dies shortly afterwards, William asserting precedence to the last.

The Dorrit family and Clennam have invested their all in Merdle's enterprises, which now fail, wiping out the capital of anyone involved and in addition getting Clennam clapped in the Marshalsea as a debtor. Amy returns to England, implausibly putting up at the de luxe hotel (the present Claridge's, so renamed just before *Little Dorrit* came out) where her father had stayed on his brief London trip. Her main purpose is to visit Clennam in the Marshalsea.

Rigaud, as he is now known (though he calls himself alternately Rigaud Blandois and Rigaud Lagnier Blandois), tries blackmailing Mrs Clennam over her family history. It seems Arthur Clennam's father, a timid fellow, was commanded by his forceful uncle Gilbert to marry Gilbert's choice of bride, the present Mrs Clennam. But the timid fellow had fathered Arthur on a girl he had gone through a form of marriage with. Mrs Clennam bullied the girl into surrendering Arthur for her to bring up. She also suppressed a codicil in Gilbert Clennam's will leaving money to more than one possible beneficiary, the sole person to qualify now being Amy Dorrit. Mrs Clennam employed Amy as seamstress to compensate her for having kept her out of her legacy.

The codicil was taken by Flintwinch's lunatic-asylum-warder twin brother Ephraim (in whose keeping Arthur's true mother, by then mad with grief, had at one time been placed) to Antwerp. There Rigaud, an acquaintance of Ephraim's, had found it after his death. The revelation of all this cures Mrs Clennam of her wheelchair-bound paralysis. She rushes off to the Marshalsea to find Amy Dorrit, for whose attention Rigaud has left a package explaining the above should Mrs Clennam refuse him £2,000 hush money. Mrs Clennam now tells Amy all, thus cutting the ground from under Rigaud's feet. They return to confront him at the Clennam family's ancient house in the City of London. As they approach, it collapses, burying Rigaud. Flintwinch has escaped earlier, taking what cash and valuables he can lay his hands on and setting up in Amsterdam as 'Mynheer von Flyntevynge'.

It is extraordinary that so late in his career Dickens should have patched together such a farrago of outrageous coincidences and hokum stage furniture, not least a missing will, a device he had used thrice already, in *Oliver Twist*, *Nicholas Nickleby* and *Bleak House* (and was to use again – two of them, moreover – in *Our Mutual Friend*). The Clennam business involves sufficient plot for another novel, yet Dickens loads it onto the tail end of his original one. The new creaky burden nearly brings down the excellent main theme of William Dorrit's debtor decay, rather as rotten beams and joists do the Clennams' house.

Amy marries Arthur Clennam, having first tricked him, her eyes 'glistening', into burning the codicil. She thus refuses her legacy, and at a moment when she has no grounds for thinking Clennam possesses money of his own. A quixotic action, the episode suggests first that Amy is just as careless about money as her father was and, second, that she will as wife be just as manipulative of Clennam as her sister Fanny is of Edmund Sparkler. Doyce returns from abroad a rich man and as his business partner Clennam will benefit, so perhaps Amy's improvidence, appetite for subterfuge and power-hunger hardly matter. And were they not in any case the product of all those Marshalsea years? Food for thought there.

Little Dorrit did pretty well in the standard magazine serial format, the first number, that of December 1855, selling 38,000 copies. It subsided to 35,000 each in the middle passage (1,000 more than *Bleak House* at the same stage) and with the two last ones (combined in a single issue of June 1857) something under 30,000. The critics started off favourable, but later grew less impressed. They hadn't been thrilled by *Bleak House* either, yet that is now considered one of the greatest Dickens novels. Dickens himself affected to despise critics and seldom read their reviews of his work.

A Tale of Two Cities

Magazine format 1859
Book published 1859

'Darnay ... was taken ... to the guard-house, where ... patriots in rough red caps were smoking, drinking, and sleeping, by a watch-fire.' (Ch XXXI). Illustration by Phiz.

Characters

Barsad, John (see also Pross) Chief Crown witness against Charles Darnay at his 1780 treason trial in London, but his credibility destroyed by Stryver's cross-examination; later suspected by M and Mme Defarge in Paris of spying on them; by 1792 has joined Paris revolutionaries.

Carton, Sydney

Bibulous and unambitious but very competent barrister, as which devises arguments and cross-examination tactics used in court by his friend Stryver, hence less the jackal to Stryver's lion, as Dickens claims fellow lawyers see him, than the puppet-master to Stryver's marionette; Old Salopian (no trivial point this, since Shrewsbury old boys have shone as lawyers, e.g. Judge Jeffreys, who despite the Bloody Assizes was a good judge and a better advocate, while the Old Salopian Sir Philip Sidney, who after being mortally wounded in battle famously renounced a drink of water in favour of another wounded soldier, clearly inspired Dickens to name Carton 'Sydney' as the kind of selfless paragon who would take Charles Darnay's place under the guillotine). Played by Ronald Colman in the 1935 film; Dirk Bogarde in the 1958 one; Peter Wyngarde in the 1957 BBC TV adaptation; Charles Dance in the 1989 BBC Radio 4 one.

Cly, Roger Darnay's former servant; testifies against Darnay at latter's 1780 treason trial, his testimony being so undermined by Carton's suggested line of cross-examination, used at the trial by Stryver, that Darnay is acquitted and the impression left on spectators' minds that Cly is a government spy or agent provocateur.

Cruncher, Jerry (formally Jeremiah) Odd-job-man at Tellson's Bank; moonlights as a 'resurrectionist' (i.e. body-snatcher, his trade in fresh corpses filched from new-dug graves finding a ready market with medical students and more seasoned anatomists). Played by Alfie Bass in the 1958 film.

Cruncher, Mrs Pious wife of above.

Cruncher, 'young' Jerry Son of above two.

Darnay, Charles; aka the Marquis St Evrémonde

Toff-with-a-conscience, being nephew and heir to the wicked old Marquis, following whose murder he would normally inherit the title and estates, but

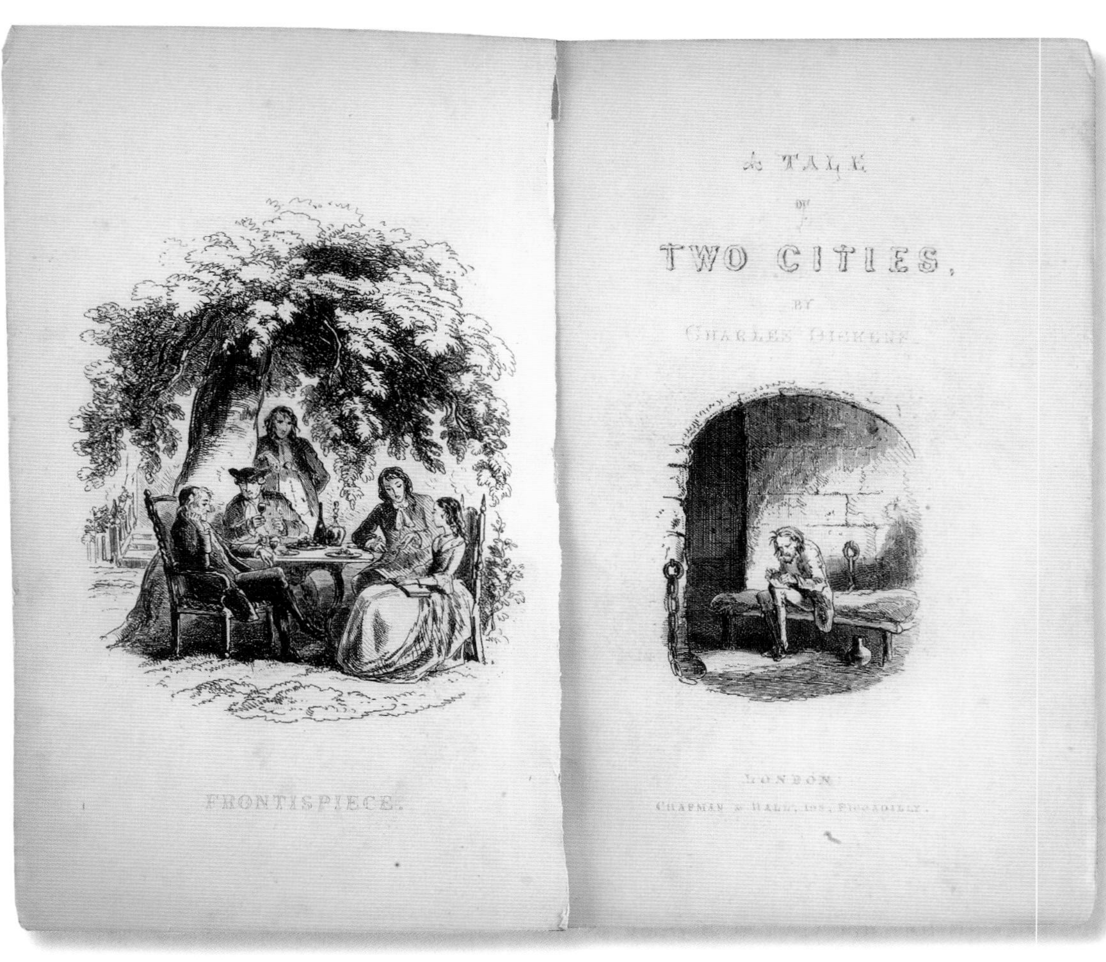

A Tale of Two Cities *title pages with illustrations by Phiz, 1859.*

prefers to work in England as a French language tutor and translator, having earlier expressed to his uncle his distaste for the St Evrémondes' history of cruelty and disregard of their peasants' welfare; aged about 25 in 1780; 'Darnay' an anglicised version of his mother's maiden name, D'Aulnais.

Defarge, Ernest, aka Jacques Four

Ex-servant of Dr Manette long before the Revolution, later Paris wine shop proprietor; from at least 1780 draws up with his still more vengeful wife a list of obnoxious aristocrats and their hangers-on for liquidation come the Revolution; when it does come, develops into a prominent agitator of the Faubourg St Antoine (where the Bastille was situated); in his relations with Lorry shows faint signs of abating his revolutionary grimness.

Defarge, Mme (Thérèse)

Wife of above and still more prominent revolutionary, heading her own women's cadre; perennially knitting, partly as a hobby, but mostly since it lets her keep a list of revolutionary victims coded according to the type of stitch; turns out to be sister of the girl raped by the St Evrémonde brothers years before the Revolution, to attend on whom in her ravings Dr Manette was summoned by the St Evrémondes then clapped at their instigation in the Bastille to prevent him blabbing. Played by Rosalie Crutchley in the 1958 film; Billie Whitelaw in the 1980 made-for-TV film.

Gabelle, Théophile Postmaster and tax functionary of village at base of the St Evrémondes' château.

Gaspard Father of a child run over and killed by the old Marquis St Evrémonde, who tosses him a coin in compensation; out of revenge stabs St Evrémonde in his bed and is hanged 40 feet high above the fountain of the village near the St Evrémondes' château.

Jacques One, Two, Three and Five Revolutionaries under Defarge; the name 'Jacques' (James or Jim) was in France akin to the English 'Hodge', meaning a witless rustic; a *jacquerie* or peasants' insurrection had special resonance in French revolutionary lore ever since one such north of Paris in the late 14th century.

Joe London–Dover mail coach guard.

Lorry, Jarvis

Functionary with Tellson's Bank; helps bring Dr Manette to London from Paris in 1775 and becomes friends with him and his daughter Lucie, also helping them get out of Paris in 1793. Played by Nigel Stock in the 1980 BBC TV adaptation; John Mills in the 1989 Granada TV one; Richard Pasco in the 1989 BBC Radio 4 one.

Manette, Alexandre

Paris doctor, so long imprisoned in the Bastille that Lucie thinks him dead, while he himself on release answers only to the appellation 'One and Five, North Tower', his prison number. Played by Peter Cushing in the 1980 made-for-TV film.

Manette, Lucie

His daughter. Played by Edna May Oliver in the 1935 film; Dorothy Tutin in the 1958 one.

Pross

Her maid; gruff but affectionate towards Lucie, calling her 'Ladybird'. Played by Athene Seyler in the 1958 film; Flora Robson in the 1980 made-for-TV film; Anna Massey in the 1989 televisation.

Pross, Solomon, aka John Barsad Brother of above, as which stole all her property to speculate with.

St Evrémonde, Marquis

Charles's uncle through St Evrémonde's dead younger twin-brother; elegant, polite, sneering, heartless, epigrammatic ('Detestation of the high is the involuntary homage of the low'), the complete *ci-devant* French aristo of popular tradition. Played by Basil Rathbone in the 1935 film; Christopher Lee in the 1958 one.

Stryver

Barrister; just over 30 but looks 50 due to self-indulgence.

Tom Drives London–Dover mail coach.

Vengeance, The Female revolutionary.

A Tale of Two Cities

Story Commentary

Let it be stated at once that the two cities in question are London and Paris. Yet less of London gets described there than in almost any other Dickens novel. Soho, the Old Bailey environs, Tellson's Bank in Holborn, a minor episode on Shooter's Hill. Paris likewise: the Faubourg St Antoine, the St Germain quarter and but a prison or two – their insides at that.

As with *Barnaby Rudge*, its predecessor, the story opens in 1775. As with *Rudge*, it assembles the principal actors then moves on a few years to the main and very violent action. Among those actors is Dr Manette, who, like William Dorrit, has been so long in prison that he is ill at ease once free.

Writing huge books, one coming after the other with relative rapidity, meant Dickens often carried over surplus fictional dough from story A to knead into story B. That is why a confessedly historical novel about the French Revolution followed on from a pseudo-historical one like *Little Dorrit*, and why each covers the same things: prisons, France and the free daughter–confined papa relationship. Dickens even has Dr Manette take to cobbling again after his daughter's wedding to Charles Darnay, as forgetful of all that has happened since his Bastille imprisonment as William Dorrit had been over his post-Marshalsea life when breaking down at Mrs Merdle's Rome dinner party.

Again as with *Barnaby Rudge*, the pace only picks up when the background involves violence. In late summer 1792, when the French Revolution is about to enter its most savage phase, Darnay, long happily married and living in London, chances upon a letter addressed to him from France. The writer is Gabelle, his family's rent-collector. Gabelle has been imprisoned as a lackey of the aristos, even though he long ago stopped taking rents from locals due to their poverty. His prison is L'Abbaye, on Paris's Left Bank, where the September Massacres of a few weeks later are soon to commence. Darnay resolves to go to Paris to try and free him. He tells no one.

Once in France he is arrested, taken to Paris under guard and confined in the prison of La Force. The latter will have had even more sinister connotations to Dickens's generation than L'Abbaye, it being where Marie-Antoinette's close friend the Princesse de Lamballe was incarcerated about the same time as Darnay before being especially brutally raped, or so it was long said, as an *hors d'oeuvre* to her mutilation and murder.

Darnay's wife and daughter come to Paris to look for him and for a while get some protection from Lorry, who is in Paris on Tellson's Bank business, and Lucie's father Dr Manette, who as an ex-Bastille prisoner and medical man is respected by the mob. Darnay is held in La Force till December 1793, 15 months later. He is then tried and with Dr Manette's help gets off. Gabelle has by now been freed also. Then Darnay is rearrested.

Sydney Carton now turns up in Paris. Using his formidable cross-examining powers he extracts from Barsad that Barsad is a turncoat spy. Carton can thus intimidate Barsad into helping Mme Darnay and her daughter leave Paris. Carton contrives Charles Darnay's escape from prison by changing clothes with him on a visit to his cell. He then mounts the tumbril in which he will proceed to the guillotine, having through his extraordinary facial resemblance to Darnay (signalled at Darnay's trial 13 years before) run what in racing circles is called 'a dead ringer'.

Carton is credited in film versions of *A Tale*, notably that of 1935 featuring Ronald Colman as Carton, with one of the most famous exit lines in literary-cum-cinematic history, namely 'It is a far, far better thing that I do, than I have ever done; it is a far, far better rest that I go to, than I have ever known.'

But although Dickens puts the words in quotes, he states before doing so that they are Carton's thoughts, not a speech. So let us recall another slightly earlier passage by Dickens: 'They said of him [Carton], about the city that night, that it was the peacefullest man's face ever beheld there.'

Dickens and his magazine, All the Year Round.

A Tale of Two Cities came out in 1859 in Dickens's magazine *All the Year Round*, which had a phenomenal circulation of up to 120,000 ordinarily and with Christmas issues could reach 300,000. It was first a weekly serial, then got repackaged as a monthly bumper issue containing four weekly ones. As recently as the eve of World War I it had sold well, but no more. Since then it has notched up world-wide sales of around 200,000,000, putting it in the top half dozen mega-sellers of all time. Yet not only is it far from being Dickens's best novel, it is not even his best historical novel. Its commercial success presumably derives from its being made a set book in schools, a role it is ideal for since it not only lacks humour, so runs no danger of amusing those made to study it, yet conveys a history lesson as well as being a slice of yer genuine literature. *Tale* also contains nice neat teachable themes. But there are better reasons for reading Dickens than because he is the Education Department's favourite son. Try his other novels first.

There were three silent film versions (1911, 1917 and 1922) apart from those mentioned in 'Characters' above. There have been several broadcast adaptations, including two on radio other than those mentioned in the 'Characters': a 1938 one in America with Orson Welles and a BBC one of 1950 scripted by Terence Rattigan and John Gielgud. A BBC TV adaptation other than those mentioned in the 'Characters' was broadcast in 1965. A 1968 musical, *Two Cities, the Spectacular New Musical*, starred Edward Woodward. A 2006 musical, *Two Cities,* had as setting the Russian Revolution. A Broadway musical production under the same title as the book was mounted in 2008. There have been two productions as musicals in Japan, each with all-female casts. The BBC produced an opera version of the book in 1953.

Great Expectations

Weekly serial, 1860 to 1861
Book published 1861

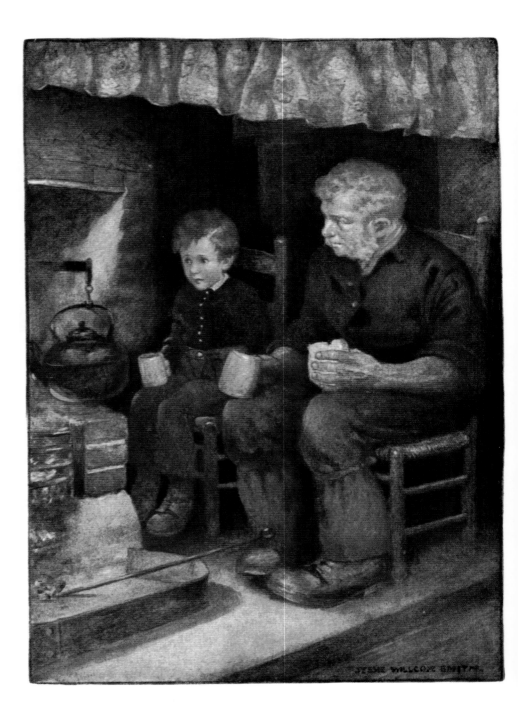

Pip, precociously resenting his 'low' milieu, with his brother-in-law Joe Gargery, an illustration by Jessie Willcox Smith.

Characters

Aged (P[arent]), The Wemmick's father, so addressed by Wemmick.

Barley, Clara Marries Herbert Pocket.

Biddy

Wopsle's second cousin, being his great-aunt's grand-daughter; orphan; eventually marries Joe Gargery.

Campbell Alias of Provis (né Magwitch) while secreted by Pip at Clara Barley's house.

Coiler, Mrs Widowed neighbour of the Pockets.

Drummle, Bentley

Unpleasant pupil of Matthew Pocket; two heartbeats away from inheriting a baronetcy; marries Estella but maltreats her and they separate; killed by a fractious horse.

Estella

Real daughter of Magwitch and Molly; adopted daughter of Miss Havisham, by whom encouraged, one might almost say 'trained', to destroy males' peace of mind through coquetry, which she certainly succeeds in doing with Pip. Played by Jean Simmons as the girl Estella and Valerie Hobson as the woman Estella in the David Lean 1946 film; previously there had been two silents (1917, 1922) and a 1934 Danish talkie; by Sarah Miles as both girl and woman Estella in the 1974 film; Gwyneth Paltrow in a 1998 film setting the story in 1990 America; Justine Waddell in the 1999 BBC made-for-TV film; Francesca Annis in a 1967 televisation; Patsy Kensit as the girl Estella in the 1981 BBC televisation.

Flopson Pockets' children's nanny.

Gargery, Joe

Village blacksmith to whom his brother-in-law Pip is apprenticed in youth. Played by Bernard Miles in the 1946 film; Joss Ackland in the 1974 one.

Gargery, Georgiana Maria

Pip's much older sister. Played by Rachel Roberts in the 1974 film.

Pip waits on Miss Havisham, by Marcus Stone.

Havisham, Miss

Elderly lady, deeply eccentric through having been abandoned just before her intended wedding years before; her residence Satis House untouched since then, especially the dining-room, where the table still laid for the wedding breakfast; benefactor in a minor way to Pip, inviting him over during his childhood once a week or so to play cards with Estella, but also to be tormented by her; later repents her manipulative ways. Played by Martita Hunt in a 1940 stage production and in the 1946 film; Margaret Leighton in the 1974 one; Jean Simmons (an earlier Estella, see above) in the 1989 one; Anne Bancroft as the Havisham character, renamed Ms Dinsmoor, in the 1998 film set in 1990 America; Charlotte Rampling in the 1999 made-for-TV film; Estelle Winwood in a 1954 televisation.

Jaggers

Aggressive London lawyer; Miss Havisham's man of business; intermediary between Pip's mystery benefactor and Pip, to whom till aged 21 (the then age of majority) he is guardian. Played by Anthony Quayle in the 1974 film.

Magwitch, Abel

Pip's convict benefactor and nemesis; an orphan, frequently jailed for vagrancy or petty theft, he has become a confirmed criminal while still a boy and on taking up with Compeyson, a gentleman forger, had all the blame for their joint forgeries by looking a villain while Compeyson looked the gent, Compeyson getting seven years and Magwitch 14 (increased to life for trying to scrag Compeyson when the two of them escape from the hulks at the time of Magwitch's encountering Pip in the churchyard). Played by James Mason in the 1974 film; Anthony Hopkins in the 1989 one; Robert De Niro as the Magwitch character, renamed Lustig, in the 1998 film set in 1990 America; Stratford Johns in a 1981 BBC televisation.

Mike Client of Jaggers.

Molly Housekeeper-cum-maid-of-all-work to Jaggers, who once represented her when tried for murder (but acquitted).

Orlick, Dolge

Joe Gargery's underling; oddly refers to himself in the third person as 'Old Orlick'; lures Pip to a nocturnal rendezvous to kill him over a string of past grievances but Pip rescued by Herbert Pocket; later breaks into Pumblechook's house and is jailed.

Pip (*né* Philip Pirrip)

Hero. Played by Marius Goring in the 1940 stage production (see Havisham, Miss); John Mills as adult in the 1946 film; Michael York in the 1974 one; Ethan Hawke, under the name Finn, in the 1998 film version set in 1990 America; Ioan Gruffudd in the 1999 made-for-TV film; Roddy McDowell in a 1954 televisation; Dinsdale Lansden in a 1959 one.

Pocket, Belinda Herbert Pocket's mother.

Pocket, Herbert

Rooms with Pip on his coming to London; Pip secretly pays half his first year's fixed income of £500, i.e. £250 (over £30,000 today) to a merchant ('or shipping broker' – Dickens is typically vague) to take Herbert into business as a partner. Played by Alec Guinness in the 1940 stage production (see Pip) and in the 1946 film, as which he allegedly gave that name to the authorities when arrested and fined 10 guineas (say £333 today) for homosexual activity in a Liverpool public lavatory the same year.

Pocket, Matthew Father of Herbert and cousin of Miss Havisham; tutors the newly prosperous Pip at his house in Hammersmith (then outside London).

Pocket, Sarah Another cousin of Miss Havisham, to whom she is later housekeeper.

Provis Magwitch's alias on returning to England.

Pumblechook

Joe Gargery's corn-chandler (grain merchant) uncle. Played by Robert Morley in the 1974 film; Frank Middlemass in the 1989 one.

Skiffins, Miss Marries Wemmick.

Startop Pleasant pupil of Matthew Pocket.

Waldengarver Wopsle's Jewish dresser in the theatre.

Wemmick, John

Jaggers's clerk. Played by Peter Bull in the 1974 film.

Wopsle Parish clerk in village of Pip's childhood; takes to professional acting.

Wopsle, Miss Wopsle's great-aunt; keeps a dame school in Pip's village.

Great Expectations

Story Commentary

Pip leaves the village; an illustration by F W Pailthorpe.

Great Expectations is the third Dickens novel running to be set well before when it was written, and if you include *David Copperfield* the fourth of five in a row. Clearly as Dickens got older he revisited his past more and more. *Great Expectations* also resembles *David Copperfield* in having an 'I' narrator. And the 'I', here Pip, is an orphan, first boy then youth, again like David.

But Pip starts several rungs below David on the social ladder, being a genuine proletarian, though of the rural variety. Under the baleful influence of Estella, a *femme fatale* even as a small girl, Pip soon resents the 'common' ways of the people he lives and works among.

Dickens's exit visa from his family was his genius. Pip's from his, and the blacksmith's forge, is hard cash. But it is of mysterious origins, for Pip has an anonymous well-wisher. Just who, and why the mystery, and why Pip mustn't inquire, are the theme of the book. A very good one too, if unlikely.

How far in the past did Dickens set *Great Expectations*? The 'King' is mentioned when Pip has for some time been 'gentle-folked', as Joe Gargery puts it. And Pip as a boy says that 'Joe's education, like Steam [*sic*], was in its infancy'. Since from the final scenes we know Dickens has paddle-steamers in mind (rather than steam locomotives, which don't feature in *Great Expectations*), we can place Pip's birth as roughly contemporary with Dickens's, or 1812, by which time the first paddle-steamers were operating. This would make his initial encounter with Magwitch around 1818 and his coming into his 'great expectations', or sudden wealth, about 1829.

But in life's journey Pip needs a guide as well as the fare. Herbert Pocket is ideal – or would be did he not invent the nickname 'Handel' for Pip, deriving from 'The Harmonious Blacksmith' hence not hugely tactful. However, no better sapper could have defused for Pip the anti-personnel devices in the minefield that is etiquette.

A tricky minefield all the same. Estella showers Pip with shrapnel: 'He calls the knaves jacks, this boy!', she says, a nymphet Nancy Mitford anticipating the U versus Non-U debate by a century, as they play the card game 'beggar my neighbour'. Herbert is gentler, telling Pip: 'in London it is not the custom to put the knife in the mouth ... and ... while the fork is reserved for that use, it is not put further in than necessary ... . Also, the spoon is not generally used overhand, but under.' He even wraps his observations on class in little epigrams, like party favours: 'I don't know why it should be a crack thing to be a brewer [as Miss Havisham's father was]: but ... while you cannot possibly be genteel and bake, you may be as genteel as never was and brew.'

Reminders of Pip's origins crop up everywhere. He acquires a boat for rowing, but his instructor casually mentions that Pip's arm is like a blacksmith's, thereby nearly losing a pupil. His former comrade Biddy in a letter writes 'My Dear Mr Pip', like a family retainer to the young master. And Pip is steeped in shame at the thought of his fellow pupils at Matthew Pocket's catching sight (or sound) of Joe. In a breakfast-table conversation Joe alternates between calling him 'Sir' and 'Pip'. It is excruciating, brilliantly observed and moving all at once.

On reaching 21, Pip comes into £500 a year (over £60,000 a year today). Jaggers stresses his imminent withdrawal from the arrangement. So Pip, who believes the benefactor is Miss Havisham, begins to think Jaggers and Miss Havisham have disagreed over her bestowing Estella on him. It is one more in his long list of misapprehensions. 'Grand Illusions' rather than 'Great Expectation' would be a more accurate story title at this stage.

Then the ghastly truth emerges. Pip's benefactor is the convict he helped all those years ago in the churchyard on the edge of the marshes, stealing for him a file, a pie and some liquor – thefts which would at that time have got Pip himself transported. Magwitch (for such is the convict's name) has made a fortune as a 'sheep-farmer, stock breeder ... [and in] other trades besides' in Australia. Magwitch visits Pip in his new set of rooms, in the Temple (nowadays exclusively barristers' chambers), on the Thames Embankment off Fleet Street.

Magwitch tells Pip that if caught he will be hanged. This intensifies Pip's agonising shame. One of Magwitch's most horrifying traits, to Pip, is using a wodge of bread to mop his gravy up with, just the sort of 'common' behaviour Pip was guilty of before Herbert Pocket took him in hand. Pip is like a maiden aunt whose scapegrace nephew uses a rude word – an apt comparison since Pip now passes off Magwitch to his cleaning women as an uncle.

Herbert is sworn to secrecy by Magwitch, who then tells the two room-mates his life history. Herbert realises that the Compeyson he mentions was Miss Havisham's professed swain, later her betrayer, and that Arthur, Compeyson's earlier pre-Magwitch accomplice, was Miss Havisham's half-brother. He intimates as much to Pip.

'Old Orlick' means murder, by F W Pailthorpe, c. 1900.

Magwitch is clearly being watched. Pip, enlisting first Herbert then Startop, spirits him down-river with a view to getting him aboard a German-bound ship. Their boat is intercepted by some customs officers accompanied by Compeyson, demanding that Magwitch be surrendered. Magwitch grapples with Compeyson. They fall in the water. Compeyson drowns. Magwitch is injured, fatally as it transpires, by a paddle-steamer.

Magwitch's death while a felon means his property is forfeit to the Crown. Pip is left with nothing. He becomes a clerk under Herbert in the latter's Cairo branch of the business, works his way up to partner and many years later revisits his childhood haunts. On the site of Satis House, now demolished, he encounters Estella. She wants the two of them to be 'friends', that eternal brush-off by a woman to a man desiring something more. But Dickens has Pip talk of seeing 'no shadow of another parting from her',

David Lean's 1946 film Great Expectations, *starring Valerie Hobson and John Mills (above and right).*

Restoration House, Rochester: original of Miss Havisham's Satis House, painted by Ernest Haslehust, from Dickens Land *published by Blackie and Son in 1911.*

which, together with his having taken her hand, is usually interpreted as meaning they will marry, if not immediately at any rate in due course.

Great Expectations represents a complete break with the earlier novels: infinitely bleaker than the slightly 'Hammer Horror' *House* of that name and with more twists as to plot than the eponymous *Oliver*, while its characters do a greater amount of shopping (of each other) than if the *Old Curiosity* emporium had mounted a post-Christmas 'Everything-Must-Go' sale masterminded by a retail titan like Sir Philip Green. Despite its sombre tone and contemporary critics' carping, *Great Expectations* sold well. The book version had gone into a fourth edition only weeks after the final number to feature it of the magazine *All the Year Round*.

In addition to the films and televisations mentioned above against individual characters, *Great Expectations* has been turned into a children's cartoon and adapted for various stage productions.

Our Mutual Friend

Monthly serial, 1864 to 1865
Book published 1865

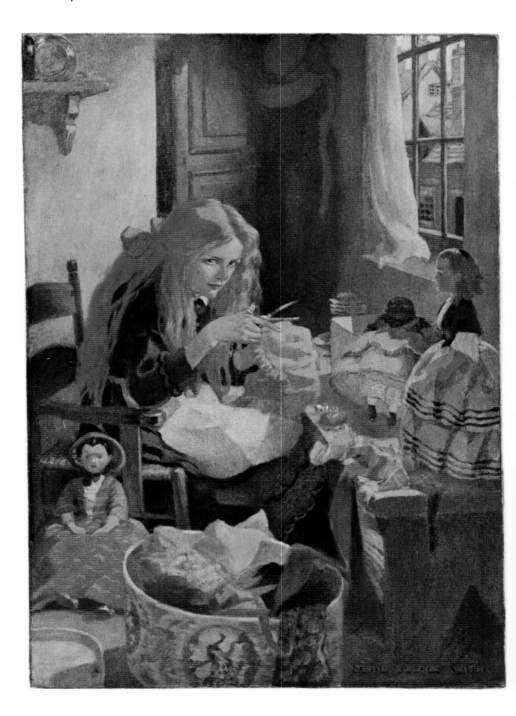

Jenny Wren, the dolls' dressmaker, as a Toyah Wilcox lookalike in this illustration by Jessie Willcox Smith.

Characters

Akershem, Sophronia Marries Alfred Lammle for his money but discovers he is badly off; joins him in helping Fledgeby to marry Georgiana Podsnap for her money but then backs out.

Blight, 'Young' Clerk to Mortimer Lightwood.

Boffin, Henrietta Wife of 'Noddy' Boffin; gives a home to the orphan Johnny.

Boffin, Nicodemus ('Noddy'), aka 'The Golden Dustman'

A simple soul; inherits old John Harmon's fortune.

Cleaver, aka 'Mr Dolls' Drunk, treated as errant child by his daughter.

Cleaver, Fanny His daughter; see Jenny Wren.

Fledgeby, 'Fascination' Secretly runs Pubsey & Co, usurers, putting in Riah as front man.

Gliddery, Bob Abbey Potterson's assistant in her pub.

Handford, Julius Alias of John Harmon when attending identification of corpse thought to be John Harmon's.

Harmon, John

Hero; marries Bella Wilfer.

Rokesmith, John Main alias of John Harmon.

Headstone, Bradley

Schoolmaster; leads a double life; loves Lizzie Hexam; befriends Charley Hexam; grapples with Rogue Riderhood (as whom he previously disguised himself to attack Eugene Wrayburn) and pulls him into the waters of a lock on the Thames, both men drowning.

Hexam, Charley Gaffer H's selfish son; becomes a schoolmaster under his mentor Headstone. Played by Jack Wild in the 1976 BBC televisation.

Hexam, 'Gaffer' (real forename Jesse) Forager in the Thames for dead bodies, appropriating any valuables he finds on them.

Hexam, Lizzie

'Gaffer''s daughter; marries Eugene Wrayburn.

Higden, Betty Child-minder in Brentford, then west of London but now absorbed by it.

Inspector, Mr Policeman, superficially competent, actually ineffective.

Johnny Betty Higden's great-grandson.

Kibble, Jacob Fellow passenger with John Harmon on his voyage from the Cape to England.

Lammle, Alfred Brand new friend of the Veneerings (they have no other kind); makes same mistake over his wife's supposed money that she does with him.

Lightwood, Mortimer

Solicitor handling old John Harmon's will; friend of Eugene Wrayburn.

Milvey, Rev Frank The Boffins' local clergyman; they seek his advice about adopting an orphan.

Milvey, Margaretta His wife.

Peecher, Emma Schoolmistress; loves Bradley Headstone.

Podsnap, Georgiana John P's daughter.

Podsnap, John Self-righteous, abrupt, pedantic, narrow-minded, snobbish, bullying; allegedly based by Dickens on John Forster, an old and close friend and his first biographer.

Podsnap, Mrs His wife.

Potterson, Abbey (originally Abigail) Upright pub landlady; helps Lizzie Hexam.

Potterson, Job Steward aboard the ship John Harmon travels from the Cape to England on.

Riah 'Good' Jew; Dickens's penance for Fagin.

Riderhood, Pleasant Daughter of 'Rogue' below; loved by Mr Venus; they eventually marry.

John Podsnap.

Riderhood, 'Rogue' (real forename Roger)

Blackmails Headstone for having passed himself off as RR when assaulting Wrayburn, hence turned on by Headstone.

Sampson, George Marries Lavinia Wilfer.

Sloppy Bastard former work-house boy now working for Betty Higden, so called since found on a wet night; falls for Jenny Wren.

Tippins, Lady Dinner guest of the Veneerings.

Twemlow, Melvin Cousin of a peer, one Lord Snigsworth, hence courted by Veneerings.

Veneering, Anastatia Wife of Hamilton V.

Veneering, Hamilton *Nouveau riche*.

Venus

Keeper of a shop selling freaks of nature (stuffed animals, preserved frogs, etc.).

Silas Wegg.

Wegg, Silas

Wooden-legged ballad-seller; plods through Gibbon's *Decline and Fall of the Roman Empire*, echoing Boffin's reference to it as 'Declining and Falling off the Rooshan [Russian] Empire'.

Wilfer, Bella

Elder daughter of 'The Cherub' below, a name she uses for him out of quasi-maternal exasperation.

Wilfer, Lavinia Younger ditto.

Wilfer, Mrs Avaricious, discontented wife of 'The Cherub' below.

Wilfer, Reginald (aka 'Rumty' or 'The Cherub') Poor clerk.

Wrayburn, Eugene

Briefless barrister; assaulted by the jealous Headstone and pitched in river; Lizzie Hexam rescues him, nurses him back to health and wins him as husband.

Wren, Jenny

Crippled dolls' dressmaker; scolds her father over his drinking.

Jenny Wren and her father, by Harold Copping.

Our Mutual Friend

Story Commentary

The phrase 'Our Mutual Friend' is a misnomer. 'Mutual' is something you and me do to each other, like shaking hands. A third party we are both fond of is a common friend. But that can sound like someone who wears socks in bed or says 'Pleased to meet you' on being introduced, as Podsnap more or less does when mistaking Twemlow for their host Veneering in Chapter II. Dickens makes Noddy Boffin utter the expression, almost certainly deliberately instead of 'our common friend', because Noddy senses that the latter might sound insulting. For Mrs Wilfer has just pointedly amended his description of Rokesmith as 'a lodger' to the less 'low' term 'gentleman'. Noddy, being a decent old fellow, takes the hint. But he is no very subtle wielder of the English language. So he comes up with this wonderfully euphemistic yet convoluted misnomer. It has stuck fast in the English language ever since, like corn-on-the-cob fibres between the teeth. Such was Dickens's power to shape our mother tongue.

Now the story. John Harmon, falling out with his father, has settled at the Cape in South Africa. His father leaves John a fortune built from 'dust' (ground-up old bones, chunks of coal and so on recycled for fuel, fertiliser and brick-making) provided he marries Bella Wilfer. John has never met her. He voyages to London. An assailant there robs him but is then murdered and his corpse flung in the Thames. Gaffer Hexam fishes it out. From items found on it people assume the corpse is John Harmon's. John exploits the mistake to look his intended bride Bella over, 'on appro' as it were, in the guise of 'Rokesmith', a lodger in her father's house.

The fortune meanwhile goes to Boffin as next heir. Boffin, an illiterate, employs Wegg to read aloud to him. Wegg sees an opportunity to relieve Boffin of his wealth. But Boffin also employs 'Rokesmith' as secretary. Further, he takes in Bella to compensate her for losing a rich husband. A classic imbroglio: hero-in-disguise, heroine-ignorant-of-hero's-identity, villain-menial's-evil-designs, villain-ignorant-of-hero's-true-identity-as-rightful-heir-to-fortune – all under one roof.

For deception is what *Our Mutual Friend* is about: deliberate (Boffin of Bella, Headstone of Wrayburn); self-deception (Lammles over each other; Wegg over Venus); the inadvertent kind (Twemlow somehow causing Podsnap to think him his host); and tacitly agreed mass deception (the hypocrisy of 'society').

But Mrs Boffin recognises 'Rokesmith'/Harmon. So Noddy Boffin graduates from deceived to deceiver, notably of Bella by pretending to be a miser and pretending to find fault with 'Rokesmith'/Harmon, sacking him. 'Rokesmith'/ Harmon departs the Bower (the Boffins' house). Bella departs it too. They marry.

Then Harmon and the Boffins reveal to Bella that they have been tricking her to test her, and 'Rokesmith' is really John Harmon. Their justification for such monstrous tactics is that Bella's missish surface hides a good heart. Whether you are more disgusted by their duplicity or their arrogant condescension in treating Bella like a laboratory hamster, to be moulded into whatever behaviour pattern pleases her husband and his lackeys, is your choice. Any girl of spirit would have slapped Harmon's and the Boffins' chops and walked out.

Bella, despite her earlier pertness, declines to rock the boat. (After all, she has done what she wanted – married a moneybags.) The episode nonetheless leaves a nasty taste in one's mouth. No wonder Dickens's own marriage disintegrated. That he thought wives could be treated as bendy toys is evidenced as far back as his first American trip in 1842, when in Pittsburgh he had hypnotised Catherine two nights running as an after-dinner party trick.

The Garden on the House Top, by Arthur Dixon.

Wegg tries blackmailing Boffin using a will he has found that is of later date than the one leaving the Boffins old John Harmon's money. Under it the Harmon fortune passes to the Crown. Boffin trumps this with a third will, still more recent, which bypasses young John Harmon and leaves everything to him and Mrs Boffin direct. Venus, hitherto pretending to support Wegg, drops the mask and denounces him. The Boffins good-naturedly or servilely (depending on your view) surrender the money to young John Harmon, keeping only old Harmon's dust heaps for themselves.

The *All the Year Round* print run of numbers including episodes of *Our Mutual Friend* started at 40,000 a month. By the tenth issue it had dropped to 28,000 and by the final one a mere 19,000. Nonetheless, Dickens made over £12,000 (£1,500,000 today) from the serialisation as a whole.

The Mystery of Edwin Drood

Magazine format 1870
Published 1870

Tartar (oars) sculls Rosa and Grewgious up the Thames; his 'man' Lobley assists (original caption 'Up the river', Ch XXII).

Characters

Bazzard Grewgious's clerk.

Billickin, Mrs Lodgings-landlady; cousin of Bazzard.

Bud, Rosa, aka 'Rosebud' or 'Pussy'

Daughter of Edwin Drood's dead father's dead best friend, the two men having long ago 'chosen' her as Edwin's future wife.

Crisparkle, Rev Sept(imus)

'Muscular Christian' Minor Canon of Cloisterham.

Crisparkle, Mrs Rev Sept's mother, called 'Ma' by him.

Datchery, Dick We never discover what he is; possibly a private detective.

Deputy, aka 'Winks' Cloisterham urchin.

Drood, Edwin

Rosa Bud's fiancé; his passion for Rosa wanes; they break off their engagement just before he disappears.

Durdles, Stony Cathedral stonemason.

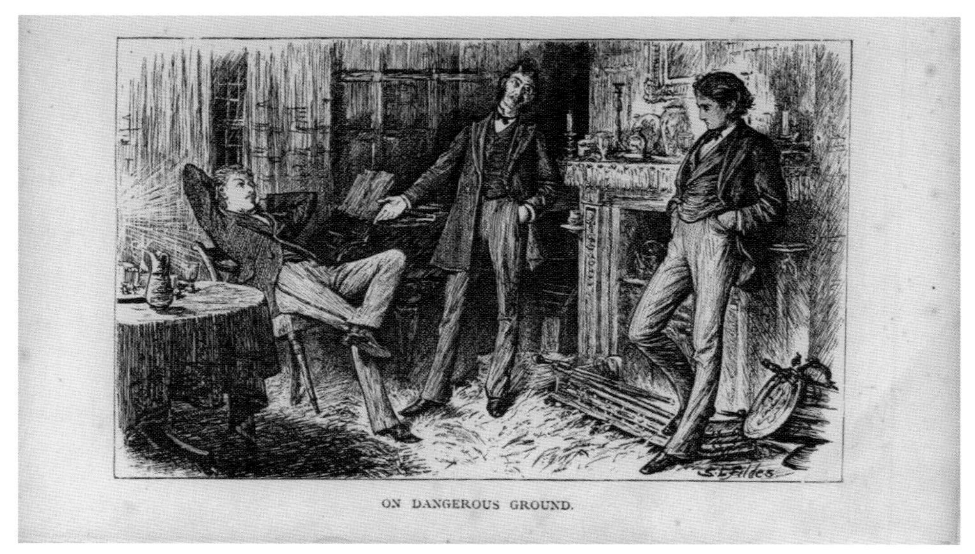

'Look at him!' cries Jasper [centre] . . . 'See where he lounges so easily, Mr Neville!' (Ch VIII). Edwin Drood, seated and flushed with wine, on the verge of racially insulting Neville Landless (right, lounging against chimney piece), over his dark complexion.

Grewgious, Hiram

Dried-up, elderly and somewhat unworldly barrister; Rosa's guardian.

Honeythunder, Rev Luke

Opinionated progressive clergyman married to Mrs Crisparkle's sister and guardian to Neville Landless; based on the radical politician John Bright.

Jasper, John Only about 26 but Drood's uncle; opium addict and Drood's murderer from jealousy over Rosa, whom he is besotted with.

Landless, Helena Rosa's self-declared new friend and twin sister of ...

Landless, Neville

Studying under Crisparkle; loves Rosa, hence quarrels over her with the slightly dog-in-the-manger-ish Drood; Ceylon-born and dark-complexioned through either long exposure to tropic sun or what used to be called a 'touch of the tar brush', hence subject of half-jocular, half-offensive digs at his ethnicity by Drood.

Sapsea Auctioneer; becomes Mayor of Cloisterham.

Tartar Neighbour of Neville Landless as student in London; ex-schoolmate of Crisparkle.

AT THE PIANO.

'Mr Jasper was seated at the piano ... and was accompanying Miss Rosebud while she sang.' (Ch VII).

Frontispiece to The Mystery of Edwin Drood *from the 1870 Chapman & Hall edition (opposite).*

Tisher, Mrs Miss Twinkleton's lieutenant.

Tope Cloisterham Verger.

Tope, Mrs Jasper's domestic.

Twinkleton, Miss Headmistress of girls' school where Rosa is educated.

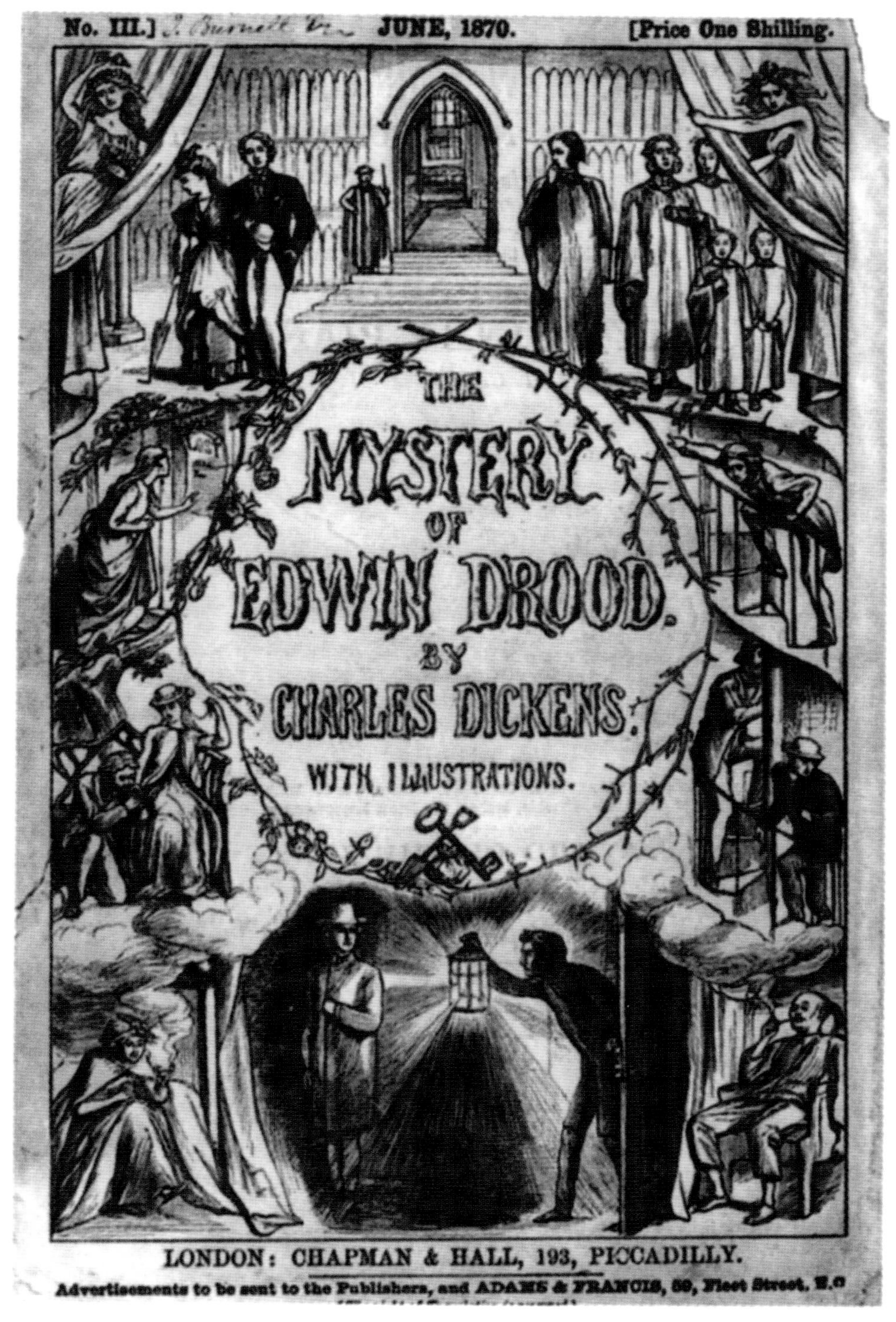

The Mystery of Edwin Drood

Story Commentary

Dickens's last fiction work, and only half-completed when he died, *Edwin Drood* involves two very modern preoccupations, drugs and racism. It opens with Jasper in an opium den, so out of it that he sees white elephants parading in front of the cathedral tower of Cloisterham (based on Rochester). Thereafter Jasper sometimes displays blanched lips, the 1870 equivalent of today's rotted septum after hoovering cocaine. Presently Jasper emerges from his den, puts on a white surplice and gets ready for vespers, for his day job is Lay Precentor of the Cloisterham Cathedral choristers.

After Drood's disappearance Neville is beset by a gang of local vigilantes convinced he is behind it because of their recent quarrel. Mayor Sapsea, before whom they hail Neville, suspects him too, chiefly because of his dark complexion. Neville is placed under house arrest. Grewgious tells Jasper that Rosa's and Drood's engagement is broken off and Jasper collapses – remorseful over having murdered his nephew unnecessarily. Grewgious begins to suspect Jasper. Drood's watch and 'shirt-pin' are found but not his corpse. Crisparkle stands by Neville.

Jasper makes advances to Rosa, hinting that if she will accept him he will call off the hunt to amass evidence against Neville, whose sister Helena is Rosa's best friend. Rosa half-suspects Jasper of Edwin's murder and detests him. A magnificent scene this, rich with Dickens's new literary style just when his money-grubbing public readings were about to kill him. And then Dickens died.

The opening number sold 50,000 copies, more than any other serialised version of a Dickens novel bar *The Old Curiosity Shop*.

Opium Smoking – The Lascar's Room, by Gustav Doré.

Dickens's Stories

As a story-teller Dickens did not confine himself to novels. Even with two early novels, *Pickwick Papers* and *Nicholas Nickleby*, he inserted into the main narrative tales told by characters but irrelevant to the plot, for instance because a group of characters are brought together in a country inn at night and kill time entertaining each other. Most of his other tales, notably the *Christmas Books*, had an existence of their own.

Nobody would deny that Dickens's novels overshadow his shorter fiction. Nonetheless, some critics place the story character Mrs Lirriper among his subtlest and warmest female creations. The market eventually reflected what might be called this lesser but effective literary skill. Though Dickens had got nothing for his earliest stories, which appeared in Captain Holland's *Monthly Magazine* (circulation 600), his late-period ones commissioned from America brought him astronomical sums (see 'Dickens Abroad'), far more in crude pounds sterling per word even than his major novels.

Dr Marigold from Doctor Marigold's Prescriptions, *which was Dickens's Christmas story for 1865 in* All the Year Round.

He wrote a great number of stories. The *Household Words* list Michael Slater gives in his biography's index of articles, *jeux d'esprit* and stories exceeds 100, the *All the Year Round* one over 40. John M L Drew, *Dickens the Journalist* (London, 2003), and Harry Stone, ed., *Charles Dickens's Uncollected Writings from Household Words* (2 vols., London, 1968), cover the subject in detail.

Hesperus Classics, a modern imprint, currently publish some of Dickens's stories in book form. They include *A House to Let*, which first appeared in 1858, the last Christmas Number of *Household Words* before Dickens resigned the editorship in spring 1859. Then there is Hesperus's *Mrs Lirriper. Mrs Lirriper's Lodgings* was the 1863 Christmas Number of *All the Year Round*, in which *Household Words* had merged. It sold 300,000 copies. Dickens revived her in *Mrs Lirriper's Legacy* for the following Christmas Number.

Hesperus also publish *Mugby Junction*. This, originally the *All the Year Round* 1866 Christmas Number, was another sell-out, its print run of 265,000 copies exhausted by late January 1867. Lastly, the Hesperus list contains *Somebody's Luggage*, *The Haunted House* and *The Wreck of the* Golden Mary. *The Wreck* had been the *Household Words* 1856 Christmas Number. Dickens collaborated on it with Wilkie Collins, newly appointed to the *Words* editorial staff.

The Haunted House is a slightly later Christmas Number, that of 1859, the first indeed of the new magazine *All the Year Round*. It consisted of seven ghost tales and one about the 'mortals' in the house. *Somebody's Luggage* was the *All the Year Round* bumper Christmas issue for 1862. It features Dickens's old

Toby Veck from The Chimes, *one of Dickens's* Christmas Books.

Boulogne friend and holiday landlord Ferdinand Beaucourt Mutuel, an ardent fan of Napoleon. Dickens had first run him in a *Household Words* essay of 1854 under the name Monsieur 'Loyal Devasseur'.

The market for stories, or short-ish fiction, was much more buoyant in Dickens's day than now. Or that is how it looked till very recently. The rise of 'compact/quick reading' devices like Kindle and the hectic pace of modern life, perhaps also shorter attention spans, seem to have revived the public's appetite for the genre. Dickens's contribution is worth exploring.

Toby Veck and his daughter Meg in an illustration by Harold Copping from The Chimes.

Dickens's Plays

Dickens was stage-struck from childhood. He at one point in early manhood nearly auditioned as an actor. A nasty cold scotched the audition itself, and through swiftly ascending the literary ladder soon afterwards he lost interest in trying again. He was a competent drama critic. But his chief enthusiasm was amateur dramatics, both as actor and director. Perhaps his best role was Bobadil in Ben Jonson's *Every Man in His Humour*.

Dickens as Bobadil in Every Man in his Humour.

In his various London residences he mounted productions of other plays, all by much lesser dramatists than Jonson, including himself. The habit started during his childhood in Bentinck Street. It reached a grand climax when he lived at Tavistock House, a substantial mansion in Bloomsbury. But he also put on plays in the country, frequently at the seats of landed friends such as the Lyttons at Knebworth in Hertfordshire or the Watsons at Rockingham Castle.

One of his first works, written when he was ten or rather more, was a tragedy, *Misnar, the Sultan of India*. Nothing of it survives. By about February of 1836, on the very eve of completing the first chapter of *Pickwick Papers*, he had ready *The Strange Gentleman*, a 'comic burletta [itself meaning a comic operetta]' as he put it, in two acts. The plot was an elaboration of 'The Great Winglebury Duel' in his *Sketches by Boz*.

The play was put on in late September 1836 at the St James's Theatre, opened only the previous year. It continued for 50 nights, a good run in those days. Dickens's most recent major biographer Michael Slater reckons the play to have been 'a triumph'. The St James's stage manager, John Pritt Harley, a good singer (counter-tenor), took the title role. Coincidentally, he had played Bobadil when *Every Man* had been revived in 1816.

Dickens almost immediately followed with the libretto to *The Village Coquettes*, a comic opera composed by John Hullah, who Dickens's sister Fanny knew at the Royal Academy of Music. It ran for 19 nights at the St James's then transferred to Edinburgh. Dickens at the time thought his contribution good, later changing his mind.

Contemporary critics shared his low matured opinion. Dickens's less recent biographer Peter Ackroyd is interesting on Dickens's limitations as dramatist, reckoning that he was overawed by the theatre. But when he adds that Dickens's talent was for 'symbolic narrative rather than ... dialogue' one can only gasp. Dickens's dialogue in novels is brilliant. That it does not translate to his plays is surely because the conventions and taste of his time favoured feeble stuff like farces and melodramas, and Dickens was acutely sensitive to the public's taste. After all, the only playwright from then still produced today is Dion Boucicault. The memorable Victorian-era ones, Wilde, Pinero, Shaw, were active long after Dickens's death. And of that four three were Irish and one, Pinero, Sephardic. It was a lean age for *echt*-Anglo-Saxon dramatists.

Is She His Wife? Or, Something Singular, a comic burletta in one act, was Dickens's third play. A production was mounted in March 1837 and continued till at least early May since it was on the seventh of that month, after watching a performance, that Dickens's adored sister-in-law Mary Hogarth died suddenly. His play-writing was fizzling out by now. *The Lamplighter*, an 'unfortunate little farce' in Dickens's own words, was never produced, though it did start rehearsals in or around 1838. Three years later he turned it into 'The Lamplighter's Story', a piece of prose fiction.

The actor William Charles Macready.

He now confined himself dramatically to collaborations. Or in one case to a minor contribution. He wrote a 48-line prologue to a five-act tragedy by J Westland Marston, *The Patrician's Daughter*. The distinguished actor William Macready, a friend of Dickens, produced it in 1842 at the Drury Lane Theatre. Macready, though conceding that Dickens read aloud as well as a professional actor, thought him 'unskilled' on stage, a judgment which has been taken to mean too much attention to detail, spoiling the overall effect.

Mark Lemon, the editor of *Punch*, thought up a farce called *Mr Nightingale's Diary*. Dickens made alterations to it, some of them considerable, before its amateur performances in May 1851. Dickens chiefly, with Lemon as part of the company, subsequently took it on tour to Bath and Bristol and in June 1855 revived it in the converted schoolroom at Tavistock House.

There followed *The Frozen Deep*. This, originally by Wilkie Collins but similarly altered by Dickens to make it run more smoothly, was put on for limited though substantial audiences in the winter of 1856 and 1857, again at Tavistock House, where the private theatre could hold around 90 people, and later in summer 1857 at the Gallery of Illustration in Lower Regent Street. The latter, as a 500-seat 'intimate' auditorium, was less disreputable than most London theatres then.

Dickens contributed another prologue, this time for Wilkie Collins's *No Thoroughfare*, first put on at the Adelphi Theatre in 1867 just after Christmas and running for over 150 nights till at least the following spring, after which it transferred successfully to Paris, though of course in translation. It had earlier been published as a joint Dickens-Collins short murder story in that year's Christmas number of *All the Year Round*.

The Frozen Deep has curiosity value for its having been seen by Queen Victoria and its being the occasion of Dickens meeting Ellen Ternan when he arranged its production in Manchester, a highly successful one as it turned out. By now the interest to us of Dickens's plays was incidental to the plays themselves. After all, he was not just primarily a novelist but the most successful one of the age. To try and conquer the theatrical world as well was going it a bit. At least he seems to have made a conquest of Ellen Ternan.

Dickens's Poetry

When Dickens devised a dummy book spine decoration for his study at Gad's Hill he used jokey titles like 'History of a Short Chancery Suit' in XIX volumes. One might add 'Dickens's Immortal Poetry'. He may have written verse, but he was not really a poet (perhaps the reason he sniped at Byron, who intermittently was). That said, Mrs Leo Hunter's 'Ode to an Expiring Frog' in *Pickwick Papers* is a joy – and rather better than T S Eliot's lines to a Persian cat, a Yorkshire terrier or a duck in the park. It is worth reproducing here:

Can I view thee panting, lying
On thy stomach, without sighing;
Can I unmoved see thee dying
On a log
Expiring frog!

Say, have fiends in shape of boys,
With wild halloo, and brutal noise,
Hunted thee from marshy joys,
With a dog,
Expiring frog!

(Surely the exclamation marks should be replaced by question marks?)

One would have liked a sample of Alfred Jingle's poetry, but Dickens ducks the opportunity. Certainly the form it took – an epic of 10,000 lines on the July Revolution of 1830 in France – would have taxed even Dickens's energy and fertility of invention. The *Spectator* should make it the subject of one of that paper's literary competitions, the challenge being to give Jingle's anacoluthon a lyrical twist.

Peter Ackroyd's biography, as if inspired from the Great Beyond by Dora Spenlow's friend Julia Mills, talks of *Oliver Twist* as exhibiting 'a poetry of barely whispered notes that sets up a deep refrain within the text'. But this is Ackroyd letting his fancy run away with him.

Those who determine to sample Dickens direct in rhyme, notwithstanding the above remarks, should consult Frederic G Kitton, ed., *Poems and Verses of Charles Dickens* (London, 1903). It is a decidedly rare work. The London Library possesses no copy. But why should it? Dickens was no true poet.

Title page from a Danish edition of a collection of Dickens works, David Copperfield and Other Stories, 1888.

Dickens's Illustrators

As with other novelists of the day, the stories Dickens wrote were accompanied by numerous pictures. For though the late-Hanoverian/early-Victorian public had to make do with books rather than television, it was as easily seduced as today's public by visual trickery. Dickens got his first break as a book-writer when Robert Seymour, Pickwick's first illustrator, went and killed himself. Seymour's successor, Phiz (Hablot Knight Browne), was a much better fit, his near-caricature figures matching Dickens's creations in their frequently deep eccentricities. Thackeray put in for the job of Seymour's successor, but Dickens rightly preferred Phiz. Thackeray as illustrator is clumsy and amateurish. Besides, the rejection turned Thackeray's ambitions predominantly to literature, a much better use of them.

OliverTwist introduced to the 'merry old gentleman', by George Cruikshank (below left).

The attempted burglary in Oliver Twist, *by George Cruikshank (below right).*

George Cruikshank, *Oliver Twist*'s illustrator, has, and had in his day, a great reputation. It is hard to see why except as the heir of Gillray and Rowlandson, that is, an outright caricaturing one-off cartoonist rather than serial embellisher of works of fiction. He was not good at females unless grotesques. A grave defect: females make up half humanity. And all heroines have to be comely, a trick Cruikshank could never

really pull off. He and Dickens did not collaborate much after *Twist* and later grew somewhat estranged.

Dickens occasionally in *Barnaby Rudge* and *The Old Curiosity Shop* alternated Phiz contributions with illustrations by Samuel Williams (Little Nell asleep in bed in the Old Curiosity Shop) and George Cattermole (Nell dead on her bed down in the country). Otherwise in his novels he stuck for over twenty years with Phiz. His middle-period ventures into book-packaging, chiefly his *Christmas Books*, involved using Dickie Doyle and John Leech, who in their way were very nearly as good as Phiz.

Marcus Stone, son of Frank below and best known as illustrator of *Our Mutual Friend*, was plucked from relative obscurity by Dickens after Phiz and he had parted company in 1859, the chief reason being a falling off in Phiz's work and his style losing favour with the public. Marcus Stone also illustrated the Library Editions of *American Notes, Pictures from Italy* and *A Child's History of England*, a series launched in the early 1860s.

Edwin Drood was predominantly illustrated by no less a figure than Luke (many years later Sir Luke) Fildes, though the dust-jacket frontispiece was the work of Dickens's son-in-law Charles Collins. Other pictorial contributors to Dickens works who, like Fildes, were predominantly painters rather than illustrators included Daniel Maclise ('Nell and the Sexton' in *The Old*

MASTER HUMPHREY'S CLOCK.

The Old Curiosity Shop.

CHAPTER THE THIRTY-EIGHTH.

IT—for it happens at this juncture, not only that we have breathing time to follow his fortunes, but that the necessities of these adventures so adapt themselves to our ease and inclination as to call upon us imperatively to pursue the track we most desire to take—Kit, while the matters treated of in the last fifteen chapters were yet in progress, was, as the reader may suppose, gradually familiarising himself more and more, with Mr. and Mrs. Garland, Mr. Abel, the pony, and Barbara, and gradually coming to consider them one and all as his particular private friends, and Abel Cottage Finchley as his own proper home.

Stay—the words are written, and may go, but if they convey any notion that Kit, in the plentiful board and comfortable lodging of his new abode, began to think slightingly of the poor fare and furniture of his old dwelling, they do their office badly and commit injustice. Who so mindful of those he left at home—

VOL. II.—27. B

The Old Curiosity Shop *serialised in* Master Humphrey's Clock *with illustrations by Phiz.*

'At Rest' by George Cattermole. 'She was dead. Dear, gentle, patient, noble Nell, was dead ... Sorrow was dead ... in her, but peace and perfect happiness were born; imaged in her tranquil beauty and profound repose ... So shall we know the angels in their majesty, after death.' The Old Curiosity Shop, *Ch XVI.*

Curiosity Shop), Frank Stone ('Milly and the Old Man' in *The Haunted Man*, one of the *Christmas Books*) and finally Clarkson Stanfield and Edwin Landseer, the latter two helping illustrate *The Cricket on the Hearth*, yet another of the *Christmas Books*.

Editions of Dickens since his death have had many able illustrators. (See the 'Story Commentary' to *Barnaby Rudge* for Harry Furniss, for instance.) George Du Maurier, best known for his novel *Trilby*, illustrated a book version of the Dickens-Wilkie Collins play *The Frozen Deep* which came out in 1875.

So great and lasting is Dickens's impact in creating characters that numerous cartoonists who have been primarily political or topical have used them, often dressed up, to make political or topical points. The list includes the *Punch* illustrators Tenniel (who had also contributed illustrations to *The Haunted Man*), Linley Sambourne and Bernard Partridge (F E Smith as Mister Jingle, for instance).

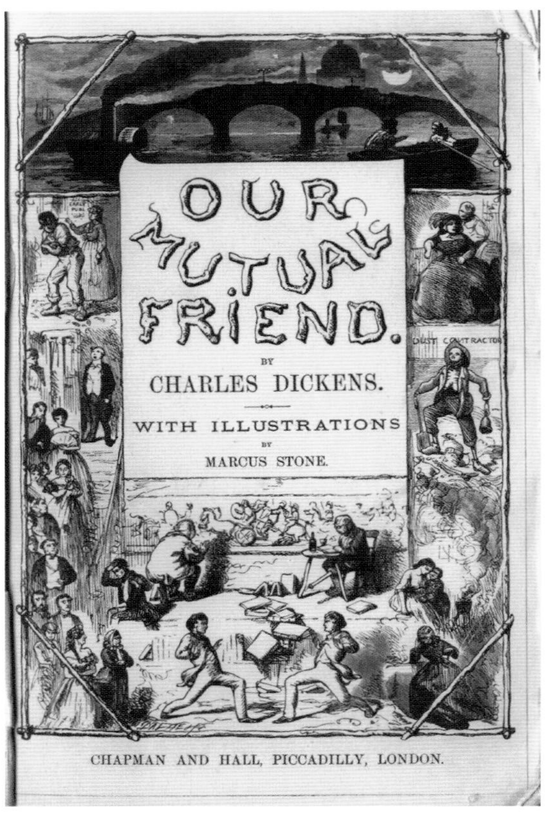

Our Mutual Friend *illustrated by Marcus Stone.*

'Mrs Gamp proposes a toast' from *Martin Chuzzlewit,* illustrated by Phiz.

Straightforward late-19th/20th-century illustrators of Dickens novels per se include Edward Ardizzone (*Great Expectations*, 1979), C E Brock (Harrap's editions of *Pickwick Papers*, *Nicholas Nickleby*, *Martin Chuzzlewit* and the *Christmas Tales* 1930–32), Mervyn Peake (Methuen's 1983 edition of *Bleak House*), Arthur Rackham (*A Christmas Carol*, 1915), Frank Reynolds, Ronald Searle (*A Christmas Carol* (1961), *Oliver Twist* and *Great Expectations* (both 1962), also art work for the 1970 film *Scrooge*) and E H Shepard, best known as illustrator of the Pooh books and *The Wind in the Willows*.

Peter Fluck and Roger Law, chiefly famous for the *Spitting Image* ITV puppet series but originally illustrators, provided the pictures for a Viking 1979 edition of *A Christmas Carol*.

Florence Dombey in Captain Cuttle's Parlour, by William Egley.

Dickens Abroad

America

By 1842 Dickens had developed something like a Special Relationship with America. He was read there, adulated there. A visit by him would be a huge success. So off he went. Unfortunately this one-man Anglo-Columbian dalliance, like all enduring affairs of the heart, had its stormy moments.

There were three problems. Dickens disliked Americans' self-assertiveness and, dare one say it, brashness. The self-assertiveness was understandable. Only 60 years earlier Americans had pulled off what no other British colony ever managed: successful all-out armed rebellion against the overlord.

In the return match, the War of 1812, they had in some post-final-whistle-fisticuffs whupped Limey again, doing so at New Orleans early in 1815. They were meanwhile vastly increasing their country's size and wealth, by purchase and conquest (including outright theft from the indigenes), using limitless raw materials, huge energy, valorous enterprise, the free labour of blacks and the very cheap labour of immigrants. By the 1840s, they had plenty to crow about.

Yet such crowing lacked the ease of manner, the beaming John Bull sense of superiority, which to Dickens may have made British self-regard tolerable. Britons also were a very boastful lot in the 19th century, something Dickens's anti-American digs in *Martin Chuzzlewit* ignored.

Americans had grounds for resentment against British literary figures generally. Fanny Trollope, mother of the novelist Anthony, had clawed them unmercifully in *Domestic Manners of the Americans* (1832). Captain (Frederick; best known for *Mr Midshipman Easy*) Marryat's *A Diary in America* (1839) had dumped on Americans too, despite Marryat's mother being American.

Two US-Canadian boundary disputes were simmering away. Since Canada was then a direct British possession, that meant an Anglo-American quarrel. The USA had never signed the international anti-slave trade agreement. The Royal Navy searched merchantmen, including US ones, and seized them if they held slaves. In 1842 defaulting on bond issues by seven US states totalled £56,000,000 ($280,000,000), much of it held by British investors.

There was the pirating of Dickens's works. The USA, with a population of over 17,000,000, was the biggest English-speaking market outside Britain. Exact sales figures of Dickens's works there are hard to compute. But at a February 1842 banquet honouring Dickens, the jurist John Duer mentioned

A daguerreotype of Dickens by Unbek, 1843

Dickens portrayed as rude and greedy (above and top opposite) in cartoons in the American press.

200,000 readers of *Pickwick Papers* in New York alone, with 500,000 in the entire USA.

A single book or magazine instalment probably got passed round among family and friends; 'readers' didn't necessarily mean each one bought a copy. But if any had, it was almost bound to be a pirated one. For no international copyright agreement existed in America till 1891. By 1842 Dickens seems to have made £350 at most in legitimate American sales (say around £44,000 today).

If we divide Duer's 'reader' figures by five to give notional book/magazine sales, Dickens had lost the proceeds of at least 100,000 sales of *Pickwick*. Add his other four novels to 1842, and you get 500,000 times Dickens's cut from each copy of an entire novel of his sold in America. Calculating this at ½ a cent on the 3–6 cents price then of a cheap monthly or weekly instalment, gives roughly 5–10 cents for each completed set of the first three novels and 53 cents for the other two (which were in weekly, not monthly, instalments). Multiplying by volume sales suggests Dickens could have foregone as much as $300,000, equivalent at the then exchange rate to £50,000 and nowadays to perhaps £6,125,000 (say $10,000,000 at today's sterling-dollar exchange rate).

Not all American editions of Dickens were dirt cheap. Adding 10 per cent to the above figures to accommodate the carriage trade gives respectively say $330,000 and £55,000 at 1842 prices and £6,740,000 and $11,000,000 at today's. By 1842 things may have improved. The relatively upright Philadelphia publishers Lea & Blanchard proposed to pay Dickens what in the event would have been a total of £750 (say £12,750 today) for each week's number of *Barnaby Rudge* and *The Old Curiosity Shop* – provided they got them before they appeared in London, a harsh condition. Lea & Blanchard soon dropped their honourable attitude. They were among the first firms to rush out a pirated edition of *A Christmas Carol* in the winter of 1843–44.

On landing in America Dickens soon raised the subject of copyright, doing so chiefly at banquets got up to honour him in Boston and New York. They were ideal forums, letting him deliver eloquent but moderate-toned pleadings before a distinguished audience that in Boston included its Mayor, Josiah Quincy Jr, and the authors Oliver Wendell Holmes and Richard Dana, and in New York American literature's founding father, Washington Irving.

Many among such audiences agreed with Dickens over copyright. Some said so publicly. Politicians who supported him included those very distinguished Senators John C Calhoun from South Carolina and Henry Clay from Kentucky. But when the press spread word of this seemingly mercenary reason for Dickens's trip, even if it was in truth one he only thought of once he had arrived in America (or so he said), he lost popularity with the masses.

Authors among his American friends also supported him, and for a very good reason. The piracy racket meant American publishers were less ready to bring out works by Americans since they would have to pay them royalties. An international copyright agreement would benefit writers in both America and Britain.

Dickens's visit began in January 1842. He travelled by one of the new steamships to New York via Boston. Touring Massachusetts, he met Longfellow (who the following autumn stayed with Dickens in London) and inspected several New England 'institutions' such as a factory, prison and lunatic asylum. He paid similar visits to their equivalents in other states.

The orderliness of such places impressed him. They were far superior to most of their English equivalents. The latter were often leftovers from the 18th century or earlier, when going to mock at lunatics or attend public executions was part of life's colourful and cruel pattern, like attending a bear-bating session or cock fight. In short, such English places were often out of date not just in design and management, but in the public idea as to what they existed for in the first place.

Yet Dickens omitted any mention of model American institutions from *Martin Chuzzlewit*. And though he wrote them up in *American Notes* (published in autumn 1842, four months after his return to England), that book, as reportage, was less read than his novels. It was also much less favourably received. Nonetheless the New York newspaper tycoon J Gordon Bennett reckoned it had sold 100,000 copies in America within a month of publication. And in Britain it netted Dickens £1,000, say today £125,000.

In New York he was feted at a 'Boz Ball'. ('Boz' was his early *nom de plume*.) Several *tableaux vivants* depicted scenes from his novels. Two others illustrated sketches by Boz. Revellers footed it to the strains of a Boz Waltz. In Philadelphia fans were said to have eyed up Dickens's flowing hair with a view to snipping off locks as keepsakes. And a confectioner called James Parkinson erected in his Chestnut Street emporium a temple made of sugar. It contained niches into which he inserted sugar statuettes of Little Nell, the Fat Boy, Pickwick and Sam Weller.

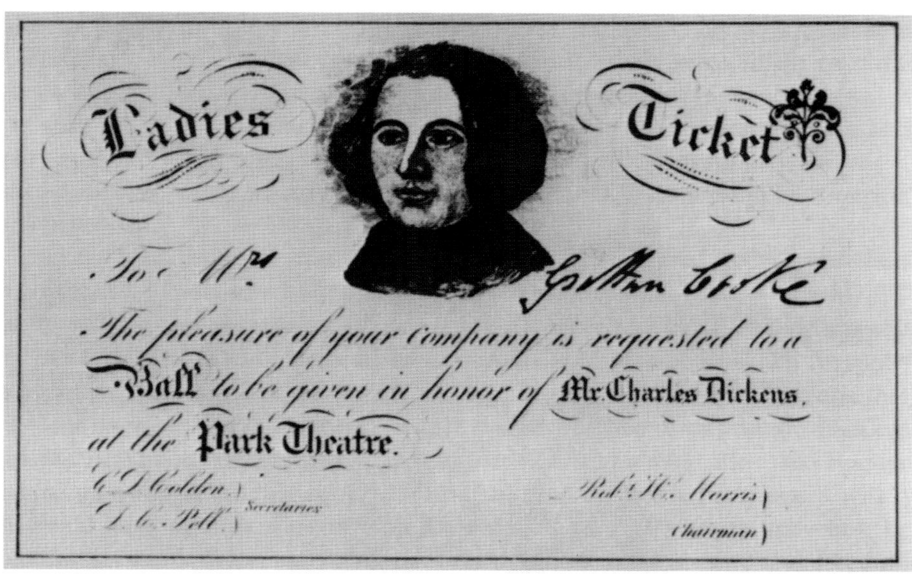
Ladies Ticket

To Mrs

The pleasure of your company is requested to a Ball to be given in honor of Mr Charles Dickens, at the Park Theatre.

Secretaries

Chairman

Ticket for the Boz Ball at the Park Theatre, New York.

But the general adulation soon annoyed Dickens. As did the press attacks, some of them highly personal as well as stressing what they considered his bad manners in banging the copyright drum while luxuriating as the nation's guest. He was finding that free speech is a tricky blessing. Moreover, he was always acutely touchy both as to criticism and what he conceived of as sharp practice at his expense. Lastly, though a radical now in the land of the free, he proved to be of the delicate English variety, a species that transplants with difficulty, often withering in its new habitat. America was a country he had hitherto admired from afar.

Dickens at a function at Delmonico's, New York, probably during his 1867–68 visit.

He found the real thing a tad sordid.

Some American practices noted by Dickens survive, for instance getting British place names and institutions slightly wrong. The character General Choke in *Martin Chuzzlewit* speaks of 'Windsor Pavilion', confusing Brighton Pavilion, then still (just) a royal residence, with Windsor Castle.

Others, mercifully, do not. In Baltimore Dickens remarked that the hotel there was the first he had been given enough water to wash with. And on his river boat trips he seems to have been the only passenger to wash at all. Americans nowadays are famous for their personal hygiene. Not then.

In Philadelphia Dickens was tricked by a Colonel Florence into shaking hands with a horde of complete strangers, mostly casual sightseers. Florence had given him to understand he would be meeting a small group of personal friends. Dickens was indignant.

From Philadelphia Dickens went to Washington, where the secretary he had taken on, George W(ashington) Putnam, drew his attention to Robert C Winthrop, then a Massachusetts Member of the House of Representatives, saying 'That, sir, is one of the most remarkable men in our country.' Dickens retorted, 'I have scarcely met a man since my arrival who wasn't one of the most remarkable men in our country.' This found its way almost verbatim into *Martin Chuzzlewit*.

Dickens next toured 'the West' (now the Mid West, but then more or less the frontier): Illinois, Kentucky, Missouri, Ohio. During the Louisville–St Louis river boat trip he went ashore to view a Kentucky giant called Porter, who stood seven foot eight high. This dwarfed Dickens, who was a bit of a titch. Porter didn't much care for Dickens's flashy clothing, especially the breastpins. They reminded him of American river gamblers. The last laugh was surely on Dickens there, a pint-sized James Garner in *Maverick*.

During the voyage down the Ohio River the boat passed Cairo, Ill., original of Eden in *Martin Chuzzlewit*. Dickens and other Englishmen had lost money investing in the settlement there. Cairo, lying at the junction of the Mississippi and Ohio Rivers, was often inundated by floods. Even when not, it was a hellhole of marsh, rank vegetation and malarial infection. Dickens worked off his spleen towards it via a venomous description in *American Notes*. And in subsequent novels he has characters losing money in foreign investments, almost as a warning to his readers.

The other chief means of transport Dickens used in America was the train. His first fictional handling of one comes in the American episode in *Martin Chuzzlewit*. Here he typically uses the carriage arrangement as yet another stick to beat Americans with, emphasising that the rearmost carriage was for blacks and appropriately painted black. This was accurate enough over segregation on the railroads, but hardly tactful.

Slavery had plenty of opponents in America. But a foreign critic like Dickens was always going to be resented. Anyway, during the Civil War Dickens supported the South. It didn't do his long-term US reputation much good.

Then there were Dickens's offensive American characters *per se*, jostling each other in *Martin Chuzzlewit* like the crowds of gawping onlookers who had spoilt his tour in the first place. The relevant numbers of *Martin Chuzzlewit* burst upon flesh-and-blood Americans, like a redcoat salvo at Bunker Hill, in spring 1843.

And like Bunker Hill, it was a hollow triumph for the perpetrating Britisher. No *Martin Chuzzlewit* American character bar Bevan has redeeming features. The awful characters are awful in the same sort of way, the females more pretentious than their menfolk, but otherwise morally indistinguishable.

Dickens had betrayed his art. The laws of hospitality too. He as ex-guest had spat in the face of a slightly farouche but nonetheless well-disposed ex-host, the American nation. Americans let off a collective Bronx Cheer in protest. And the American episode only boosted the 20,000 UK circulation figures of earlier numbers of *Martin Chuzzlewit* by 2,000–3,000.

Dickens argued speciously when defending himself, in the preface to the 1859 Library Edition of *Martin Chuzzlewit* saying, 'The American portion of this book is [merely] ... an exhibition ... of the ludicrous side of the American character. As I have never, in ... fiction, had any disposition to soften what is ridiculous ... at home, I hope ... that the good-humoured people of the United States are not ... disposed to quarrel with me for ... the same usage abroad.'

This amounted to claiming *Martin Chuzzlewit*'s parade of American scoundrels, braggarts, bogus army officers, crawling snobs, covert racists, know-nothings and know-alls (often the same people) was no worse than Dickens's gallery of the lampooned in England. It wasn't true. They were worse. Much worse. For he depicted his Americans as being representative of America. They constantly said so themselves.

His early novels' grotesques had not styled themselves representative Britons. Fagin hadn't extolled London's superior pickpocketing techniques over the Bowery's while instructing his boy thieves. Quilp hadn't defied America to show as villainous a dwarf as himself when persecuting Kit Nubbles. Pecksniff didn't claim to be John Bull while moralising on his own rectitude, meanwhile deprecating Uncle Sam's baseness.

Nor did they scold, harry and erroneously presume to set right a fictional American visitor, pointing to the degeneracy of his homeland, as Americans did young Martin Chuzzlewit. Dickens in *Chuzzlewit* showed himself unfair, ungenerous and ungrateful to his American hosts, however uncouth the habits of many (but by no means even the majority) of them.

There is a happy sequel. Its earliest sign was almost immediate, with Americans' delighted reception of *A Christmas Carol*. As a glance at the section on that work shows, its status even today in America is canonical.

Next, the financial position improved. Dickens got money from the Boston publishers Harper & Brothers for advance sight of his last five complete novels: £3,900 in all (£487,500 [$800,000] today). Add to that the $5,000 (£700–£1,000 at the then exchange rate, or today £87,500 [over $140,000]–£125,000 [over $200,000]), paid him for a short story, Hunted Down, commissioned by the *New York Ledger*, together with the £1,000 (today £125,000 [over $200,000]) that the Boston and New York publishers Ticknor & Fields paid for another short story, George Silverman's Explanation. By the eve of his second tour, the money Dickens had earned in America purely from his writings approached in modern terms £750,000 (say $1,230,000).

The real kiss-and-make-up moment had to wait till this second tour, mounted in the winter of 1867–68. It was a straightforward business venture, aimed at earning Dickens money from a series of 76 readings. And a winter it truly was, for though the readings ran from December to April, they were accompanied by snow falls right to the end.

Emotionally, relations were sunny. The Civil War had abolished slavery. No past critic of it was now going to be abused. Economically, the Gilded Age was about to commence. (In 1842 there had been something of a recession.)

Preliminary soundings by Dickens's scouts along the Eastern Seaboard showed every prospect of triumph. To be safe, Dickens softened the original preface to *Martin Chuzzlewit* for republication by his authorised US publishers Ticknor & Fields in their 'Charles Dickens' and 'Diamond' editions.

The excitement in America grew intense. A smash hit was imminent: ticket touts charging mark-ups of several thousand per cent, half-mile long queues outside the theatres, aspirant audience members camping on the sidewalks in savage cold, fortified by mattresses, blankets and pleasurable anticipation.

As before, the jamboree had its absurd side. Tobacconists dubbed their wares 'Little Nell Cigars' or 'Mr Squeers's Fine Cut'. This ignored the one indisputably accurate feature of Dickens's criticism in 1842: the American male's disgusting propensity to chew tobacco and spit out a brown dollop of juice which might (and in the case of Dickens's wife Catherine actually did) befoul an innocent bystander's clothing.

Dickens's initial reception on the 1867–68 tour was in Boston, also his point of disembarkation. It went beautifully. But he realised he couldn't possibly summon his *petite amie* Ellen Ternan to be with him, as he had hoped. His promoter-of-the-family image would be shattered. Clever literary detective work has revealed that Dickens agreed a code with Ellen before leaving England. A telegram from him to her would mean 'come' or 'don't come' according to minute variations in the wording. This fortifies the theory that Ellen was Dickens's mistress.

Dickens's support team set pickets outside his hotel rooms to stop rubbernecks hounding the great man. Another secondary market developed in the publishing field, with Ticknor & Fields putting out booklets containing the texts Dickens had selected to read from. Lithograph portrait reproductions of him sold for

£1.25 each, photographs (including one by Matthew Brady, famous for his Civil War battlefields) for between 25 cents and $3 each, depending on size. It all prefigured the celebrity merchandising we know today.

The readings schedule was stiff: two hours each on stage, four nights a week Monday to Friday (Dickens got Wednesday off). The tour lasted from 2 December to 20 April, nearly five months. Only when President Andrew Johnson was being impeached were any readings cancelled. A surviving newspaper account describes Dickens's stage costume of dandified dark suit, embellished by a red and white flower in his lapel and gold chains festooned across his vest [waistcoat]. It also mentioned his trim figure and agility in treading the stage, though he was now nearly 56.

One of the very worst nights for weather coincided with Dickens's third New York reading. Demand outran supply nonetheless. But the weather generally, and the strain of the tour, made Dickens's already poor health much worse. Between performances he recuperated in his hotel room, often with no voice at all, only to drive himself into 'finding' it again on mounting the stage that evening.

Towards the end he developed a swollen foot and the night of his last reading he could not stand on stage. The tour, and his renewed readings in Britain on his return, which numbered 75 and brought him £6,000 (say today £750,000 [$1,230,000]), were the chief contributors to his early death two years later.

He read from a condensed version of the work in question. Actually, 'read' does him poor justice. He scarcely turned the pages of the volume on the lectern in front of him, giving more of a recitation and improvising variations to the original material, even adding completely new words. Above all, he got so carried away that several times he very nearly joined in the audience's laughter. Boston houses were thought especially hard to charm. Dickens had no problem there.

Criticism was not entirely lacking. An actor called George Vandenhoff also gave readings from Dickens's books. Those who had heard both men thought Vandenhoff showed up Dickens's amateur elocution. Press accounts mention Dickens's tendency to deliver most of a sentence in something of a monotone and end it on an upward inflection, also traces of a Cockney accent and inability to throw his voice properly.

Compared with 1842, Dickens came away with very tidy pickings: $140,000, or £20,000–£28,000 at the then exchange rate (some $2,000,000/£3,250,000 today). But had he not sown for 30 years the seeds of fame with his pirated works disseminated, thanks to their cheapness, across the American nation, he would not now have reaped such a golden crop.

Dickens photographed by Gurney during his second trip to the US in 1867–68.

Australia

Every novelist has the power, nor just to bring his characters to life, but to put them to death. Dickens exploited it to the point of infanticide (Little Nell, Paul Dombey). But he also transported his characters. Hosts of them.

Transportation, or shipping people as part of a criminal sentence overseas, in Dickens's day meant Australia. From 1788 to 1868 Australia was the felons' destination of choice – not theirs but British officialdom's.

'Felon' often meant any poor wretch who had lifted a loaf of bread to feed himself, or pilfered a pair of shoes to prevent her feet bleeding on England's unmetalled roads. The standard tariff was seven years' transportation. This held good whether the felon's swag consisted of cheese to fend off starvation or quantities of manufactured goods to sell on. The latter in a rational world would have been a graver offence.

Rationality didn't come into it. You could get 10 years for as little as trousering four pennies, or 2p in modern currency and £2.50 in modern value. This is the cost of a short bus ride today. In Dickens's day it bought you a one-way ticket to the other side of the planet under an armed guard, forced labour when you got there and no turning back to the old country till a fat chunk of the rest of your life had elapsed, if then.

And going home too soon was rather more serious than turning up an hour early for a party. Magwitch in *Great Expectations*, a 'returned convict', or one who has come back to England illicitly, is in consequence a wanted man.

In fairness, transportation was devised as a humane alternative to the death penalty. This at the beginning of Dickens's life was the tariff for 100 petty offences alone. Transportation was also a cheap alternative to building more prisons. At its height it coincided with Dickens's career, the 1830s–60s. No wonder he used it so lavishly as a dramatic device.

The list of characters he despatches via transportation is a minor roll call from his works: the Artful Dodger in *Oliver Twist*, Brooker and Squeers in *Nicholas Nickleby*, Alice Marwood in *Dombey and Son*, Magwitch in *Great Expectations*. Dickens also sends blameless characters out to Australia. Augustus Moddle in *Martin Chuzzlewit* for one, who flees to Van Dieman's Land (now Tasmania) to escape marrying the ghastly Cherry Pecksniff.

Then there are Em'ly, Dan Peggotty, Mrs Gummidge, the Micawber family and Mr Mell, all from *David Copperfield*. They voyage to mainland Australia, making good there, Mr Micawber as District Magistrate of Port Middlebay, and Mell, now styled 'Doctor', as (implicitly) headmaster of Port Middlebay Grammar School.

Micawber's achievement has been found implausible by many people, given his failure back in England. But Dickens preempts such criticism by making it clear that Micawber was rather a good lawyer's clerk, not least in assembling evidence against Uriah Heep, trawling through innumerable complex business transactions. In short (Micawber's favourite phrase), he was good at the theory of finance, less so its practice. So what? He had enough grasp of law to make a bonzer beak Down Under.

Not everyone in Dickens novels benefits from being thus transplanted. Martha Endell, also from *David Copperfield*, Dickens packs off to Australia too. But she has taken to prostitution, so Dickens puts her in the Outback, 400 miles from all human society other than that of her husband. This is hell indeed.

In real life Dickens was involved in assisting the passage of reformed prostitutes from his West London Urania Cottage settlement out to Australia as well. Two of Dickens's sons, Alfred Tennyson Dickens and Edward Bulwer Lytton Dickens, named respectively after the poet and historical novelist (both friends of Dickens), emigrated to Australia. Unlike Micawber or Magwitch, neither was a business success there. They did resemble Magwitch in trying to make money at sheep-farming and Edward carved a career as a member of the New South Wales legislature.

Dickens had in the early 1860s been offered £10,000 (£1,250,000 today) to do a reading tour of Australia. In 1869 he reverted to the idea. Had he lived longer, it might have come off.

One of the world's only two statues of Dickens is in Australia (the other is in Philadelphia). It was commissioned in 1880 by Sir Henry Parkes, Premier of New South Wales. Parkes had himself been an immigrant from England and a moving spirit in getting transportation abolished. More, he was a huge Dickens fan. The statue stood in Sydney's Centennial Park till removed in 1972 owing to vandalism.

The statue of Dickens in Centennial Park, Sydney, Australia.

It then vanished, to be rediscovered just over a year ago, minus its head and a finger among other adornments, after the President of the New South Wales Dickens Society got several anonymous phone calls informing her of its whereabouts. Dickens would have loved the mystery of this, even though he was against being commemorated by such things as statues. The statue was re-erected in time for his 199th birthday on 6 Feb 2011.

Part fairyland for nice people who deserve something better than poverty or death, yet couldn't quite succeed back in the Old Country (Mr Micawber). Part Siberia, a limbo for villains and unfortunates, who Dickens can nonetheless with a flick of his pen summon back to England to ginger up the action there (Magwitch). And lastly, part tarts' oubliette. Australia is an ideal offstage parking lot for characters Dickens has no immediate use for. The wonder is that the device hasn't been more used by other novelists.

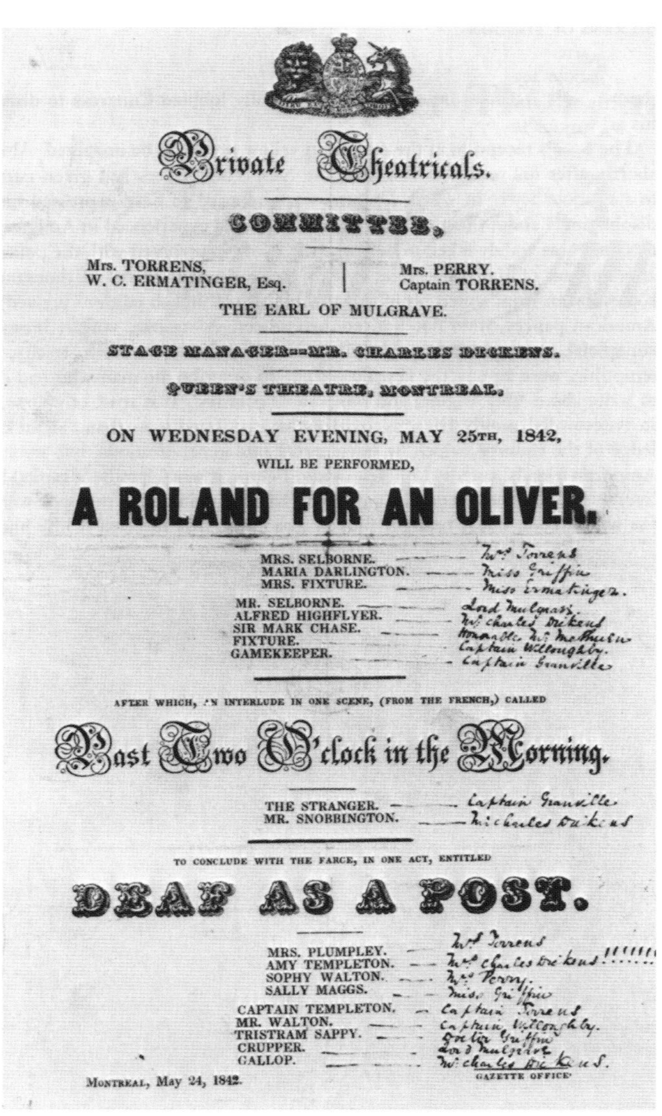

Private Theatricals.

COMMITTEE.

Mrs. TORRENS,
W. C. ERMATINGER, Esq.
Mrs. PERRY.
Captain TORRENS.
THE EARL OF MULGRAVE.

STAGE MANAGER—MR. CHARLES DICKENS.

QUEEN'S THEATRE, MONTREAL.

ON WEDNESDAY EVENING, MAY 25TH, 1842,
WILL BE PERFORMED,

A ROLAND FOR AN OLIVER.

MRS. SELBORNE. — Mrs Torrens
MARIA DARLINGTON. — Miss Griffin
MRS. FIXTURE. — Miss Ermatinger.
MR. SELBORNE. — Lord Mulgrave.
ALFRED HIGHFLYER. — Mr Charles Dickens
SIR MARK CHASE. — Honble Mr Methuen
FIXTURE. — Captain Willoughby.
GAMEKEEPER. — Captain Granville

AFTER WHICH, AN INTERLUDE IN ONE SCENE, (FROM THE FRENCH,) CALLED

Past Two O'clock in the Morning.

THE STRANGER. — Captain Granville.
MR. SNOBBINGTON. — Mr Charles Dickens

TO CONCLUDE WITH THE FARCE, IN ONE ACT, ENTITLED

DEAF AS A POST.

MRS. PLUMPLEY. — Mrs Torrens
AMY TEMPLETON. — Mrs Charles Dickens!!!!!!
SOPHY WALTON. — Mrs Perry.
SALLY MAGGS. — Miss Griffin
CAPTAIN TEMPLETON. — Captain Torrens
MR. WALTON. — Captain Willoughby.
TRISTRAM SAPPY. — Doctor Griffin
CRUPPER. — Lord Mulgrave
GALLOP. — Mr Charles Dickens.

MONTREAL, May 24, 1842.
GAZETTE OFFICE

The playbill for a play staged by Dickens in Montreal in 1842. The actors' names in longhand were added by him.

Canada

It was in Canada that Dickens first touched New World soil, stopping off at Halifax, Nova Scotia, on 20 January 1842 before disembarking altogether at Boston. Halifax did him proud. The Nova Scotia legislature's speaker came aboard Dickens's ship and paged him in person. Dickens was guest of honour at the legislature's state opening, coincidentally due that day.

He returned to Canada for a month before returning to Britain, crossing the border near Niagara Falls on 26 April. The Dickenses spent nine days at a hotel overlooking the Falls. 'Nothing but water ... and too much of that,' sniffed Catherine Dickens's maid Anne Brown.

They briefly visited Toronto and Kingston, Ontario, then Canada's capital, and spent the rest of May, bar a side trip to Quebec City, in Montreal. There a shipboard acquaintance from four months back, Lord Mulgrave (later Governor of Nova Scotia), was an officer with the British garrison. Dickens took charge of some garrison private theatricals, stage-managing, directing and performing the lead role.

Dickens's only Canadian-connected character is Edmund Sparkler in *Little Dorrit*, Mrs Merdle's son by her first husband, a British army office. Sparkler, Dickens tells us, was born at Saint John, New Brunswick. 'Tip' Dorrit in the same book is intended for Canada as a black sheep member of the family but never gets nearer than Liverpool before giving up and walking back to London. Dickens's son Francis was a Mountie for 12 years.

France

Dickens visited France on about 20 occasions, the first in 1837, the last in 1868. They weren't all pleasure trips. Not even Paris, for most people the ultimate pleasure destination. He worked there on *Dombey and Son* in 1847, killing off little Paul in between visits to the Morgue (a place he found fascinating), and on *Little Dorrit* in the winter of 1855–56. He gave three readings at the British Embassy in 1863, slipping mysteriously away between whiles, probably to Ellen Ternan, who between roughly 1862 and 1865 he seems to have kept at Condette, a village near Boulogne.

Dickens was almost as famous in France as in Britain. He sat for Ary Scheffer, a Paris-based painter of appropriately 'literary' subjects. He mixed with various French writers, including George Sand. Railway station bookstalls

An illustration of Porte Saint-Denis in Paris, c.1840.

displayed his works. He mounted a play in Paris with his favourite, the actor Charles Fechter (like Scheffer predominantly French, despite their German-sounding names).

But Dickens had a restricted artistic outlook. Paris, so rich in classic drama, museums, art galleries and opera, was for Dickens more a pantomime, her citizens its cast. He expressly regarded visiting French cathedrals and the like as chores. In Britain such narrowness was unremarkable. In Paris, the 19th century's hub of civilisation, it diminished him.

He liked the freedom of France, although arranging most of his visits under the Second Empire, an illiberal regime. But 'freedom' to Dickens, a notoriously dressy man, meant wearing whatever clothes he fancied without being mocked, and the right to make his French characters homicidal (Hortense in *Bleak House*, Blandois in *Little Dorrit*, the Defarges in *A Tale of Two Cities*). The French figuratively shrugged their shoulders over this.

Dickens varied his technique with French characters when they spoke English. Retaining French constructions worked quite well, giving dialogue a plausible flavour of foreignness. And Dickens's grasp of French by his middle period had got good enough to do this. But he translated some idioms literally, with unfortunate results. Thus on Blandois' lips the curse

'*Sacré bleu!*' becomes the risible 'Holy blue!'.

France supplied something else, the backdrop to sexual irregularity. Unlike his great French rival Balzac, Dickens in novels avoided adultery. Close calls – yes. But very few: Mrs Pott and Winkle (*Pickwick Papers*), Louisa Bounderby and Jem Harthouse (*Hard Times*). Lastly, Edith and Carker in *Dombey and Son*. (Always the wife wavers, never a husband.)

The Dijon apartment where Edith awaits Carker after leaving Mr Dombey is almost what the Rouen cab was to be for Madame Bovary: humdrum provincial urban setting within which wife-of-a-dull-husband gives herself to a seducer. Actually, Edith bottles out. But the episode had to suggest eroticism, however furtively planned, and however frustrated as to outcome. So Dickens needed a French locale.

And when he needed to depict the lesbian-tinged Miss Wade–Tattycoram relationship in *Little Dorrit*, he started in Marseilles and finished in Calais, spanning the country's entire land mass. For to British minds France long remained a lubricious place, giving its very name to sexuality. A couple exchanged French kisses, the man donned a French letter and to spice things up the woman might dress as a French maid. Paris was where newlyweds honeymooned, Mr and the second Mrs Dombey among them. France for Dickens was more than a frequent holiday destination. It eroticised his art.

Italy

France represented to Dickens a civilisation different to Britain's but equally valid. In Italy he was essentially a tourist, and of that most miserable kind, the ex-pat slinking abroad to economise.

He settled in Genoa between 1844 and 1845, renting for his family first a villa then a palazzo. Genoa was really a base. He mounted from it excursions that in total lasted three months, taking in the main northern cities then Florence, Rome and Naples.

Nine years later, in the autumn of 1853, he did a six-week return tour, accompanied by the painter Augustus Egg and the novelist Wilkie Collins. Dickens wrote back to England that he scorned staying anywhere more than a week. Just like the whirlwind package tourists of today, really. Although after his mid-1840s stay he had written with conventional admiration of Italy's art works, this time he expressed an oafish disdain for Florentine paintings, rather as Gradgrind in *Hard Times* might have. But Dickens had before his Genoa stay learnt Italian (though in *Little Dorrit* he clumsily translates what will have been Cavalletto's imprecation '*Madonna mia!*' as 'Lady of mine!').

Dickens wrote two of his Christmas works in Italy, *The Chimes* (an attack on utilitarianism) of 1844 in Genoa, and in Venice in 1853 *Nobody's Story*, an elaboration of the sort of homeless wretch's plight he had covered in *Bleak*

House. He went one better with *Pictures from Italy*, a travelogue published in 1846. In it, foreshadowing E M Forster's *A Room With a View* 60 years on, he guyed the sort of tripper whose insincere 'appreciation' of art parrots guide books or tour guides.

The Coast of Genoa, by Jasper Francis Cropsey.

Switzerland

Dickens had first experienced Switzerland en route to Italy in 1845 and visited it a last time on his Italian tour of 1853, recalling the then laborious traversing of the Great St Bernard Pass into Italy in *Little Dorrit*.

When back in 1846 he had renewed his economy drive by letting his London house and moving abroad again, he chose Lausanne, on Lake Geneva. Catherine seems to have had some say in the decision – for once.

Dickens describes the long coach journey there in *The Uncommercial Traveller* (1861, enlarged edition 1868). The Dickenses rented a lakeside villa called Rosemont. Although they inhabited Switzerland only between June and November 1846, Dickens's creativity was prodigious. He composed the first three monthly episodes of *Dombey and Son*, a retelling of the New Testament for family use (published in 1934 as *The Life of Our Lord*) and his Christmas Book for that year, *The Battle of Life*. The last sold 23,000 copies on publication and made Dickens 4,000 guineas (well over half a million pounds today). The economy drive had hit pay dirt.

Russia

Though revered in Russia, Dickens never went there. But his novels wielded great influence, mostly before the 1917 Revolution. Gogol has been suggested as one disciple, notably in the way *Dead Souls* (1842) echoes the picaresque element in *Pickwick Papers*, parts of which were translated into Russian as early as 1838.

A safer bet is Dostoevsky, whose niece translated Dickens into Russian for a living and who himself read Dickens assiduously. Dostoevsky frequently mentions Dickens as inspiration and even interviewed him for a periodical in 1861. Steerforth has been suggested as model for Stavrogin in *The Devils* (see also the *Barnaby Rudge* 'Story Commentary', Gashford having been suggested model for Peter Verkhovensky), as have Rosa Dartle (Daria Shatov) and Betsey Trotwood's relationship with Mr Dick (Mme [Varvara] Stavrogin's with Stepan Verkhovensky).

Other Dostoevsky novels whose major characters allegedly reflect Dickens characters include Prince Myshkin and Nastasia Filippovna in *The Idiot* (respectively John Harmon and Edith Dombey), Raskolnikov in *Crime and Punishment* (Bradley Headstone) and Nellie in *The Insulted and Injured* (Little Nell). Dostoevsky thought *The Old Curiosity Shop* a masterpiece.

Tolstoy as editor in 1866 published *A Christmas Carol* in the magazine *Posrednik* ('The Intermediary'). Like Dostoevsky, he had a Dickens-translator niece (Vera). She produced free versions of *A Christmas Carol*, part of *David Copperfield*, *Little Dorrit* and *Great Expectations*. Her complete *Great Expectations* (1895) had as title 'The Daughter of the Convict, or From the Forge to Wealth', thus revealing Estella's origins.

Tolstoy, like Dickens, sugared his novels with sentimentality. Not all Russians swallowed this. Lenin in 1922, at a dramatisation of *The Cricket on the Hearth* (originally one of Dickens's *Christmas Books*), stalked out halfway through, disgusted by its petty-bourgeois mawkishness. Yet *The Cricket* had broad appeal throughout the Slavonic world. In the Balkans it was a hit as an opera by Karl Goldmark, better known for his *Rustic Wedding Symphony*. Back in Russia, Tchaikovsky learnt enough English to read *Pickwick Papers* and *David Copperfield*. A pity he never went further, turning out a deliciously sombre ballet of *Bleak House*, say.

Dostoevsky in 1879 (above).

A portrait of Leo Tolstoy in 1887 by Ilya Efimovich Repin (below).

Among twentieth-century Dickens-influenced novelists, Yevgeny Zamyatin and Mikhail Bulgakov have been suggested. Zamyatin, who at one point lived in Newcastle, praised Dickens's social realism. Solzhenitsyn read him too, though of so gloomy a personality one hesitates to say 'with pleasure'.

Between 1894 and 1944 some 3,000,000 copies of Dickens's novels were printed in Russia/the USSR. This excludes any breakdown between pre-1917 years and post-1917 ones. An important point that, since from the Revolution on he was an 'approved' author, as showing up the evils of capitalism (but did *Pickwick*?). Evidence as to Dickens's true popularity is therefore bedevilled by politics. Not only did ideologically 'correct' books like his enjoy massive print runs and low pricing, but 'incorrect' rivals were banned. In the period 1935–36 new Soviet editions of *Pickwick*, *Dombey and Son* and *Bleak House* sold 160,000 copies, though the regime favoured the extra-gritty *Hard Times* most, so promoted it hardest.

for settlement by later novelists such as George Gissing and H G Wells a generation after him and Alan Sillitoe and John Braine a whole century on. He was English literature's Robespierre.

Dickens introduced in his late novels frequent use of the present tense, in modern writers' hands too often a tiresome affectation but with him still echoing the true 'historic present', developed for a rapid sequence of dramatic events. It was Dickens who began the use of dialogue without indicating a speaker, stripping out the 'he saids'/'she saids'. Again this was late in his development. Earlier he was as clumsy as any neophyte, using 'rejoined Snooks', 'Joe Soap protested' after direct speech.

His prose could be so impressionist as to approach obscurity, notably in the passage ending *Great Expectations*. *Edwin Drood* shows signs of carrying this further, anticipating 20th-century developments both in narrative and dialogue. In Chapter II of *Drood* occurs the following: 'No, but really; – isn't it, you know, after all?' Try that, the true author's name unseen, on Eng. Lit. dons and 99 per cent will answer 'Henry James'.

Dickens influenced an impressive list of successor novelists. They include the A-list highbrow-approved Franz Kafka, together with our home-grown Sir Angus Wilson. Dickens has proved a singularly tough nut actually to imitate. James Joyce, the Alpha Double Plus of the A-lister highbrows, is thought by some people to have had a crack via the Oxen of the Sun passage in *Ulysses*. Even a short wrestle with those jungly prose thickets shows any such thing to be either very ineptly done – odd, given Joyce's technical facility with the English language – or, more probably, a take-off of Rabelais and the mock heroic voice.

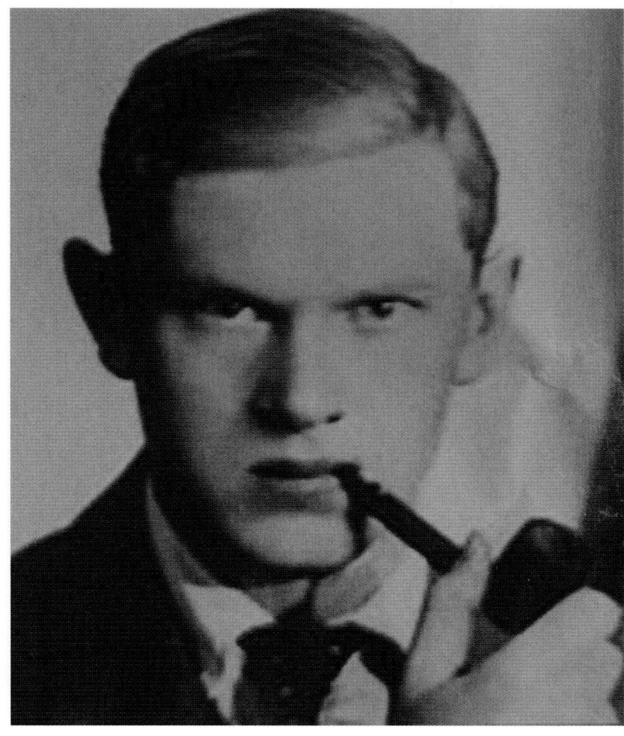

Evelyn Waugh.

Dickens's most interesting literary heir, because superficially such a contrast, is Evelyn Waugh. Arthur Waugh, Evelyn's father, was Managing Director of Chapman & Hall, Dickens's publishers and part-copyright holders. Dickens's literary earnings therefore put Evelyn Waugh through Lancing, where he was taught to express himself by J F Roxburgh, later first headmaster of Stowe, and Oxford, where he first drew a bead on his own special literary quarry, the upper classes, completing Dickens's demolition of them but much more subtly inasmuch as he appeared to share their values. Evelyn Waugh, in short, extended the satirical side of Dickens, dropping the sentimentality and refining the macabre element.

Similarities abound. Trivial, perhaps. But trivia when abundant constitute solidity. The two novelists had virtually identical nicknames: 'Boz' for Dickens; for Waugh, 'Boaz'. Each man nearly always put a prison or other forcible detention in his novels. Waugh lifts at least two plot devices from Dickens. First, Tony Last towards the end of *A Handful of Dust* reading aloud Dickens novels to Mr Todd when a captive in Amazonia (based on a trek Waugh made in Guyana, Dickens's Demerara). This power play echoes Martin Chuzzlewit, in his unregenerately selfish days, getting Tom Pinch to read to him. Second, one partner in a firm using the other partner's supposed hardheartedness to exploit a victim. Spenlow, of Spenlow & Jorkins, lies to David Copperfield, pretending that though

Charles Dickens giving a public reading, 1861

he himself is sympathetic to David's wish to renegotiate his articles, Jorkins (in actuality a cipher) wouldn't hear of it. Benwell, Adam Fenwick-Symes's publisher in *Vile Bodies*, does the same to get Adam to sign a grossly unfavourable contract, the absent partner in question having long ceased to help run the publishing house.

Mr Stiggins, to Dickens the archetypal evangelical, by Kyd.

There is Waugh's frequent use of Dickens character names, sometimes slightly modified: Miss Flite the dotty *Bleak House* litigant and Flyte the *Brideshead* peer's family; Fagin in *Oliver Twist* and Fagan in *Decline and Fall*; Mrs Jellyby in *Bleak House*, Prof Jellaby in *Scoop* and the Jellaby servants in *Work Suspended*; Steerforth, both David Copperfield's schoolfellow and Master of the *Caliban* in *Pinfold*. Others (the first of a pair a Dickens character, the second a Waugh one; single names are common to both) include Crupp/Crump, Greenacre, Grime/Grimes, Jaggers/Jagger, Jorkins, Podgers/Podger's, Pott/Potts, Sniggs, Stiggins, Tippins/Tipping, Trotter. This echoing reverberates all the more because both novelists choose silly names for many characters, and to an extent no other novelist of comparable stature does.

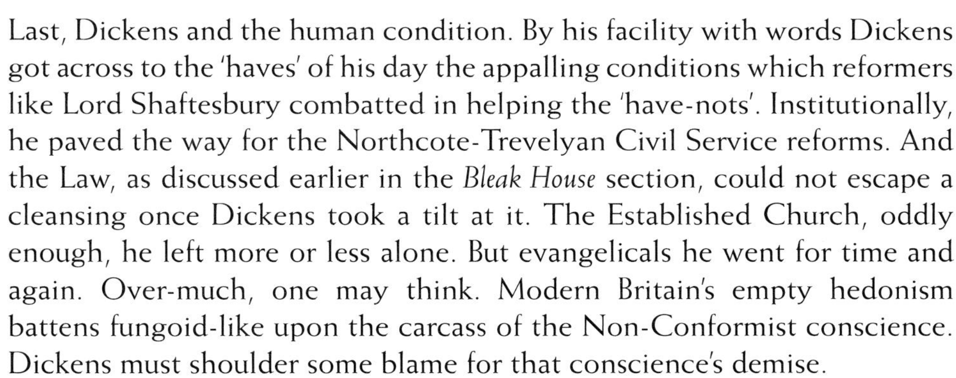

Last, Dickens and the human condition. By his facility with words Dickens got across to the 'haves' of his day the appalling conditions which reformers like Lord Shaftesbury combatted in helping the 'have-nots'. Institutionally, he paved the way for the Northcote-Trevelyan Civil Service reforms. And the Law, as discussed earlier in the *Bleak House* section, could not escape a cleansing once Dickens took a tilt at it. The Established Church, oddly enough, he left more or less alone. But evangelicals he went for time and again. Over-much, one may think. Modern Britain's empty hedonism battens fungoid-like upon the carcass of the Non-Conformist conscience. Dickens must shoulder some blame for that conscience's demise.

Dickens, along with Shakespeare, is a literary name that resonates with millions around the world. Most unusually, he is nearly as familiar to those who haven't read him as to those who have. In this he outshines Shakespeare. That said, even those who have sampled Dickens in print have often undergone the experience only as adolescents, during some school project in which they 'did' an approved text such as *Bleak House*, in consequence retaining into later life memories at worst resentful, at best confused, albeit lurid.

If this present celebration of Dickens can induce anyone to return to him of their own free will, or have a go as a rookie reader, it will rescue a colossus of letters from that mortuary slab to which dim teachers (the Gradgrinds of our day) have relegated him. And on the exceptionally slanderous charge of being a 'study text'.

Selected Bibliography

The leading versions of Dickens's works for readers wanting detailed notes, scholarly readings of variations in earlier texts and so on are the Norton Critical Edition (www.wwnorton.com/college/english/nce_british.htm), also the Oxford Clarendon Edition and paperback Oxford World's Classics (ukcatalogue.oup.com/). The Penguin Classics are another good paperback equivalent.

More de luxe versions are the modern Nonesuch Dickens (www.nonesuch-dickens.com/) and the splendidly compact but elegant Collector's Library volumes (www.collectors-library.com/). The two last concentrate on the novels.

Michael Slater (Emeritus Professor of Victorian Literature, Birkbeck College, London), *Charles Dickens* (New Haven and London, 2009), provides the standard and most recent biography. He is also author of *Dickens and Women* (London, 1983) and *An Intelligent Person's Guide to Dickens* (London, 1999). He has edited *The Dickensian* (see below) and *The Dent Uniform Edition of Dickens's Journalism* (3 vols. [vol. 4 co-ed. John Drew], 1994–2000).

The next most recent biography is Peter Ackroyd's *Dickens* (London, 1990). This is useful since it is by a fellow creative writer. But Ackroyd is ill-served by his publisher, whose deplorable indexing frequently lists the wrong pages and misleading subject matter.

Fred Kaplan's *Dickens: A Biography* (New York) appeared in 1988. Much older biographies include G K Chesterton's *Charles Dickens* (London, 1906), also by a creative writer hence still useful, and Dickens's friend John Forster's *The Life of Charles Dickens* (3 vols., London, 1872–76, ed. J W T Ley, 1928). Ley, in *The Dickens Circle* (London, 1918), discusses among other things the originals of various Dickens characters.

Forster destroyed many of Dickens's letters. Those that survive run to 12 vols.: *The British Academy Pilgrim Edition of the Letters of Charles Dickens* (ed. Madeline House, Graham Storey & Kathleen Tillotson, Oxford, 1965–2002).

For reminiscences see Philip Collins, ed., *Dickens: Interviews and Recollections* (2 vols., London, 1981). For more general information see Paul Schlicke, ed., *Oxford Reader's Companion to Dickens* (Oxford, 1999).

The Dickensian is the journal of the Dickens Fellowship. This now comprises mainly enthusiasts for his writings and is involved in running The Charles Dickens Museum, at 48 Doughty Street, London WC1N 2LX (www.dicken-smuseum.com/). Among the latter place's treasures are a range of novelty items in its little shop that include a plastic 'Charles Dickens Action Figure with quill pen and removable [top] hat! [*sic*]' (£8.99) and a gift-packaged pot of dipping ink (£4.50).

Dickens was so much a multi-media entertainer himself that it is absurd to confine a bibliography to books. In addition to broadcast/film adaptations (see the 'Characters' section of each novel), the actor-playwright Emlyn

Williams for well over 30 years recreated Dickens's readings in a one-man show. Simon Callow followed suit on TV and in a London stage production, *The Mystery of Charles Dickens*, 2000–01. Miriam Margolyes (see 'Characters' of *Oliver Twist* and *Little Dorrit*) reprised various Dickens female characters in a one-woman London stage production, *Dickens's Women* (1991).

Charles Dickens as a young man by George Cruikshank.

Index

An index of characters in Dickens's works starts on page 238.
CD = Charles Dickens.
Index entry names of characters in brackets refer to persons not active in a novel, for instance because they died before the action begins.
Numbers in **bold** refer to the timeline pages.
Numbers in *italics* refer to picture captions.
Numbers in (brackets) indicate a page lacking a printed number, for example because it is a map in colour plate form.
Where two or more characters have the same or very similar name the title of the novel he/she appears in is given in brackets.

Abbot, Russ, plays Fagin 52
Abraham, F Murray, plays Scrooge 101
Ackland, Joss, plays Joe Gargery 183
Ackroyd, Peter, CD biographer 7, 147, 232
  admires *Martin Chuzzlewit* 116
  inspired by Julia Mills? 206
  on CD's limitations as dramatist 204
Administrative Reform Association **24**
Adrian, Max, plays Fagin 52
Adventures of Chichikov, The **24**
Africa 150
Ainsworth, William Harrison, friend of CD 37
Albert, Prince 8, **23**
Alderton, John, plays Christopher Casby 167
Alexander II of Russia, Tsar **24**
Alfred the Great, CD admires 21
Ali Baba (among CD's favourite childhood tales) 105
Alice in Wonderland 20
All the Year Round 18, **25**, 181, *181*, 189, 202
  phenomenal circulation 181
Allen, Keith, plays Jonas Chuzzlewit 112
Allen, Lily 112
America 12, 212–19
  CD's fame consolidated by *Old Curiosity Shop* 116
  Crummles emigrates to 64
  Gilded Age 218
  lax banking system, CD attacks via Scrooge 105
  Littimer tries fleeing to 135
  Martin Chuzzlewit (Jr) seeks fortune in, nearly dies 118–19
  North, US portion of 27
  power to instil virtue via adversity softens CD's satire 112
American Civil War **25**, 218, 219
American Notes 11, 209, 215
Americans 10, 20
Amsterdam, J Flintwinch absconds to 175
Andersen, Hans Christian **23**
Anderson, Gillian, plays Lady Dedlock 148
Andover–Devizes–Warminster triangle
  Pecksniff home in? 114
Andrews, Anthony, plays Mr Murdstone 137
Anglers' Inn (*Our Mutual Friend*) (30), (31)
Anglo-Bengalee Disinterested Loan and Life Assurance Company 111, 112, 113, 118
Anglo-French tension **25**
Annis, Francesca, plays Estella 183
Anthony, Lysette, plays
  Agnes and Rose Fleming 53
  Florence Dombey 123
Antwerp (32), (33), 175
Appleton, Honor C,
  CD illustrator *101, 104, 105, 106, 107, 109*
Arbus, Diane, freak photos, matched in prose in *The Old Curiosity Shop Ch XIX* 83
Arctic, setting for CD–Wilkie Collins drama collaboration 27
Ardizzone, Edward, CD illustrator 211
Armstrong, Alun, plays Flintwinch 169
Atkins, Eileen, plays Jane Murdstone 137
Atkinson, Rowan, plays Fagin 52
Attenborough, Richard, plays Tungay 139
Austen, Jane 20
Australia 27, (33), 134, 220–1
  CD offered huge sum to do reading tour of 221
  two of CD's sons settled 221

Baddeley, Hermione, plays
  Mrs Bardell 39
  Mrs Cratchit 99
  Ninetta Crummles 63
Balkans, The 226
Baltimore, Maryland, USA (32), 216
Balzac (Honoré de) 9, 224
  Illusions perdues, homosexual character Herrera 82
Bancroft, Anne, plays Miss Havisham 184
Barbados (32), 122, 128, 129
Barclay and Co, their porter beer 86
Baring's Bank 131
Barnaby Rudge 18, 20, **22**, **23**, (28), (30), (31), 116, 180, 209, 210, 214, 225
  sales 94
  television 1960 95
Barnard Castle, Co Durham 67
Barnet, Hertfordshire (30), (31), 56
Barrow, Charles (CD's grandfather) 13
Barrow, Janet (CD's aunt) *title page*
Barrow, John (CD's uncle) 15
Barrymore, John, plays Scrooge 100
Barrymore, Lionel, plays
  Dan Peggotty 137
  Scrooge 100
Bart, Lionel, creator of musical *Oliver!* 51, 52
Bartholomew, Freddie, plays David Copperfield 133
Bass, Alfie, plays
  Bob Cratchit 99
  Jerry Cruncher 177
Bastille, the 178, 179, 180
  Dr Manette long imprisoned in 179
  Dr Manette old lag has status with Paris mob 181
  'One and Five, North Tower', prison number 179
Bateson, Timothy
  cameo role in Polanski-directed *Oliver Twist* 94

plays
  Lord (Frederick) Verisopht 69
  Mr Dick 134
  Mr Fezziwig 100
  Sim Tappertit 95
  William Guppy 149
Bath, Avon (in CD's day Somerset) (30), (31), 39, 40, 42, 45, 48, 78
  Assembly Rooms 39
  servants 'swarry' at 44, 45
Battle of Life, The 225
Beadnell, Maria (CD's first love) 17
Beaucourt Mutuel, Ferdinand (holiday landlord) 203
Belgium 27, (32), (33)
  Blandois/Lagnier/Rigaud born there 167
Bellingham, Lynda ('Oxo Mum'), plays Mrs Lupin 113
Bengal (33), 39
Bennett, J Gordon 215
Bentley's Miscellany, CD edits **23**
Bible, King James, influence 14
Birmingham 45, 85
  'Black Country' near 85
blacking warehouse **22**, 115
Bleak House 14, 18, **22**, **24**, (28), (30), (31), (32), (33), 68, 95, 114, *154*, 175, 189, 211, 223, 224–5, 226, 231
  commences unusually powerfully 155
  debate re when set 148
  first edition copies of 36, *35*
  sales 159
  silent film of 1922 148
  success induces CD Harper's deal America 159
  television 1959 149
  television 1985 147
  television 2005 148
  why title 154
Bleak House, Broadstairs, Kent 154, *155*
Bleak House (John Jarndyce's Hertfordshire residence) (30), (31), 150, 151, 154, 158
Blue Dragon inn (30), (31), 113, 115, 117, 118
Blunderstone, Suffolk (*David Copperfield*) (30), (31), 133
Bogarde, Dirk, plays Sydney Carton 177
Boston, Massachusetts 215, 217, 218, 222
  CD feted 1842 (32), 214
  CD readings 1867–1868 **25**, (32), 219
  Old State House *26*
Botany Bay, New South Wales, Australia (33)
Boucicault, Dion 205
Boulogne, Nord-Pas-de-Calais, France 12, (32), (33), 203, 222
Bovary, Madame 224
Bow Bells, sound of 12
Bow Street Runner(s) 51, 61
Bower, The (Boffins' residence) (29)
Bowes Academy, inspired Dotheboys Hall 69
'Boz' (CD's early *nom de plume*) **23**, *36*
Brady, Mathew 218–219
Braine, John, debt to CD 229
Brecht, Bertholt, *A Threepenny Novel* 118
Brentford 192
Bright, John 198
Brighton, Sussex (30), (31), *120*, 123
  boarding house at 126
  Downs 130
Britain 215
Britten, Benjamin 108
Broadstairs, Kent 12, (30), (31), *155*
Brock, C(harles) E(dmund), CD illustrator 211
Bron, Eleanor, plays Mrs Merdle 171
Brooks's (club) 42
Brown, Captain 11
Browne, Hablot Knight; *see* 'Phiz'
BT TV ads involving Maureen Lipman 162
Buffalo, NY, USA (32)
Bulgakov, Mikhail 226
Bull, John 212
Bull, Peter, plays
  Serjeant Buzfuz 39
  Wemmick 185
Bunny, Bugs 108
Burdet-Coutts, Angela (Baroness) 9, 11
Bury St Edmunds, Suffolk (30), (31), 44, 45
Byron, Lord **22**, 41, 85, 86, 138, 151, 170
  dog Lyon inspires Gowan's Lion 170

Caine, Michael, plays Scrooge 100
Cairo, Egypt (32), (33), 188
Cairo, Illinois, USA (32), 216
Calais, Nord-Pas-de-Calais, France (32), (33), 224
Calhoun, John C, US Senator South Carolina 214
California, rough gold-diggers in, touched by Little Nell's fate told in Bret Harte's poem **25**
Callow, Simon, one-man show re CD, *The Mystery of Charles Dickens* 233
Canada 27, (32), (33), 212
  CD son Mountie in 222
  Halifax, Nova Scotia (32), (33), 222
  Kingston, Ontario (32), (33), 222
  Montreal, Quebec (32), (33), 222, *222*
    CD mounts theatricals at garrison 222, *222*
  Nova Scotia legislature honours CD 222
  Quebec City (32), (33), 222
  Saint John, New Brunswick (32), (33)
    Edmund Sparkler born there 222

  'Tip' Dorrit intended for 222
  Toronto, Ontario (32), (33), 222
Canning, George **23**, 46
Canterbury, Kent (30), (31), 138, 139
Cape (of Good Hope) (32), (33), 192, 194
Carême 10
Carol, A Christmas 6, 10, **24**, (28), 52, 95, *103*, 211, 214, 217, 226
  most reworked item by posterity in CD's fiction 107
  MS., sample page *103*
  numerous film (cartoon and human), gramophone, made-for-TV film, musical, film musical, made-for-TV musical and radio dramatisations 99–101
  other genres, reworkings in 108
  public readings, CD chooses for first of 107
  religious revival shown in, flourishing of 104
Carradine, John, plays Scrooge 100
Carrey, Jim, plays Scrooge 101
Carson, John, plays Mr Dombey 124
Castle, Roy, plays Sam Weller 45
Catholic Emancipation Act **23**
Catholic Relief Bill 89
Cattermole, George, CD illustrator *96, 97*, 209, *209*
Ceylon (32), (33), 198
Chalk, Kent (30), (31)
Chaney, Lon, plays Fagin 52
Chapman & Hall, CD publisher 46, 87, 174, *199*, 229
Characters, CD, London streets named after 15
Charing Cross (railway) Station, London **25**
Charitable Grinders, The 126
Charles Dickens Museum, The **23**, 232
Charles X King of France **22**
Chartism 18
Chatham, Kent *21*, 84
  CD, family lived **22**, (30), (31)
Chatto, Daniel, plays 'Tip' Dorrit 169
Chelsea Bindery *36*
Chertsey, Surrey (30), (31)
Chesney Wold, Lincolnshire (30), (31), 149, 151, 154, 158
Chesterton, G(ilbert) K(eith), biography of CD 232
Chigwell, Essex (30), (31), 89, 90, 92, 97
Child Characters from Dickens *8*
Child's History of England, A 20, 209
Chimes, The *10*, *203*
China (33), 131, 168
Christ, Jesus 107
Christianity, Muscular 197
Christ's Hospital (school), W Sussex 126
Christmas, 106, 107, 109, 224
  Christian festival, a 107
  Manor Farm, Dingley Dell, Kent, at 39, 48
  'merry' 8, 102
  Nativity story cold-shouldered on TV 109
  Twelfth Night 106
  Victorian 8, **23**
Christmas Books 10, 11, 116, 202, *203*, 209, 210, 226
Christmas Carol, A; *see Carol, A Christmas*
Cincinnati, Ohio, USA (32)
Circumlocution Office (*Little Dorrit*) 15, 18, 167, 171
  CD has Treasury in mind 167
Clay, Henry, US Senator from Kentucky 214
Cloisterham (*The Mystery of Edwin Drood*) (30), (31), 97, 199, 200
Coaches/coachmen 11, 41, 45
Coalbrookdale 164
Cobden, Richard 102
Cobham, Kent (30), (31)
Cockney characters 12
Coketown (*Hard Times*) (30), (31), 161, 162
Coleman, Gary, plays Ghost of Christmas Past 99
Collins, Charles, CD illustrator 209
Collins, Joan, sometime wife of Anthony Newley (qv) 52
Collins, Phil, plays The Artful Dodger 52
Collins, Wilkie
  tours Italy, Switzerland with CD 224
  works with CD on *The Frozen Deep* 27, (32), (33), 205
Colman, Ronald, plays
  Sydney Carton 177
  Scrooge 100
  famous Sydney Carton exit line and 181
Columbus, Ohio, USA (32)
Comet, paddle steamer **22**
Condette, near Boulogne (32), (33), 222
Congress' (US), 'Member of 114
Continent 131
Coogan, Jackie, plays Oliver Twist 54, *54*
Cooling, Kent (30), (31)
Cope Bros & Co, cigarette card publishers 39
Copping, Harold, CD illustrator *46, 48, 50, 61, 71, 81, 83, 99, 101, 106, 123, 126, 136, 142, 144, 145, 173, 193, 203*
Corby, Northamptonshire (30), (31)
Cornwall 106
Cornwell, Judy, plays Clara Peggotty 137
Courtenay, Tom, plays
  Newman Noggs 67
  Daniel Quilp 79
  William Dorrit 169
Cranford 11
Crewe, Lord, employs CD's grandparents 13, 114
Cricket on the Hearth, The *11*, 210, 226
  disgusts Lenin 226
'crim con' 48

Crimean War, bungling of, Board of Enquiry into **25**
Crisp, Quentin, likeness to Ghost of Christmas Past 99
Cromwell, Oliver, CD admires 21, 56
Cropsey, Jasper Francis *225*
Cruickshank, Andrew, plays John Jarndyce 150
Cruikshank, George, CD illustrator *36, 58*, 208, *208*, *233*
Crutchley, Rosalie, plays Mme Defarge 178
Cukor, George 133
Curry, Tim, voices Scrooge 99, 101
Cusack, Cyril, plays Frederick Dorrit 168
Cusack, Sinéad, plays Em'ly 134
Cushing, Peter, plays Dr Manette 179

Daily News 10, **24**
Dale, Jim, plays Scrooge 101
Daltrey, Roger, plays Scrooge 101
Dana, Richard 214
Dance, Charles, plays
  Sydney Carton 177
  Tulkinghorn 153
D'Aulnais, Charles Darnay's mother's name 178
Davenport, Nigel, plays Dan Peggotty 137
David Copperfield 14, 19, **23**, (28), (30), (31), (33), 41, 51, 52, 91, 95, 104, 114, 125, 161, 185, *207*, 220, 221, 226
  Blunderstone in, based on Blundeston 133
    latter's rectory inspired 'The Rookery' 133
  cartoon musical of 1993 133
  CD dedicated it to friends the Watsons 151
  critics and 145
  film 1935 133
  film 1969 133
  long-term popularity 144
  made-for-TV film 2000 133
  reckoned by CD his best novel 140
  sales of 145
  screen version 1974, little-known 134
  television 1999 133
De Niro, Robert, plays Magwitch-figure (Lustig) in free version *Great Expectations* 184
Dead Souls **24**, 225
Dedlock Arms (*Bleak House*) (30), (31)
Delmonico's, New York *216*
DeLuise, Dom, voices Fagin 53
Demerara 41, 43, 79, 122
  slave labour, resting on, most commerce in 43
  slave revolt in **22**, (32), 47
Devils, The 225
Devon 70, 74, 75, 85, 133
Devonshire Terrace, CD resides **23**, (28)
De Vries, Peter, American novelist 20
Dickens, Catherine, *née* Hogarth (CD's wife) *8*, 11, 17, (28), (30), (31), (32), (33), 225
Dickens, Charles John Huffam, 8, 9, 11, 13, 14, 15, *181*, *213*, *214*, *215*, 227, 232
  actors then mostly despised in novels of 40
  adultery, CD avoids in novels 224
  agitates against official incompetence **24**
  amateur actor 8, 204
  American tours 212–19
    1842 **24**, (30), (31), 116
    1867–1868 **25**, (30), (31), *216*, *219*
  anxiety to be thought a gentleman
    David Copperfield's, CD's, Pip's 15
  Anglo-centric tendency 18
  aristocrats and 14
  background colour, visits
    Preston, Lancashire, in search of **24**
    Yorkshire in search of **23**
  'baddies', Early Period, two-dimensionality of 13
  birthplace *12*, (30), (31)
  begging-letter-writers and 11
  benevolence, practised and preached 11
  blacking factory/warehouse and 17
  book editor 8
  book packager 8, 14, 36
  book production in time of 34
  brilliance transformed to genius 86
  business dealings 19
  campaigner 8
  cardboard cut-out characterisation, youthful vice 13
  centenary penny stamp (1912) *19*
  characters, nasty, appropriately nasty faces 14
  child characters, handling of 82
  childhood reading of imposed by CD on Scrooge 105
  children, CD's 10 8
  Cockney, not a true 12
    Cockney wit, possessed 12
  comedy of manners 12
  commits cardinal sin of story-telling 157
  contradictions in character of 15
  copy-editor 8
  cosmopolitan, extent to which 27
  creepy side to 131
  David Copperfield based on self 133
  death at 58 9, *228*
  debunks Byron legend **22**
  descendants *19*
  dialogue,
    archaic terms in 14
    gift for 8
  divorce in CD's day 134

- Dickens, Charles (*continued*)
  - domestic detail, love of, wider novelist's purpose, can defeat 104
  - dramatist 8
  - dressiness of 15, 223
  - earnings in America on eve of 1867–1868 tour 218
  - earnings in lifetime 228
  - editions of works by 34
    - market in 37
    - Nonesuch Dickens *35*, 36, 232
  - editor's duties 11
  - Ellen Ternan and 16, 17, **25**
  - English literature's Robespierre 229
  - evangelical characters, humbugging 11, 40, 44, *44*
  - family of, petty bourgeoisie, from 13
  - fashion and 15
  - feeler rather than thinker 19
  - foreign sojourns/trips (32), (33)
  - Garter, Order of the, CD on 21
  - Grand Guignol 10
  - helped destroy Non-Conformist conscience 231
  - historian, shortcomings as,
    - yet strong sense of passing time 20
  - honeymoon (30), (31)
  - hottest literary property in Britain, world too? 87
  - ignorance of finance 118, 131
  - illustrators/illustration and 34
  - influence on posterity's speech/thought patterns 16, 228
  - influences other writers **23**
  - inventor of
    - mystery tale 10
    - private investigator 10
  - journalist 8, **23**
  - last fiction words *228*
  - libel suit, threat by a Mrs Hill, re Miss Mowcher 136
  - lived in past 17, 186
  - lower-middle class, skill in handling 15
  - magazine editor 8, **23**
  - magazine serial format, works first appearing in 35, *35*
  - marriage **23**, **25**, (28)
  - melodrama 12, 19
  - medieval church, on 21
  - migration with family to Continent 116
  - minor characters more nuanced 86
  - mistress, putative; *see* Ternan, Ellen
  - mobs and 18
  - mortally wounded 'silver fork' novels 228
  - murder, fascination with 10
  - 'neat' high praise with CD 150
  - negotiator, tough 14
  - nepotism and 14
  - newspaper editor 8
  - novels as serials 9
  - novels lose early sparkle, have yet to develop weight 116
  - novels join grand European tradition 129
  - paternal grandparents' servant status 13
  - paternalism, political outlook towards, tendency of 18, 105
  - philistine streak of CD detectable on Paris trips 223
  - pirating of CD's works 116, 212–19
  - play director 8, 204
  - playwright 204–5
  - 'political incorrectness' of in *Oliver Twist* and *The Old Curiosity Shop* 83
  - politics of 18
  - popularity as author in America 116
  - portrait of, age 18 *title page*
  - power to shape our speech 194
  - praised by Engels 228
  - productivity slows 116
  - project-manager 14
  - privately cool re, publicly lauds Harriet Beecher Stowe **24**
  - professional actor manqué 204
  - prosperity couldn't match businessmen's 19
  - prostitutes, and 11, **24**
  - public as swayed by visual trickery as today's 208
  - public readings 8, 12, **24**, **25**, *230*
    - contributed to early death 200
  - public speech reporter 8, 15, **23**
  - residences **22**, **23**
  - restlessness 12
  - retorts to critics 47
  - retrenchment 116
  - sales of works in USSR owed how much to politics? 227
  - savage streak 10
  - self-pity 19
  - sentimentality 10
  - serials 11
  - servants, sense of status among 13, 127
  - separation from wife 8
  - sex in novels and 82
  - showed you could earn a fortune by your pen 228
  - solicitor's clerk, work as **23**
  - stage manager 8, 204
  - stories, number CD wrote 202
  - stories, late-period, earned most per word of all writings 202
  - summer resorts, favourite (30), (31)
  - strain on, tight writing schedule of 84
  - sympathy with children 12
  - technical innovations 229
  - tendency continue themes from one story to successor 180
  - theatricals, amateur (32), (33), 204–5
    - at Knebworth, Rockingham Castle 204
  - travel writer 10, 11
  - vision, chief defect of 14
  - walker 9
  - workers, less convincing in portraying 13
  - writer, becomes full-time **23**
- Dickens, Charley (CD's eldest son) 21
- Dickens, Elizabeth (CD's mother) *13*, (28), 135
  - model for Mrs Nickleby? 66
- Dickens, Fanny (CD's sister), **23**, 102, 204
  - husband Henry Burnett model for Nicholas Nickleby? 66
- Dickens, John (CD's father) *13*, 14, **22**, (28), 172
  - original of Mr Micawber 14, 136
- Dickens, Katey (CD's daughter) 8, *9*, 11
- Dickens, Mamie (CD's daughter) *9*
- 'Dickens in Camp', Bret Harte poem **25**
- Dickens Fellowship, The 232
- *Dickens Land* *189*
- 'Dickensian' (term), 'Victorian' contrasted with 17
- Dijon, Burgundy, France (32), (33), 131, 224
- Dimbleby, Jonathan 109
- Dingley Dell (*Pickwick Papers*) (30), (31), 39, 44, 47, 48
- Dinner at Poplar Walk', 'A **23**
- Disraeli, Benjamin 102
- Dixon, Arthur, CD illustrator *55*, *85*, *108*, *133*, *195*
- Doctors' Commons, Faraday Building 14, (28), 133, 139, 143
- Dombey and Son 125, 126, 128, 129, 131
- *Dombey and Son* 11, 13, 14, **22**, **24**, (28), (30), (31), (32), (33), 53, 116, 140, 145, 220, 222, 224, 225, 226
  - first edition copy with extra illustrations 35
  - first of CD's later novels to show maturity 128
  - sales 131
  - televisation 1969 124
  - televisation 1983 123
- Doré, Gustave 201
- Dors, Diana, plays Charlotte 51
- Dorset, Dorrits formerly prominent in 172
- Dostoevsky, Fyodor **22**, **24**, **25**, 97, 225–226, *226*
  - mentions CD as inspiration, not least certain characters 225
  - thought *The Old Curiosity Shop* a masterpiece 226
- Dotheboys Hall (*Nicholas Nickleby*) (30), (31), 67, 69, 70
- Doughty Street, CD's house in 15, **23**, (28)
  - *see also* Charles Dickens Museum, The
- Dover, Kent (30), (31), 134, 143
  - mail coach between and London 179
- Doyle, Richard ('Dickie'), CD illustrator 209
- Drake, Charlie, plays Grandfather Smallweed 152
- Drew, John M L 202
- Dreyfuss, Richard, plays Fagin 52
- Du Maurier, George, CD illustrator 210
- Duck, Daffy 108
- duelling, taboos governing 72
- Durham, Co 67, 69
- East Anglia 132
- East India Company (33), 39, 123
- Eatanswill, corrupt constituency 47
- *Eatanswill Gazette*, English newspaper 43
- *Eclipse, L'*, French newspaper *7*
- Eden, USA (*Martin Chuzzlewit*) (32), 111, 113, 114, 215
- Edgar, David, dramatises *Nicholas Nickleby* 64, 69
- Edinburgh 204
- education, primary, legislation introducing nationwide **25**
- Egg, Augustus, painter, tours Italy, Switzerland with CD (32), (33), 224
- Egley, William, CD illustrator *211*
- Eliot, T S 206
- Elliott, Denholm, plays John Jarndyce 150
- England 46, 64, 75, 119, 131, 167, 168, 174, 220, 224
  - Charles Darnay settles in 178
  - John Harmon voyages from Cape to 192
- Established Church 231
- Eton, CD sends eldest son Charley to 21
- Evans, Edith, plays Betsey Trotwood 139
- Eve, Trevor, plays Mr Murdstone 137
- exchange rate, pound sterling/dollar 1840s 111
- Fagin, Bob, CD's workmate blacking factory 58
- Faraday Building (*see also* Doctors' Commons) (28)
- Fechter, Charles 223, 228
- Field, Sally, plays Betsey Trotwood 139
- Fielding, Henry, among CD's favourite childhood authors 97
- Fielding, Sir John, blind beak 97
- Fields, W C, plays Mr Micawber 136
- Fildes, Sir Luke, CD illustrator 34, *196*, *197*, *198*, 209
- Finney, Albert, plays Scrooge 100
- Fleet Prison (28), 41, 42, 43, 44, 45, 49
- Fletcher, Cyril, plays Alfred Mantalini 66
- Flintstones, The 108
- Florence, Col 215
- Florence, Italy (32), (33), 224
  - CD's philistine tendencies when in 224
- Fluck, Peter, CD illustrator 211
- Forster, E(dward) M(organ) 225
- Forster, John, CD's old friend 192
  - his biography of CD 232
- Fortnum & Mason 99
- 43rd (Monmouthshire) Regiment of Foot 42
- Fox, Edward, plays Mr Brownlow 51
- Fox, Emilia, plays Clara Copperfield 133
- Fox, James, plays 'the single gentleman' (*The Old Curiosity Shop*) 79
- Foy, Claire, plays Little Dorrit 168
- France, 134, 180
  - Blandois/Lagnier/Rigaud's mother French national 167
  - CD and 27, (32), (33), 222–3
  - CD technique with French characters' dialogue 223–4
  - Dan Peggotty seeks Em'ly in 137
  - epitomises eroticism for 19th-century Britons 224
  - French CD characters often homicidal 223
  - 'Jacques', significance of 179
  - Second Empire (1852–70) 172, 223
    - end of **25**
  - sexual irregularity for CD and 224
  - Sir Mulberry Hawk flees to 64
- Franklin, Pamela, plays Dora Spenlow 137
- Franks, Philip, plays
  - Rick Carstone 147
  - Tom Pinch 114
- Fraser, Bill, plays Christopher Casby 167
- Frederick, Duke of York 44
- French, Dawn 134
- French Revolution **22**, **25**
- Frith, William Powell, painter *93*, *227*
- *Frozen Deep, The*, CD–Wilkie Collins play collaboration 27, 210
- Furniss, Harry, CD illustrator 95, 210
- *Gabriel Vardon, The Locksmith of London* 94
- Gad's Hill Place, Kent *9*, 11, **25**, (30), (31)
  - CD uses dummy book spine titles as decoration 206
  - Swiss châlet *228*
- Gaskell, Mrs 11
  - specialist Alan Shelston 95
- Geneva, Lake **24**, 225
- Genoa, Italy 12, (32), (33), 167, 224, *225*
  - *The Chimes* written in 224
- George III, 44
  - his madness **22**
- George IV 17, **22**, **23**
- *George Silverman's Explanation* (CD short story) 218
- Germany
  - CD traverses 27
  - Pip tries shipping Magwitch to 188
- Gibbon, Edward 193
- Gielgud, John; *see Tale of Two Cities, A*
- Gill, André, caricaturist *7*
- Gillray, James 208
- Gingold, Hermione, plays Miss Tomkins 44
- Gissing, George, debt to CD 229
- Gladstone, like CD a prostitute-rescuer 9, 11
- Glasgow–Greenock paddle boat service **22**
- Glover, Julian, plays Mr Dombey 124
- Gogol, Nikolai **23**, **24**
- Goldberg, Whoopi, voices Ghost of Christmas Past 99
- Golden Globe award 52
- Goldmark, Karl 226
- Gordon Riots, subject of *Barnaby Rudge* **22**, 89
- Goring, Marius, plays Pip 185
- Grammer, Kelsey, plays Scrooge 101
- Grant brothers, models for Cheerybles 72
- *Great Expectations* 15, 17, 18, **22**, (28), (30), (31), (32), (33), 111, 169, 211, 220, 226, 229
  - 'common' ways disgust Pip 186
  - different from earlier novels 189
  - film 1946 183, *188*
  - film 1974 183
  - film 1989 184
  - film 1998 with 1990 American setting 183
  - first edition copies of 36
  - how far in past book set 186
  - made-for-TV film of 1999 183
  - other forms of entertainment, adapted for 189
  - sales 189
  - silent films 1917, 1922 183
  - stage production 1940 184
  - 'talkie' (Danish) 1934 183
  - televisation 1954 184
  - televisation 1959 185
  - televisation 1967 183
  - televisation 1981 183
- Great Ormond Street Children's Hospital **24**
- Great St Bernard Pass, Switzerland (32), (33), 225
- Green, Sir Philip 189
- Green, Poll 115
- Greenwood, Joan, plays Mrs Clennam 168
- Grenfell, Joyce, plays Mrs Leo Hunter 40
- Greta Bridge, N(orth Riding of) Yorkshire/Co Durham (30), (31), 69
- Grimaldi, Joey, clown, memoirs of 8
- 'Growlery', John Jarndyce's 150
- Gruffudd, Ioan, plays Pip 185
- Guinness, Alec, plays
  - Fagin 52
  - Marley's Ghost, Scrooge 100
  - Herbert Pocket 185
  - William Dorrit 169
- Gurney, Jeremiah *219*
- Guyana (32), 41
- Haggard, H Rider, novelist, stamp design-approver *19*
- Hall, William, publisher 46
- Hammersmith 17, (28), 185
- Hampshire, Susan, plays Agnes Wickfield 139
- *Hard Times* 19, (30), (31), 224, 226
  - CD's earnings from 165
  - first edition copies of 36
  - numerous textual variants show CD poor speller 164
- Hardwicke, Cedric, plays Ralph Nickleby 67
- Haredale family **23**
- Harley, John Pritt 204
- Harper & Brothers, Boston publishers 217
- Harte, Bret **25**
- Hartnell, William, plays cabby (*Pickwick Papers* film) 46
- Harwood, Ronald, scripts Polanski *Oliver Twist* 53
- Haslehust, Ernest, topographical painter *189*
- Hathaway, Anne, plays Madeline Bray 63
- *Haunted Man, The* 210
- Havers, Nigel, plays Nicholas Nickleby 66
- Hawke, Ethan, plays Pip-figure *Great Expectations* variant 185
- Hayes, Patricia, plays Affery Flintwinch 169
- Helen (of Troy), invoked by Tom Moore, Dick Swiveller 86
- Hemmings, David, plays Dick Swiveller 79
- Hendon, CD sends Bill Sikes to 17
- Henley-on-Thames, Oxfordshire (30), (31)
- Henshall, Ruthie, plays Nancy 54
- Hertfordshire 150
- Hesperus Classics 202
- Hicks, Seymour, plays Scrooge 100
- Highland clearances, CD ignores 18
- Hiller, Wendy, plays Mrs Micawber 135
- Hobson, Valerie, plays adult Estella 183, *188*
- 'Hodge', English equivalent of French 'Jacques' 179
- Hogarth, Catherine; *see* Dickens, Catherine
- Hogarth, Mary (CD's wife's sister) 9, 11, **23**, 205
- Holdsworth, Sir William 148
- Holland, Captain, owned *Monthly Magazine* 202
- Holloway, Stanley, plays Vincent Crummles 64
- Holmes, Oliver Wendell 214
- Hop Pole, Tewkesbury (*Pickwick Papers*) (30), (31)
- Hopkins, Anthony, plays Magwitch 184
- Hordern, Michael, plays
  - Little Nell's grandfather 78
  - Marley's Ghost, Scrooge 100
- Hoskins, Bob, plays Mr Micawber 136
- *Household Words* 21, **24**, **25**, 202, 203
- Howes, Sally Ann, plays Kate Nickleby 66
- Hudd, Roy, plays Fagin 52
- Hudson, George, the 'Railway King' 11
- Hugo, Victor, poem 'Tristesse d'Olympio', Charles Swann on; applicability to Little Nell and Quilp 82
- Hullah, John 204
- Humphries, Barry, plays Sowerberry 54
- Hungerford Bridge 17
- Hunt, Martita, plays Miss Havisham 184
- *Hunted Down* (CD short story) 218
- Huntingdon, Cambridgeshire (to CD Huntingdonshire) (30), (31), 56
- Hurley Lock, Berkshire (30), (31)
- Illinois 216
- India (33)
- Inimitable', 'The, CD self-styled 9, 159
- *Inside the Whale*, Orwell in on CD 104
- *Insulted and Injured, The*, signs of being inspired both by *Barnaby Rudge* and *The Old Curiosity Shop* **25**
- Ipswich, Suffolk (30), (31), 40, 42, 45, 48
- Ireland 56
  - likely origin name Fagin in CD's day 58
- Irish potato famine, CD ignores 18, **24**
- Irving, Henry, centennial staging *Pickwick Papers* 1938 41
- Irving, Washington **24**, 214
- Isle of Man, CD's dishonest grandfather absconds to 13
- Italian unification, CD supports 18
- Italian–Swiss trip, CD's second **24**
- Italy **22**, **24**, 27, (32), (33), 125, 134, 224–5, 228
  - CD sojourns 1844–1845, revisits 1853 224
  - Dan Peggotty seeks Em'ly in 137
  - Dorrits travel to 173
- Jacobi, Derek, plays
  - Arthur Clennam 168
  - Little Nell's grandfather 78
- Jacobinism, Robert Rouncewell exudes to Dedlocks 151
- Jacob's Island (28), 53
- *jacquerie*, resonance of in France 179
- Jamaica 122
- James, Henry 229
  - pans *Our Mutual Friend* **25**
- Jarley's Waxwork 78
- Joel, Billy, voices The Artful Dodger 52
- Johns, Stratford, plays Magwitch 184
- Johnson, US President Andrew, impeachment of, scotches CD's Boston readings 1868 **25**
- Jones, Davy, plays/voices The Artful Dodger 52
- Jones, Freddie, plays Barkis 133
- Jonson, Ben, *Every Man in His Humour* 204, *204*
  - CD Bobadil in 204, *204*
- Joyce, James 229
- Judaism 90
- July (1830) Revolution (France) **23**, 41
- Kafka, Franz 229
- Kemp, Ross, plays London loan shark Eddie Scrooge 109
- Kenge & Carboy 149
- Kennet, Brackley 91
- Kensit, Patsy, plays small girl Estella 183
- Kent 11, 12, 39, 46, 131
- Kentucky 216
- Kim Jong Il, of North Korea 95
- King Charles's head, origin of phrase 134
- Kingsley, Ben, plays Fagin 52
  - Wackford Squeers 69
- Kindle 203
- Knightly, Keira, plays Rose Fleming 53
- 'Kyd' (Joseph Clayton Clarke), illustrator *39*, *40*, *42*, *47*, *48*, *49*, *57*, *60*, *73*, *81*, *84*, *87*, *115*, *119*, *127*, *130*, *142*, *144*
- 'Ladybird', Pross nickname for Lucie Manette 179
- Lamballe, Princesse de, raped (?), mutilated, murdered 180
- Lancing 229
- Landor, Walter Savage 147
  - *Imaginary Conversations* device used by Ackroyd 147
  - model for Lawrence Boythorn 147
- Landseer, Edwin, CD illustrator 210
- Lane, Nathan, plays Vincent Crummles 64
- Langella, Frank, plays Scrooge 101
- Lansden, Dinsdale, plays Pip 185
- Lausanne, Switzerland **24**, (32), (33), 151, 225
  - Villa Rosemont, CD and family's habitation at 225
- Law, Roger, CD illustrator 211
- Law, the 231
  - *Bardell v Pickwick* 40, 42, 44, 48
  - Bloody Assizes 177
  - Common Law 156
  - Court of Chancery, **24**, (28), 150, 152, 154, 156
    - brief history of 155–6
    - 'Chancery Division' 156
    - 'a monument of Chancery practice' 157
    - 'Chancery suit ... ornament to a gentleman's existence' – Sir Leicester's view 158

Law, the *(continued)*
Court of Appeal in Chancery set up 156
Court of Chancery Act 1842 156
Elizabeth I's reign 156
High Court of Justice 156
Jarndyce and Jarndyce 147, 148, 149, 152, 153
costs swallow assets 159
Lord Eldon 156
'Lord High Chancellor' 156
Six Clerks' Office **24**, 148
Slough of Despond in *Pilgrim's Progress* 156
Supreme Court of Judicature Acts 156
Vehmgericht 156
Vice-Chancellor instituted 1813 156
Westphalia 156
Equity 148
estate of Magwitch at death goes to Crown 188
'His Majesty's High Court' 142
Inns of Court 39
Insolvency Court 42
Jeffreys, Judge 177
need for copying 151
Norton v Melbourne 48
re debt 49
Lea & Blanchard, Philadelphia publishers **23**, 214
Leamington Spa, Warwickshire (30), (31)
Lean, David, director films
Oliver Twist 52
Great Expectations 51, 52, 54, *188*
Leather Bottle inn (*Pickwick Papers*) (30), (31)
Leavis, F R 6
Lee, Christopher, plays the Marquis St Evrémonde 179
Leech, John, illustrates *A Christmas Carol* 36, *108*, 209
Leigh Hunt, James Henry 151
Leighton, Margaret, plays Miss Havisham 184
Lemon, Mark, collaborates with CD on farce 205
Lenin's epigram 172
Lennon, John 133
Lennon, Julian, voices cat *David Copperfield* 133
Lester, Mark, plays Oliver Twist 54
Life of Our Lord, The 225
Lincoln, US President Abraham **25**
Lincolnshire 147, 148, 158
Lincolnshire Wolds (30), (31)
Linnell, John, portraitist *56*
Little Dorrit 15, 17, 20, **22**, **24**, 27, (29), (32), (33), 49, 67, 78, 79, 144, 222, 223, 224, 225, 226, 233
chronology of, CD muddled 172
film 1988 167
German 'talkie' 1934 167
missing will plot device overused by CD 175
pseudo-historical, contrast to *A Tale of Two Cities* 180
sales and critical response 175
silent films 1913, 1922 167
television 2008 167
title page (illustrated) *174*
William Dorrit, not Clennam, novel's true male lead 173
Liverpool, Lancashire (30), (31)
Alec Guinness's run in with law in 185
slave-trade and 43
Liverpool, Lord **23**, 46
Lolita, no true comparison Nell's fate
Old Curiosity Shop 82
London 12, 14, 52, 56, 63, 70, 74, 82, 84, 85, 86, 131, 143, 165, 174, 192, 194, 198, 225, 228
Belgravia–Chelsea border
Cadogan Place 69
Blackfriars Bridge 146
Blackheath (28)
Bloomsbury 171
CD lives as adult in 15, **24**, (28)
Gower St, CD's mother ran school in (28)
Tavistock House, Tavistock Sq, CD lives once rich **24**, (28), 204
Thomas Coram's Foundling Hospital 171
Borough (28), 45
Camden Town 135
Bayham St (28), 99
CD's family live **22**
Cratchits live 99, 106
Houghton Place, Ampthill Sq (29)
Johnson St (now Cranleigh St) (28)
Somers Town, CD's family live **22**
Toodles live 127
Susan Nipper, 'Richards'/Polly Toodle secretly take Dombey infants to visit 121
Chelsea, St Luke's (church) (28)
City (of London), The 45, 70, 89, 92, 100, 115, 123, 125, 128, 175
Billiter Street 123
Cornhill (28), 100
East India House 123
Leadenhall St (28), 123
Lime Street 123
Monument, The (Great Fire London broke out 1666) (28)
Newgate Gaol (28), 92
Queen Victoria St (28)
St Martin's Le Grand 112
Stock Exchange 112
Clerkenwell (28), 92
Covent Garden
Clare Market (probable site Tom-all-Alone's) (28)
Drury Lane Gdns, Drury Lane (28)
Tom-all-Alone's 154
CD's unrivalled knowledge of 15
Deptford
Brig Mews (Capt Cuttle's Brig Place in *Dombey*?) 122
Drury Lane, Theatre Royal 67
Dulwich (28), 45, 49
East End 57
Embankment, Thames 187
Buckingham St (28), 133
Strand, the 133
Temple (28), 112, 187
Finsbury
Goswell St (now Rd) (28)
Windsor Terrace, City Rd, Micawber's lodgings 135
Fitzrovia
Cleveland St, CD lives as child/youth (28)
Fleet Street 112
Greater, Dickens's oyster 16
gutters, Brasses scavenge in 87
Hammersmith (28)
Lyric Theatre stages *Nicholas Nickleby* 63
Holborn 180
Bleeding Heart Yard 27, 167, 171
Cook's Court, Cursitor Street 152
Farringdon St (site of Fleet Prison) (28)
High Holborn
Furnival's Inn (28), 115
Lincoln's Inn (28), 150, *157*
Lincoln's Inn Fields, shop Portugal St off, no genuine link with *Old Curiosity Shop* 80
Kingsway (28)
Saffron Hill (28)
in 1775 97
Islington 114, 126
Kentish Town
Maiden Lane (29)
Lambeth 74
Lord Mayor of 91
mail coach between Dover and 179
Mayfair 123
Brook Street 123, 129
Claridge's 174
Marylebone
Bentinck St, CD lives as child/youth (28), 204
Bryanstone-square 123
Harley St (28)
Margaret St, CD resides as child/youth (28)
Portland-place 123
northwest, Dickens installs Ellen Ternan in 17
Norwood 15, (28)
Old Bailey, the 180
one of the two cities *A Tale* treats of 180
Oxford Street 123
Parliament, Houses of 96
parts Dickens ignores, sexual guilt and 15
Peckham (Windsor Lodge, Linden Grove), CD keeps Ellen Ternan in 16, (29)
Pentonville 135, 171
Pool of 17
Regent's Park (28)
Richmond-upon-Thames
Petersham (28)
Richmond Green
Maids of Honour Row (28)
Tracy Tupman retires celibate to 44
rookeries 14
Rotherhithe, Jacob's Island at, Bill Sikes's end on 17, (28)
St George's Fields 96
Seven Dials 66
sexual overtones and certain parts of 15
Shooter's Hill 180
Shoreditch 135
Soho 66, 70, 180
Golden Sq (28)
Manette St (28)
southeast
Blackheath 133
Southwark 45, 172
inns generally in 16
Marshalsea in *18*, 172, 173, 174, 175, 180
White Hart Inn in *16*, 45, 47
Spitalfields *163*
streets named after Dickens characters 15
'Theatre Land'
Adelphi, CD/W Collins's *No Thoroughfare* staged 205
Aldwych 64
Gallery of Illustration 205
Lyceum 41
St James's Theatre 204
musical *Pickwick* staged in 41, 43
Patrick Stewart's *Christmas Carol* readings 107
theatre manager from assesses talent Portsmouth 72
Tottenham Court Rd
Boot, The, off 96, 97
Tower (of London) Hill (28), 78
Twickenham (28)
Tyburn (near present Marble Arch), place of execution 90
western outskirts 114
Whitechapel 91
Bevis Marks (28)
Longfellow, Henry Wadsworth 215
Louis XVIII **22**
Louis-Napoleon, Prince-President of France **24**, 172
Louis-Philippe King of the French **23**
Louisville, Kentucky, USA (32)
Loutherbourg the Younger, Philipp-Jakob *164*
Lunghi, Cherie, plays Mrs Steerforth 138
Lyndhurst, Nicholas, plays Uriah Heep 134
Lyons, 'Canut' revolt in **23**

McDowell, Roddy, plays
Pip 185
Scrooge 101
Macfadyen, Matthew, plays Arthur Clennam 168
McKellen, Ian, plays
in *Marley Was Dead* 109
Creakle 133
Maclise, Daniel, CD illustrator 209
Macready, William Charles, actor 36, 71
produced CD's work, opinion CD's acting ability 205
Macrone, John, CD publisher 94
Magoo, Mr 108
Maidstone, Kent (30), (31)
Man, Isle of 15
Manchester 72, 102
Manor Farm (*Pickwick Papers*) (30), (31), 39, 44
Marceau, Marcel 108
March, Fredric, plays Scrooge 100
March of Death 11
Margolyes, Miriam, plays
Flora Finching 169
Mrs Corney/Bumble 52
one-woman performance re CD female characters *Dickens's Women* 233
Marie-Antoinette 180
Marley Was Dead, BBC Radio 4 'screwball comedy' 109
Marryat, Captain (Frederick) 212
Marseille, Bouches-du-Rhône, France (32), (33), 167, 171, 224
Marshalsea debtors' prison 15, 18, **24**, (28), 167, 168, *168*, 169
Marston, J Westland 205
Martigny, Switzerland (32), (33)
Martin Chuzzlewit 10, 11, (28), (30), (31), (32), (33), 96, 102, 105, 116, *210*, 211, 212, 215, 216, 217, 218, 220
first edition copies of, with/without author's signature 34
problem its 'villains' 117
sales disappointing, hurt CD's reputation
America 116, 119, 217
television 1994 111
Mason, James, plays Magwitch 184
Massey, Anna, plays
Jane Murdstone 137
Mrs Bedwin 51
Pross 179
Master Humphrey's Clock *36*, 80, 87, 94, *209*
Mastroianni, Marcello 108
Matthau, Walter, voices Scrooge 100
Maypole Inn (*Barnaby Rudge*) (30), (31), 89, 90, 91, 92, 97, *97*
Medway Valley *21*
Melbourne, Lord **23**, 48, 56
Mendes, Sam, directs revived musical *Oliver!* 51
Merchant Navy 131
'Merry England' 11
Merrylegs, performing dog 162
'Micawber Principle' in Soviet Bloc state planning 226
Middlemass, Frank, plays
Mr Brownlow 51
Pumblechook 185
Milan, Italy (32), (33)
Miles, Bernard, plays
Joe Gargery 183
Newman Noggs 67
Miles, Sarah, plays girl and woman Estella 183
Mills, John, plays
Jarvis Lorry 179
Old Chuffey 111
Pip 185, *188*
Mississippi River 216
Missouri 216
Mitford, Nancy, Estella foreshadows 186
Molière's *Tartuffe*, shows hypocrites' inherent wordiness 117
Monkees, The 52
Moody, Ron, plays
Fagin 52
Scrooge 101
Uriah Heep 134
Moore, Thomas, 'Drink of this Cup' poem, quoted by Dick Swiveller in *The Old Curiosity Shop* 86
moppet-molesting 82
More, Hannah 85
Morley, Robert, plays
Lord Decimus Tite Barnacle 167
Pumblechook 185
Mouse, Mickey 108
Muggleton, Kent (*Pickwick Papers*) (30), (31), 47
Mulgrave, Lord 222
murder 10
Murdstone & Grinby 137
Murray, Bill, takes Scrooge role 101
Musgrave, Thea 108
Mystery of Edwin Drood, The (30), (31), (32), (33), 148, 209, *228*, 229
modern subject matter: drug-taking race *197*, 200
sales exceed other CD novels bar *Old Curiosity Shop* 200

Nabokov, Vladimir, overwritten, preening tone *Lolita* 82
Naples, Italy (32), (33), 134, 224
Napoleon (I), Emperor of the French 203
Napoleon III of France, Emperor **24**
New England 215
New Orleans, Battle of **22**, 212
New Poor Law **23**, 56
New South Wales 221
New South Wales Dickens Society 221
New World 61
New York (City), (32), 111, 112, 214, 215, *215*, 218
Bowery 217
Boz Ball in 1842 (32), 215
Martin Chuzzlewit (Jr) and Mark Tapley in 115
musical *Pickwick* staged in 39, 43, 45
readings by CD 1867–1868, tidy pickings (32), 219
readings of *A Christmas Carol* by Patrick Stewart 1988 107
New York Ledger 218
New York Rowdy Journal 111, 112
Newcastle (on Tyne) 226
Newgate Calendar 60
Newley, Anthony, plays
the Artful Dodger 52
Daniel Quilp 79
Newton, Robert, plays Bill Sikes 54
Niagara Falls (32), (33), 222
Catherine Dickens's maid's opinion of 222
Nicholas I of Russia, Tsar **24**
Nicholas Nickleby 11, 15, 18, **23**, (28), (30), (31), (33), 46, 78, 101, 118, 167, 175, 202, 211, 220
dramatisation 1927 63
dramatisation 1980 64, 69
film 1947 64, 66, 67, 68, 69
film 2002 63, 64, 67
first edition copies 34, *37*
pop musical version *Smike*, televised 1973 68
sales 75
television 1977 66
97th (Earl of Ulster's) Regiment 43, 44
Nonesuch Press *35*
Northcote-Trevelyan Civil Service reforms 231
North Country 161
Northamptonshire 51
Norton, Caroline 48
Norton, George 48

obesity hypoventilation ('Pickwickian') syndrome 41
Ohio 216
Ohio River 216
Old Country 221
Old Curiosity Shop, The **23**, (28), (30), (31), (32), 46, 67, 69, 72, 74, 114, 116, 154, 189, 209, *209*, 210, 214, 226
anonymous characters: 'the bachelor', Gandfather, 'The Marchioness', 'the single gentleman' 80
CD repeats himself in, strain, sign of 84
grandfather leaves London, money woes, like Sol Gills 125
dwarves and giants, mocked in 83
film 1975 78, 79
story New Yorkers mobbed UK ships for news Nell 116
reason CD chose nickname 'The Marchioness' 87
Nell, Little, function of in 81, 83
Punch and Judy showmen in 83
radio broadcast 1998 79
sales 81, 87, 94
sexual overtones, further dark, intrusion of 84
television 1979 79
television 1995 79
television 2007 78
Oliver & Company 52, 53
Oliver, Edna May, plays
Betsey Trotwood 139
Lucie Manette 179
Oliver Twist 15, 18, **23**, (30), (31), (33), 46, 175, 189, 208, *208*, 209, 211, 233
Sam Weller's coinage 'artful dodge' used by CD in 45
film cartoon 1974 52
film cartoon 1988 52
Fagin, references to, unacceptability of 57–58, 83
film 1948 51, 54
film 1968 51, 52, 54
film (Australian) 1982 52
film 2005 52
first edition copies 34, *36*, 37
made-for-TV film 1997 52
musical *Oliver!* original production 52, 54
Broadway production 1963, also 1977, 1994 and 2009–2011 revivals there and elsewhere 51, 52, 53, 54
silent film 1922 54
televisations 1962, 1985, 1999, 2007 51, 52, 53
Olivier, Laurence, plays
Alfred Jingle 41
Creakle 133
Scrooge 100
opium consumption *201*
Orwell, George 104
Oscar
nominations 52
winner 54
O'Sullivan, Maureen, plays Dora Spenlow 137
Our Mutual Friend **25**, (28), (29), (30), (31), (32), (33), 175, 209, *210*
deception persistent theme 194
print run dropped, but CD earned well from 195
television 1976 191
title misnomer: how it came about 194
Oxford 229

Pailthorpe, F W, CD illustrator 186, *187*
Palance, Jack 108
Palmerston, Lord **24**, 27
Paltrow, Gwyneth, plays Estella-figure
Great Expectations variant 183
Parfitt, Judy, plays Mrs Clennam 168
Paris, France (32), (33), 79, 177, 181, 222, *223*
area north of witnessed medieval *jacquerie* 179
British Embassy readings by CD 222
CD kills off little Paul Dombey in 222
Dr Manette's native city 179
Jarvis Lorry gets Manette out of, 1775 and 1793 179
L'Abbaye prison, on Left Bank 180
La Force prison, Darnay held in 180, 181
Morgue, CD fascinated by 222
Porte Saint-Denis *223*
revolutionaries 177
River Seine as it flows through 79
St Antoine, Faubourg 178, 180
St Germain Quarter 180
September Massacres 1792 180
other of two cities *A Tale* treats of 180
wine shop in, Defarge owns 178
Parkes, Sir Henry 221
Partridge, Bernard, inspired by CD 210
Pasco, Richard, plays Jarvis Lorry 179

Peacock, Trevor, plays Daniel Quilp 79
Peake, Mervyn, CD illustrator 211
pederasty 82
Peel, Sir Robert **23**, 56, *56*
dubbed 'Orange Peel' 56
Pennsylvania, USA 114
Pewsey Down, Wiltshire (30), (31), 114
Philadelphia, Pennsylvania, USA **23**, (32), 214, 216
'Phiz' 34, 35, 41, 66, *139*, 151, *153*, 154, *158*, 172, *176*, *178*, 209, *209*, *210*
his semi-caricatures a good fit with CD's characters 208
Pictures from Italy 11, 209, 225
Pickwick Papers 11, 13, 15, 20, **22**, **23**, **24**, (28), (30), (31), (32), (33), 41, 69, 72, 78, 86, 125, 138, 202, 211, 214, 224, 225, 226
'corrected' edition 46
film (1952) 39, 40, 44, 45
first edition copies 35
musical 1965 (titled *Pickwick*) 39, 43, 45
Pickwick Club in 39, 42, 43, 45
televisation 1985 43
tone of changes 49
Pinero, Arthur Wing 205
Plummer, Christopher, plays Ralph Nickleby 67
Poe, Edgar Allan **23**, **24**, 90, 147
his Auguste Dupin fiction's first armchair sleuth 147
tale *The Murders in the Rue Morgue* 147
Polanski, Roman, director film *Oliver Twist* 53
'Pompey' 15
Port Middlebay, Australia 220
Porter, Eric, plays Fagin 52
Portsmouth, Hampshire 12, **22**, (30), (31), 64, 70, 72
Portsea, outskirts Portsmouth *12*, (30), (31)
Powell, Anthony, shrewd CD critic 14, 19
'Prentice Knights 89, 92, 95
Preston, Lancashire (30), (31), 161
Prince Regent, idol of Mr Turveydrop **22**
Prior, model for Quilp 79
Proctor 143
Proctors' firm 138
prostitutes 9, 14, 53, 134, 221
prostitution 9, 134
Protestant Association 90, 91
Protestant Manual 92
Proust, Marcel 82
Prussia, triumphs Franco-Prussian War **25**
Pryce, Jonathan, plays Fagin 52
Pückler-Muskau, Prince (Hermann) **23**
Punch 210
Putnam, George W, CD's secretary in US 1842 216

Quayle, Anthony, plays Jaggers 184
Quincy Jr, Josiah, Mayor of Boston 214

Rabelais and mock heroic voice 229
Rackham, Arthur, CD illustrator 211
Radcliffe, Daniel, plays young David Copperfield 133
railways 11
boom 1840s **24**, 127
Carker, death 131
CD's first fictional mention of in *Martin Chuzzlewit* 216
Folkestone–London line 13
Great Northern Railway 148
Lincolnshire, CD *Bleak House* says absent from 148
London–Birmingham express 11
Staplehurst accident 1865 *11*, **25**
Stockton and Darlington **22**
Rampling, Charlotte, plays Miss Havisham 184
Randall, Tony, plays Scrooge 101
Rathbone, Basil, plays
Marley's Ghost, Scrooge 100
Marquis St Evrémonde 179
Mr Murdstone 137
Rattigan, Terence; *see Tale of Two Cities, A*
Raven', 'The, Poe poem **24**, 90
Reading, Berkshire 148
Redgrave, Corin, plays Steerforth 138
Redgrave, Michael, plays Dan Peggotty 137
Redman, Amanda, plays Mrs Merdle 171
Reed, Carol, director film *Oliver!* 54
Reed, Oliver, plays Bill Sikes 54
Regency 15, **22**, 141, 148
Reid, Beryl, plays Mrs Squeers 68
Repin, Ilya Efimovich *226*
Representatives, US House of 114
'resurrectionist', i.e. body-snatcher 177
Revolution, French 177, 180
Defarges prepare for 178
memories of jacquerie help stoke 179
most savage phase, about to enter, summer 1792 180
Sydney Carton's noble subterfuge in 181
The Vengeance leading embodiment of rancour in 179
Reynolds, Frank, CD illustrator 211
Rhind-Tutt, Julian, plays Monks 53
Rhys Jones, Griff, plays Fagin 53
Richardson, Ian, plays Lord Chancellor 148
Richardson, Ralph, plays
Mr Micawber 136
Scrooge 100
Richmond, Virginia, USA (32)
Rigg, Diana, plays Lady Dedlock 148
Roberts, Rachel, plays Georgiana Gargery 183
Robson, Flora, plays Pross 179
Robey, George, plays Tony Weller 45
Robinson, Muriel Spark's, Jimmie Waterford in, speech of 14
Rochester, Kent (30), (31), 44, 47, 84, 148, 200
Minor Canon Row childhood home to Sybil Thorndike 148
Restoration House original of Satis House *189*
Rockingham Castle, Northamptonshire (30), (31), 151, 159
Rockingham, Northamptonshire (30), (31)
Rodgers, Anton, plays Alfred Jingle 41
Rome, Italy **23**, (32), (33), 174, 180, 224
and *Little Dorrit* (32), (33)
Rookery, The 140
Room With a View, A, debt to CD 225
Rouen 224
Rowlandson, Thomas 208
Roxburgh, J F 229
Royal Academy of Music **22**, 204
Royal Navy pay office 13
royalty deal, new in US publishing, Washington Irving's **24**
Russell, Ken, director film *The Boyfriend* 72
Russia (32), (33), 225–227

St Albans, Hertfordshire (30), (31), 151, 159
Cathedral 154
St Giles's, rookery in *14*
St Marylebone, CD's family resides **22**
St Petersburg (32), (33)
Salem House (28), 133, 135, 137, 138, 139, 143
Salisbury, Wiltshire (30), (31), 114
Salopian, Old 177
Sambourne, Linley, inspired by CD 210
Sand, George 222
Saracen's Head, Towcester (30), (31)
Sandling, Kent (30), (31)
Satis House, Miss Havisham's 'home' (30), (31), 184, *189*
Savannah, Ga., British held American War Independence 92
Sawalha, Julia, plays Merry Pecksniff 114
Scheffer, Ary 222
Scofield, Paul, plays old Martin Chuzzlewit 112
Scots, Mary Queen of 85
Scott, George C, plays
Fagin 52
Scrooge 100
Scott, Sir Walter 228
Scottish potato famine 18
Screw 115
Searle, Ronald, CD illustrator 211
Secombe, Harry, plays Mr Pickwick 43
Mr Bumble 51
Senator, US 114
September Massacres (French Revolution) **22**
Seyler, Athene, plays
Miss La Creevy 64
Pross 179
Seymour, Robert, CD illustrator, killed self 46, 207
Shaftesbury, Lord 231
Shakespeare 231
Shatner, William, plays Ghost of Christmas Present 99
Shaw, George Bernard 205
Shaw, William, vicious Yorkshire headmaster 69
Shelley (Percy Bysshe)
Leigh Hunt sponger upon 151
Steerforth's watery end resembles death of 138
Shepard, E(rnest) H(oward), CD illustrator 211
Shepherd's Bush, where home for fallen women 9, 11
Shrewsbury (public, i.e. private, school) 177
educated Sydney Carton, Judge Jeffreys, Sir Philip Sidney, as alumni 'Old Salopians' 177
Shropshire 149
Siberia 221
Sidney, Sir Philip 177
Sillitoe, Alan, debt to CD 229
Sim, Alastair, plays, voices Scrooge 100
Simmons, Jean, plays
girl Estella 183
Miss Havisham 184
Sims, Joan, plays Betsey Prig 114
Sketches by Boz **23**, 46, 204
Slater, Michael, CD biographer 7, 202, 204, 232
slave trade **22**, 43, 128
slavery **23**, 43, 128
Slough, Berkshire (Buckinghamshire in CD's day) (30), (31)
CD settles Ellen Ternan in cottage at **25**
smallpox 150, 158
Smith, Arthur, CD illustrator *140*
Smith, F E 210
Smith, Jessie Willcox, CD illustrator *59*, *65*, *76*, *98*, *120*, *132*, *141*, *143*, *190*
Smith, Maggie, plays Betsey Trotwood 139
Smorltork, Count, Prince Pückler-Muskau based on **23**
Socrates 124
Solzhenitsyn, Alexander 226
Sondes, 2nd Baron 151
Sotheby's, signed CD first edition and 36
South (Confederacy in American Civil War), CD openly supports **25**
secession by, Lincoln winning Presidency brings nearer **25**
South Africa (32), (33)
South America 41
Spall, Timothy, plays
Fagin 53
Charles Cheeryble 63
Augustus Folair 64
Wackford Squeers 'Junior' 69
Spectator 206
Spenlow & Jorkins 133, 138, 139, 143
spontaneous combustion, CD defensive about 150
spunging house 150
Sri Lanka (32), (33)
Stanfield, Clarkson, CD illustrator 210
Star Trek 108
Staunton, Imelda, plays Mrs Micawber 135
steam power **22**, 126
Stewart, James 108
Stewart, Patrick 106, 109
TV film interpretation *A Christmas Carol* 1999 106–7
one-man performance *A Christmas Carol* 1993–1994 106–7
one-man readings *A Christmas Carol* 1988 107
Stock, Nigel, plays
Jarvis Lorry 179
Mr Pickwick 43
Stone, Frank, CD illustrator 210
Stone, Harry 202
Stone, Lewis, plays Mr Wickfield 139
Stone, Marcus, CD illustrator 34, *184*
Stowe (public, i.e. private, school) 229
Stowe, Harriet Beecher **24**
Suffolk 39, 40
Sunday ban on pleasure, CD hated 10
Sunday papers, gossip re rich, even in CD's day 126
Swan inn, The, Muggleton (30), (31)
Switzerland **22**, 27, (32), (33), 134
and *Little Dorrit* (32), (33)
Blandois/Lagnier/Rigaud's father native of 167
CD and family sojourn 1846 225
Dan Peggotty seeks Em'ly 137
Sydney, New South Wales, Australia 221, *221*
CD statue in Centennial Park 221, *221*

Tale of Two Cities, A 20, **22**, (28), 43, 51, 64, 91, 95, 97, 99, 111, *178*, 181, 223
among CD's novels, rating 181
as historical novel 181
film 1935 177
film 1958 177
made-for-TV film 1980 178
Two Cities, the Spectacular New Musical (1968) with Edward Woodward 181
musical version called *Two Cities* 2006 with Russian Revolution background 181
musical under original book title 2008 181
musicals (two), all-female cast, Japan 181
opera 1953 181
radio play 1989 177
radio versions 1938, 1950, respectively by Orson Welles, Terence Rattigan–John Gielgud collaboration 181
sales, colossal world-wide 181
silent films 1911, 1917, 1922 181
televisation 1957 177
televisation 1965 181
televisation 1989 179
Tasmania (33), 220
Tchaikovsky, Piotr Ilyich 226
Tellson's Bank 177, 179, 180
Tenniel, John, inspired by CD 210
Ternan, Ellen, CD's putative mistress 16, 17, **25**, (28), (30), (31), (32), (33), 218, 222
CD met through a production in Manchester 205
Tewkesbury, Gloucestershire (30), (31)
Thackeray, William Makepeace, hoped to illustrate CD 208
Thames, River 15, 17, 86, 96, 143, 193
Gaffer Hexam forages in 192
Surrey bank 172
Tartar rows Rosa and Grewgious on *196*
Thorndike, Sybil, plays
Lady Dedlock 148
Mrs Squeers 68
Through the Year with Dickens *10*
Ticknor & Fields 218
Toad, Mr, Jingle in danger of resembling 46
Tolstoy, Leo **23**, 226, *226*
had CD-translator niece 226
published *A Christmas Carol* in his magazine 226
Tong, Shropshire (30), (31), 86
Towcester, Northamptonshire (30), (31)
transportation, penal (to Australia) **22**, **25**, (33), 75, 125, 220
Trevor, William, wrote 1979 TV script *Old Curiosity Shop* 79
Trilby 210
Trollope, Fanny 212
Troy (Missouri?), USA 112
Tutin, Dorothy, plays Lucie Manette 179
Tyler, US President John **24**

Ulysses, 'Oxen of the Sun' passage in 229
Uncle Tom's Cabin **24**
Uncommercial Traveller, The 225
United Bull-Dogs, The (Protestant bigots) 92
Urania Cottage, fallen women's refuge 9, 11, **24**
Utilitarian 162

Vale of Taunton, Vholes's father's part of the world 157
Van Dieman's Land (33), 220
Vandenhoff, George 219
Venice, Italy 12, (32), (33)
and *Little Dorrit* (32), (33), 174
Nobody's Story written in 224
Santa Maria del Rosario, Church of *26*
Victoria, Queen 17, 18, **23**
CD lends American Civil War battlefield photos to **25**
Victorian Age 18
convention's restraints on CD re Carker 131
interplay of death and desire fascinating to 83
Victorian Britain 19
prison treadmill less degrading to than transportation 87
Villiers, James, plays Mr Brownlow 51

Waddell, Justine, plays adult Estella 183
Wall, Max, plays Flintwinch 169
Walsh, Kay, plays Nancy 54
Walters, Julie, plays Mrs Mann 53
Wanamaker, Zoë, plays
Jane Murdstone 137
Mrs Jarley 78
War of American Independence 92
War of 1812 **22**, 212
Warner, David, plays Bob Cratchit 99
Warren, The (Haredales' seat, *Barnaby Rudge*) (30), (31), *88*, 90
Warren's Blacking Warehouse 19, 58
Warwick Castle, Warwick, Warwickshire (30), (31), 129
Warwick where Quilp stalks Nell *Old Curiosity Shop?* 85
Washington, DC **22**, (32), 216
water transport **22**
Watertoast 112, 113, 114, 115
National Hotel at 112, 113
Watson, Hon Richard 151, 159
Watson, Lavinia 151
Waugh, Arthur 229
Waugh, Evelyn, chief CD disciple 9, 15, 229–30, *229*
copies/twists CD character names 231
lifts plot devices 230
introduces involuntary confinement to novels often 230
Welles, Orson, plays Scrooge 100
Wells, H(erbert) G(eorge), debt to CD 229
West, Timothy, plays Sir Leicester Dedlock 148
West Indies 61
West Malling, Kent (30), (31)
West Point, NY, USA (32)
Westminster Abbey, CD buried **25**
Whig (party) 151
White House, The **22**, **24**
Whitelaw, Billie, plays Mme Defarge 178
White's (club) 42
Whittington, Dick 129
Who, Dr 46
Who, Dr 108
Wilcox, Toyah *190*
Wild, Jack, plays
The Artful Dodger 52
Charley Hexam 191
Oscar nomination 52
Wilde, Oscar Fingal O'Flahertie Wills 205
inspired re 'Miss Prism' *Importance of Being Earnest* by Mrs General's shibboleths 'prunes' and 'prism'? 169
Wilkinson, Tom, plays
Narrator (*David Copperfield*) 114
Pecksniff 114
William IV 17, **23**
Williams, Emlyn 134
one-man recreation of CD's readings 233
Williams, Samuel, CD illustrator 209
Wilson, Angus 7, 229
Wilson, Sandy 72
Wiltshire 118
Wind in the Willows, The 47
Windsor, Berkshire (30), (31), 152
Winkler, Henry, plays Scrooge role 101
Winthrop, Robert C 216
Winwood, Estelle, plays Miss Havisham 184
Wodehouse, P G 14, 20, 69, 79
idiom foreshadowed by Toots/'Game Chicken' 122
his Madeline Bassett inspired by Julia Mills 136
Olympian Jeeves–ill-informed Wooster relationship foreshadowed by Littimer to David Copperfield 135
worldly, epigrammatic Jeeves–unworldly plain-speaking Wooster relationship foreshadowed by Sam Weller to Pickwick 45
Wolfit, Donald, plays Serjeant Buzfuz 39
Woodward, Edward, plays Ghost of Christmas Present 99
see also Tale of Two Cities, A
workhouse(s) 51, 53, 54, 56
Wyngarde, Peter, plays Sydney Carton 177

Yarmouth, (Great), Norfolk (30), (31), 134, 136, 137, 140
York, Michael, plays Pip 185
York, Susannah, plays Mrs Cratchit 99
Yorkshire schools, CD investigates **23**
Yorkshire 63, 69, 70, 154, 159
Yuletide 12

Zamyatin, Yevgeny 226

Dickens's Characters

Adams, Captain 63
Aged (P[arent]), The 183
Akerman 89
Akershem, Sophronia 191, 194
Allen (later Winkle), Arabella 39, 41, 45, 48
Allen, Ben (33), 39, 43
Anny 51, 53
Arthur 187
Ayresleigh 39

Badger, Bayham 147
Badger, Mrs 147
Bagnet, Joseph Mat(thew) 147, *147*, 158
Bagstock, Major Joe ('Old Joey'/'Old Josh'/'Joseph') 121, *121*, 124, 125, 126, 129, 129
Bailey/Bailey 'Junior', Benjamin/Uncle Ben/ Uncle Barnwell 111, *111*
Bamber, Jack 39
Bangham 167
Bantam, Angelo Cyrus 39, 44
Baptist', 'Mr; *see* Cavalletto
Barbara 77, 86
Barbary, Miss 147, 149, 150, 151, 152
Bardell, Martha 39, *39*, 40, 43, 48, 49
Bardell, Tommy 39
Barkis, C P 133
 catch-phrase 'say that Barkis is willin'' 133
Barley (later Pocket), Clara 183
Barnacle 167
Barnacle, Clarence 167, 170
Barnacle, Lord Decimus Tite 27, 167, 171
Barnacle, Ferdinand 167
Barnacle, Tite 167, *167*
Barnacle upper-class sinecurists 15
Barney 51
Barsad, John (see also Pross) 177, 181
Bates, Charley 51, 60
Bazzard 197
Bedwin, Mrs 51
Belle (Scrooge's one-time fiancée) 105
Belvawney, Miss 63
Benjamin 89
Berinthia ('Berry') 121
Bet/Betsy (*Oliver Twist*) 51
Betsy (*Pickwick Papers*) 39
Bevan, Dr 111, 217
Bib, Julius Washington Merryweather 111
Biddy (later Mrs Joe Gargery) 183, 187
Billickin, Mrs 197
Bitherstone, Master 121
Bitzer 161, 163
Blackpool, Stephen 161, 165
Blandois/Lagnier/Rigaud (32), (33), 167, 170, 171, 174, 175, 223
Blathers 51
Blight, 'Young' 191
Blimber, Cornelia 121
Blimber, Dr 13, 121, *121*, 124, 126, 127
Blimber, Mrs 121
Blinder, Mrs 147
Blockitt, Mrs 121
Blockson, Mrs 63
Blotton 39
Bob (turnkey) *166*, 167, 174
Bobster, Cecilia 73
Boffin, (Nicodemus) 'Noddy', aka 'The Golden Dustman' (29), 191, 194, 195
Boffin, Henrietta 191, 195
Boldwig, Captain 39
Bolo, Miss 39
Borum family 63
Bounderby, Josiah 19, 161, 162, 163, 165
Boythorn, Lawrence 147, 158
Brass, Sally (28), 77, 78, 84, 86, 87, 117
Brass, Sampson (28), 77, 78, 79, 84, 86, 87, *87*, 117
Bravassa, Miss 63
Bray, Madeline 13, 63, 64, 69, 73, 74, 75
Bray, Walter 63, 64, 73
Brick, Jefferson 111, *111*
Briggs 121
Brittles 51
Brogley 121
Brooker (33), 63, 75, 85, 220
Browdie, John 63, 67
Brown, 'Good' Mrs; alias Marwood 121, 125, 130, 131
Brownlow, Mr 15, 18, 51, 52, 53, 60, 61, 61
Bucket 147, *147*, 148, 151, 153
 fiction's first policeman sleuth 147
Bud, Rosa, aka 'Rosebud' or 'Pussy' *196*, 197, 198, 199, 200
Buffum, Oscar 111
Bullamy 111
Bumble 51, *51*, 52, 54, 56, 57, 61
 catchphrase 'the law is a [sic] ass.' 61
Bunsby, John ('Jack') 122
Buzfuz, Serjeant 39, *39*, 48, 49

cabby 46
Campbell; *see* Magwitch
Carker (later Morfin), Harriet 122, 131
Carker, James 16, (28), (32), (33), 121, 122, 124, 125, 126, 129, 130, 131
Carker, John 122, 131, 224
Carstone, Richard/Rick 147, 148, 149, 150, 153, 157, *157*
Carton, Sydney (32), (33), 91, 177, 181
Casby, Christopher 167, *167*, 171
Cavalletto, John Baptist/Gian Battista, aka 'Mr Baptist' 27, (32), (33), 167, 224
Chadband 148, *148*, 151, 159
Chancellor, Lord 148, 149
 historically either Lord Cranworth, Lord Lyndhurst or Lord St Leonards 148
Charlotte 51, 52
Cheeryble brothers 18, 69, 73, 74, 75, 101, 106
 Charles 63, 72, 73, 74
 Ned 63, 72
Cheeryble, Frank 63, 67, 74, 75
Cheggs, Alick 77, 79
Cheggs, Miss 77
Chester, Edward 89, 90, 96
Chester, John (later Sir John Chester, MP) *88*, 89, 91, 94, 96, 97
Chick, John 122
Chick, Louisa, *née* Dombey 122, 127
Chicken', 'The Game 122, 122
Childers, E W B 161
Chillip 133
Chitling, Tom 52
Chivery 168, 173
Chivery, 'young' John 168, 173, 174
Chivery, Mrs 168, 173
Choke, Cyrus (General) 111, 215
Chollop, Hannibal 111
Chowser, Colonel 63
Christmas Past, Ghost of 6, 19, 99, 105
Christmas Present, Ghost of 99, 102, 105, 106
Christmas Yet to Come, Ghost of 99, 106
Chuckster 77
Chuffey, 'Old' 111
Chuzzlewit, Anthony 111, 112, 113, 115, 118, 124
Chuzzlewit, George 112, 115
Chuzzlewit, Jonas 111, 112, 113, 114, 115, 117, 118, 119, 124
 CD implies he beats Merry once married to her 118
Chuzzlewit, Mrs Ned 112, 115
Chuzzlewit, old Martin *110*, 111, 112, 113, 114, 115, 117, 118, 119
Chuzzlewit, young Martin (30), (31), 111, 113, 114, 115, 117, 118, 119, 129, 230
Cicero 112
Clare, Ada 147, 148, 150
Clarke, Susan 39
Claypole, Noah 51, 52, 59, 60
Cleaver, aka 'Mr Dolls' 191, *193*
Cleaver, Fanny; *see* Jenny Wren
Clennam, Arthur 15, 168, *168*, 169, *169*, 171, 173, 174, 175
(Clennam, Gilbert 175)
Clennam, Mrs 168, 169, 174, 175
Clennam Sr (Arthur's father) (32), (33)
Cluppins, Elizabeth 39
Cly, Roger 177
'Coavins' 150
Cobb, Tom 89
Codger, Miss 112
Codlin, Thomas/Tom/Tommy 77, 77, 78, 84
Coiler, Mrs 183
Compeyson 184, 187, 188
Copperfield, Clara 133, 137, 142
 her sexual absorption in Murdstone 140
Copperfield, David 15, 17, (28), 131, 132, 133, 133, 135, 136, 136, 137, *140*, *141*, 142, 143, 144, *144*, 145, 230
Corney (later Bumble), Mrs 52, 54
Crackit, Toby 52
Cratchit, Belinda 99, *108*
Cratchit, Bob *98*, 99, 100, 102, 105, *106*, *108*, *109*
Cratchit, Martha 99, 106
Cratchit, Mrs 99, *99*, 106
Cratchit, Peter 100, 106, *108*
Craddock, Mrs 39
Creakle 133, 135
Crewler, Rev Horace 133
Crewler, Sophy 133
Crimple (*né* Crimp), David 112
Crisparkle, Rev Sept(imus) 197, 200
Crisparkle, Mrs 197
Crowl 63
Crummles, Ninetta, aka 'The Infant Phenomenon' 63
Crummles, Vincent (30), (31), *62*, 65, 67, 68, 70, 71, 72
Cruncher, Jerry (formally Jeremiah) 177
Cruncher, Mrs 177
Cruncher, 'young' Jerry 177
Crupp, Mrs 14, 133
Crushton, Hon Mr 39
Curdle, Mr 64
Curdle, Mrs 64
Cuttle, Captain Edward ('Ned') 122–3, *123*, 125, 130, *130*, 131, *211*

Daisy, Solomon 89
Darnay, Charles, aka the Marquis St Evrémonde (32), (33), *176*, 177–8, 180, 181
Dartle, Rosa 134, 225
Datchery, Dick 197
David 64
Dawkins, Jack/John; *see* The Artful Dodger
Dedlock, Lady (Honoria) (28), (32), (33), 147, 148, 149, 150, 151, 152, 153, 157, 158, *158*, 159
Dedlock, Sir Leicester 14, 147, 148, 149, 151, 153, 158, 159
Dedlock, Volumnia 148
Defarge, Ernest, aka Jacques Four 95, 177, 178, 223
Defarge, Mme (Thérèse) 95, 177, 223
Dennis, Ned 89, 90, 91, 97
Deputy, aka 'Winks' 197
Devasseur, Loyal 203
Dick (*Oliver Twist*) 52
Dick, Mr (*David Copperfield*) 134, 225
Digby', 'Mr (Smike's stage name) 67
Dilber, Mrs 100
Diver, Colonel 112, 114
Dodger, The Artful 6, (30), (31), (33), 46, 51, 52, *52*, 57, *58*, *59*, 60, 60, 61, 220
Dodson 40
Dodson & Fogg (28), 40, 45, 48, 49
Dombey, Edith (*née* Skewton, then Granger last Dombey) (30), (31), (32), (33), 121, 122, 123, 124, 125, 126, 129, 130, 131, 224, 226
Dombey, Fanny 123, 126
Dombey (later Gay), Florence (33), *120*, 121, 123, *123*, 124, 126, 127, 128, 129, 130, 131, 168, *211*
Dombey, Mr (Paul) 11, 15, 19, (30), (31), (32), (33), 121, 122, 123, 124, *124*, 125, 126, 127, 128, 129, 130, 131
Dombey, (Little) Paul (30), (31), *120*, 121, 122, 123, 124, *124*, 126, 127, 128, 129, 220
Donny 148
Dorrit (later Sparkler), Fanny (32), (33), 168, 169, 171, 172, 173, 174, 175
Dorrit, Frederick (32), (33), 168, 173, 174
Dorrit, Little (Amy) 15, (28), (32), (33), *166*, 167, 168, *168*, 169, 170, 171, 172, 173, *173*, 174, 175
Dorrit, 'Tip' (Ted) (32), (33), 168, 169, 171, 173, 174
Dorrit, William (28), (32), (33), 168, *168*, 169, 171, 172, 173, 174, 175, 180
Dowler 40
Doyce, Daniel 15, **24**, (32), (33), 169, 175
Drood, Edwin 197, *197*, 200
Drummle, Bentley 183
Dubbley 40
Duff 52
Dunkle, Ginery (Dr) 112
Durdles, Stony 197

Eastlake, John (30), (31)
Edwards, Miss 77
Em'ly (33), *132*, 134, 135, 136, 137, 138, *142*, 143, 220
Emma 40
Endell, Martha (33), 125, 134, 136, 221
Estella (28), 183, 184, 186, 187, 188

Fagin 14, (28), 51, 52, 52, 53, 54, 57–61, 58, 61, 85, 117, 191, *208*, 217
 Jewishness of 57, 58, 59
 natural teacher 59, 60
 purpose for CD literary as embodying criminal brains 58
Fan (Fanny/Frances; Scrooge's sister) 105
Fang 53
Feenix, 'Cousin' Lord 14, 124, 125
Fezziwig, Mr 100, 105, *108*
Finching, Flora 17, 144, 167, 169, *169*
Fips 112
Fitz-Marshall, (Capt) Charles 40
Fladdock, General 112
Flasher, Wilkins 40, 43
Fledgeby, 'Fascination' 191
Fleming, Agnes 53
Fleming, Rose 53
Flintwinch, Affery 169, *169*
Flintwinch, Ephraim 175
Flintwinch, Jeremiah 169, *169*, 175
Flite, Miss 149, 150
Flopson 183
Fogg 40
Folair, Augustus 64
Fred (Scrooge's nephew) 100, 102, 106

Gabelle, Théophile 178, 180, 181
Gamfield 53
Gamp, Mrs (Sarah/Sairah/Sairey) 111, 112, 113, 114, 115, *119*, 210
Gander 112
Gargery, Georgiana Maria 183
Gargery, Joe *182*, 183, 184, 185, 186, 187
Garland, Abel 77
Garland, Mr 77, 78, 80, 86
Gashford 89, 97
Gaspard 178
Gay, Walter (32), (33), 121, 122, 123, 124, 125, 129, 130, 131
Gazingi, Miss 64
General, Mrs 169
George (*Nicholas Nickleby*) 64
George (*The Old Curiosity Shop*) 77
George, Mr 147, 149, 152, 158, 159
George, Mrs (but not wife of preceding) 77
Gilbert, Mark 89
Giles, Mr 53
Gills, Solomon ('Old Sol') (28), (32), 121, 122, 123, 124, 125, 126, 128, 130
Gliddery, Bob
Goodwin 40
Gordon, Lord George 89, 90, 96, 97
Gowan, Henry 6, (32), (33), 167, 168, 170, 171
Gowan, Mrs 170
Gradgrind (later Bounderby), Louisa 160, 162, 165, 224
Gradgrind, Mrs 162
Gradgrind, Thomas/Tom 160, 161, 161, 165, 224
Gradgrind, Tom, junior 161, 162
Graham, Mary 110, 113, 117, 118, 119
Grandfather, Little Nell's 74, 76, 77, 78, 82, 83, 84, 85, 87, 114, 125
Granger, Col 125
Grannett 53
Gregsbury 64, 67
Grewgious, Hiram 196, 198, 200
Gride, Arthur 64, 67, 73, 74
Gridley 149, 157
Grimwig 53, 56
Grinder 78
Grip 6, 90, *90*
Groffin, Thomas 40
Groper, Colonel 113
Groves, Jem/Jemmy 78, 79
Grudden, Mrs 64
Grueby, John 90
Grummer, Daniel 40
Gulpidge 134
Gummidge, Mrs (33), 134, 220
Gunter 40
Guppy, William 149, *149*, 150, 152, 158, *158*, 159
Guster 149
Gwynn 40

Haggage, Dr 170
Handford, Julius 191
Haredale, Emma 89, 90, 92, 97
Haredale, Geoffrey *88*, 90, 91, 96, 97
Haredale, Reuben 90, 92
Harmon, John (32), (33), 191, 192, 194, 195, 226
(Harmon, 'old' John 191, 192)
Harris (*Pickwick Papers*) 40
Harris, 'Trotters' or 'Short' (*The Old Curiosity Shop*) 78, *78*, 79
('Harris', 'Mrs 112)
Harry 78, 79, 84
Harthouse, James or 'Jem' 162, 224
Havisham, Miss (30), (31), 183, 184, *184*, 185, 187
Hawdon, Capt (28), 149, 158
Hawk, Sir Mulberry (28), 63, 67, 69, 72
Headstone, Bradley (30), (31), 191, 192, 193, 194, 226
Heep, Uriah 134, *134*, 139, 220
Hexam, Charley 191
Hexam, 'Gaffer' (real forename Jesse) 191, 192, 194
Hexam, Lizzie (30), (31), 191, 192, 193, *195*
Higden, Betty 192, 193
Hominy, Mrs 113
Honeythunder, Rev Luke 198
Hopkins, Jack 40
Hortense 149, 155, 223
Hugh 90, 91, 96, 97
Humm, Anthony 40
Hunter, Mrs Leo 40, 44
 her 'Ode to an Expiring Frog' 206
Hutley, John/Jem, aka Dismal Jemmy 40

Inspector, Mr 192

Jackson 40
Jacques One, Two, Three and Five 179
Jaggers 184, 187
Jarley, Mrs *76*, 78, 79, 85, *85*
Jarndyce, John 18, 147, 149, 151, 152, 154, 158
Jasper, John 197, 198, *198*, 200
Jellyby (later Turveydrop), Caddy 150, 153
Jellyby, Mrs **24**, 150
Jemima 125
Jenny 150
Jerry 78
Jingle, Alfred 20, (30), (31), (32), 40, *40*, 44, 46, 47, 48, 49, 170, 210
 alias in Suffolk 40
 Byronic melancholy, look of 41
 detaches Rachael Wardle from Tupman 45
 his epic on July Revolution 206
 like Frankenstein's monster, might have overwhelmed creator 47
 idiosyncratic speech 40
 mendacity of 41
 sinister side 41
 take-off of Byron? 41, 138
Jiniwin, Mrs 78
Jinkins 113
Jinks 41
Jip 6, 135, 161
 first fictional dog to forward plot 135
 superiority over Lady Bertram's Pug in *Mansfield Park* 135
Jo (*Bleak House*) *146*, 149, 150, 152, 159
Jobling, John 113
Jobling, Tony (no kin to above) 150
Joe (the 'Fat Boy', *Pickwick Papers*) 41, *41*, 48, 215
 catch phrase 'I wants to make your flesh creep' 41
Joe (*A Christmas Carol*) 100
Joe (*A Tale of Two Cities*) 179
Johnny 191, 192
Johnson', 'Mr (Nicholas Nickleby's stage name) 64
Jones, Mary 90
Joram, Dick 135, 137
Jowl 78, 79, 85
Jupe, Sissy 162, 163

Kags 53
Kedgick, Captain 113
Kenge, 'Conversation' 150, 157
Kenwigs 64, 66, 67
Kenwigs, Morleena 64, *65*, 66, 67
Kenwigs, Susan 64, *65*, 66, 67
Kettle, La Fayette 113
Kibble, Jacob 192
Kidderminster 162
Knag, Miss 63, 64
Knag, Mortimer 63, 64
Krook 150, 152, 159

La Creevy, Miss (later Mrs Linkinwater) 64, 65
Lammle, Alfred 191, 192, 194
Landless, Helena (32), (33), 198
Landless, Neville (32), (33), *197*, 198, 200
Langdale 91
Ledrook, Miss 65
Leeford, Edward 53

Leeford, Edwin 51
Lenville 65, 71
Lenville, Mrs 65
Lewsome 113, 119
Lightwood, Mortimer 191, 192
Lillyvick 64, 65
Limbkins 53
Linkinwater, Tim 65, 72, 75, 101
Lion (dog in *Little Dorrit*) 6, 170
Lion, The (human innkeeper in *Barnaby Rudge*) 91
Lirriper, Mrs 202
List, Isaac 78, 79, 85
Littimer 135, 136
Lively 53
Liz 150
Lobley *196*
Lorry, Jarvis 178, 179, 180
Losberne 53, 61
Lowten 41
Lumbey 66
Lupin, Mrs 113

MacStinger, Mrs 122, 125, 130
Maggy 170
Magnus, Peter 41
Magwitch, Abel 18, (33), 183, 184, 186, 187, 188, 220, 221
Maldon, Jack 135, 138, 144
Mallard 41
Manette, Dr Alexandre (28), 178, 179, 180, 181
Manette (later Darnay), Lucie 179, 181
Mann, Mrs 52, 53
Mantalini, Alfred 66, *66*, 67
Mantalini, Madame 64, 66, 67
Marchioness', The 78, *81*, 86, 87, 168
Markleham, Mrs 135
Marley, Jacob, Ghost of 100, *100*, 104
  pre-ghost deathbed 105
Martha 51, 53
Martin, Mr 41
Martin, Tom 42
Marton (schoolmaster in *The Old Curiosity Shop*) 78, 84, 85, 86
Marwood, Alice (33), 121, 125, 130, 220
Mary 42, 86
Maylie, Harry 53
Maylie, Mrs (30), (31), 51, 53, 61, 85
Maylie, Rose 52, 54, 60
M'Choakumchild 162
Meagles, Mr (29), 170, 171
Meagles, Mrs (29), 170, 171
Meagles (later Gowan), 'Pet' (Minnie) (29), (32), (33), 168, 170, 171
Mell, Mr (33), 135, 138, 220
Merdle, Mr (28), 170, 171
Merdle, Mrs (28), 168, 171, 174, 180, 222
Micawber, Emma (33), 135, 138, 220
  catch-phrase 'I never will desert Mr Micawber' 135
Micawber, Wilkins (33), 134, 135, *135*, 136, 138, 140, *144*, 220, 221
  catch-phrases 'if anything turns up' and 'Annual income twenty pounds, annual expenditure nineteen nineteen six, result happiness. Annual income twenty pounds, annual expenditure twenty pounds ought and six, result misery.' 136
Miggs 91, 96
Mike 184
Miller 42
Mills, Julia (33), 91, 136
Milvey, Rev Frank 192
Milvey, Margaretta 192
Mivins 42
Moddle, Augustus (33), 113, 119
Molly 183, 184
Monflathers, Miss 78
Monks 51, 52, 53, 54, 60
Montague, Tigg 111, 113, 114, 115, 117, 118, 119
Morfin 121, 126
Mould 113, 115
Mould, Mrs 113
Mowcher, Miss 136
Murdstone, Miss Jane 135, 137, 140, 143
Murdstone, Mr 104, 133, 134, 136, *136*, 139, 140, *140*, 142, 143
Mutanhed, Lord 39, 42, 69, 96
Muzzle 42

Nadgett 10, 113, 114, 119
Namby 42, 44
Nancy 14, 51, 52, 53, 54, 61
Nandy, John Edward ('Old') 171
Neckett, Charley 150, 151
Neckett, Emma 151
Neckett, Tom 151
Neckett/'Coavins' 147, 149
Neddy 42
Nell(y), Little (30), (31), *76*, 78, 79, 80, 82, 83, *83*, 84, 85, *85*, 86, 87, 114, 129, 168, 209, *209*, 215, *215*, 220, 226
Nemo (*see also* Hawdon, Capt) (28), 148, 149, 150, 151, 157, 158, 159
Nickleby, Kate 13, 63, 64, 65, 66, 67, 68, 69, 70, 72, 73, 74, 75, 125
Nickleby, Mrs 64, 65, 66, 70
Nickleby, Nicholas *62*, 63, 64, 65, 66, 67, 68, 69, 70, 71, 72, 73, 74, 75, *75*, 129
Nickleby, Ralph (28), 63, 64, 66, 67, 68, 69, 70, 72, 73, 74, 75, 117
Nipper (later Toots), Susan 121, 124, 126
Noddy 42
Noggs, Newman 63, 64, 67, 67, 72, 73, 74

Norris family 112, 113
  racism of 113
Nubbles, Kit 78, 83, 86, 87
  sexual awakening of 86
Nubbles, Mrs 78, 85
Nupkins, George 41, 42
Nupkins, Henrietta 42
Nupkins, Mrs 42

Omer 137
Omer, Minnie 137
Orlick, Dolge 184, *187*

Pancks 27, 170, 173
Pardiggle, Mrs 151
Parkes, 'Long' Phil 91
Pawkins, Major 114
Payne, Dr 40, 42
Peak 91
Pecksniff, 'Cherry' (Charity) (33), 113, 114, 118, 119, 220
Pecksniff (later Chuzzlewit), 'Merry' (Mercy) 114, 118
  calls Jonas Chuzzlewit 'Griffin' 118
Pecksniff, Seth (30), (31), *110*, 112, 113, *113*, 115, 116, *116*, 117, 118, 119, 217
Peecher, Emma 192
Peerybingle, Mr and Mrs 11
Peggotty, Clara (30), (31), 133, 134, 137, 140, *141*
Peggotty, Dan (30), (31), (33), 134, 137, *137*, 138, 140, 142, 220
Peggotty, Ham (30), (31), 134, 137, 140
Pegler, Mrs 163
Pell, Solomon 42
Peps, Dr Parker 124, 125
Perch 126
Perker 41, 42, 45, 49
Petowker (later Lillyvick), Henrietta 65, 67
'Phib' (Phoebe) 67
Phunky 42
Pickwick, Samuel 11, *16*, (28), (30), (31), *38*, 39, 40, 41, 42, 42, 44, 45, *46*, 48, 80, 215
  censoriousness 42
  ignorance human psychology, legal procedure, defects include 43
  implausibly soft-hearted given business success 43
  scientific bent 41
  vanity 41
  wealth, source of — slaves? 43
Pilkins 126
Pinch, Ruth 114, 115
Pinch, Tom 11, *110*, 112, 114, *114*, 115, 117, 118, 230
Pip (*Martin Chuzzlewit*) 114
Pip (*né* Philip Pirrip) (*Great Expectations*) 15, (28), (30), (31), (32), (33), *182*, 183, 184, *184*, 185, 186, *186*, 187, 188
  Estella shames by ridiculing his vocabulary 186
  Herbert Pocket's tactless nickname for 186
Pipchin, Mrs 121, 124, 126, *126*
Plornish, Sally 171
Plornish, Thomas 171
Pluck 67
Pocket, Belinda (28), 183, 185
Pocket, Herbert (28), (32), (33), 183, 184, 185, 188
Pocket, Matthew (28), 183, 185, 187
Pocket, Sarah (28), 183, 185
Podsnap, Georgiana 191, 192
Podsnap, John 192, 192, 194
Podsnap, Mrs 192
Pogram, Hon Elijah 114, *114*
Pott 43, 44
Pott, Mrs 40, 43, 48, 224
Potterson, Abbey (originally Abigail) 191, 192
Potterson, Job 192
Price 43
Price (later Browdie), 'Tilda 63, 67
Prig, Betsey 114
Pross 179
Pross, Solomon, aka John Barsad 179
Provis; *see* Magwitch
Pugstyles 67
Pumblechook 184, 185
Pyke 67

Quilp, Betsy (28), 78, 79
  S&M relationship with husband? 83–4
Quilp, Daniel 15, (28), 78, *78*, 79, 82, 84, 85, 86, 87, 117, 128, 217
  financial carelessness of 83
  sexual allure of 83
Quinion 137

Rachael (later Chadband), Mrs (*Bleak House*) 151
Rachael (*Hard Times*) 161, 163, 165
Raddle, Mr 43
Raddle, Mrs Mary Ann 39, 43
Riah 191, 192
'Richards'/Polly Toodle 121, 124, 125, 126, 127
Riderhood (later Venus), Pleasant 192
Riderhood, 'Rogue' (Roger) (30), (31), 191, 192, 193

Rob the Grinder; *see* Toodle, Rob
Rogers, Mrs 43
Roker, Tom 43
Rokesmith, John; (alias of John Harmon, *qv*) 194, 195
Rosa 149, 151, 158, 159
Rouncewell, Mrs 149, 151, 159
Rouncewell, Robert 151, 158
Rouncewell, Watt 151, 158
Rudge, Barnaby 6, 90, 91, *91*, 92, 96, 97
Rudge, Mary 92, 95, 96
Rudge Senior 90, 92, 96
Rugg 171

St Evrémonde, Marquis ('wicked old', Darnay's predecessor in the title) 177, 179
(St Evrémonde, younger brother of above 177)
Sally 51, 53, 54
Sampson, George 193
Sanders, Susannah 43
Sapsea 198, 200
Sawyer, Bob (Robert) (33), 39, 40, 42, 43, *43*
Scadder, Zephaniah 114
Scadgers, Lady 163
Scaley 67, 69
Scott, Tom 79
Scrooge, Ebenezer 19, (28), 99, 100, *101*, 104, *104*, 105, *105*, *106*, *107*, *109*, 161
  catch phrase 'Bah!', 'Humbug!' 102
  coffin bears pregnant letters RIP in Patrick Stewart TV film version, suggesting ritualist conversion 107
  doctrinaire utilitarian 102
  health, poor, explains hallucinations? 104
  religious reaction to ghosts 106
  Rotarian matiness, materialism, one-man Welfare State, deteriorates to 106, 107
  Sunday shop-closing laws and 105
  utilitarian doctrine re population 105
Sharp 137
Short 79
Sikes, Bill 6, 14, (28), 51, 52, 53, 54, *54*, 58, 60, 61, 117, 129
  pseudo-Miltonic-Shakespearean imprecations of 14
Simmery, Frank 43
Simmonds, Miss 67
Simmons, Henrietta 79
Simmons, Will/Bill 114
Simpson 43
single gentleman', 'the 79, 84, 85, 86
Skettles, Sir Barnet 126
Skewton, The Hon Mrs 123, 124, 126, 127, 129, 130
Skiffins (later Wemmick), Miss 185
Skimpin 43
Skimpole, Arethusa 151
Skimpole, Harold 150, 151, 151, 152, 153
Skimpole, Kitty 151
Skimpole, Laura 151
Slackbridge 163
Slammer, Dr 40, 41, 43, 44
Sleary 161, 163
Sleary, Josephine 163
Sliderskew 67, 74
Sloppy 193
Slout 54
Slum 79
Slurk 44
Slyme, Chevy 115, 119
Smallweed, Bart(holomew), aka 'Young'/'Chick' 150, 152, 159
Smallweed, Grandfather 149, 152, 155, 158, 159
Smallweed, Judith/Judy 152, 159
Smangle 44
Smauker, John 44
Smike 63, 67, *67*, 70, 71, 74, 75, 85
Smithers 44
Smorltork, Count 23, 44
Smouch 43
Snagsby 149, 152
Snagsby, Mrs 152, 159
Snawley 63, 68, 74, 75
Snevellicci, Miss 68, 70
Snevellicci, Mr 68
(Snigsworth, Lord 193)
Snobb, The Hon Mr 68
Snodgrass, Augustus (30), (31), 44, 49
Snubbin, Serjeant 41, 44
Snuphanuph, Dowager Lady 44
Sowerberry 51, 52, 54, 57
Sowerberry, Mrs 54
Sparkler, Edmund (32), (33), 167, 168, 171, 174, 175
Sparsit, Mrs (née Scadgers) 161, 162
Spenlow, Clarissa 137
Spenlow (later Copperfield), Dora 6, 17, (28), 135, 136, 137, 140, 144, 168
Spenlow, Francis 135, 137, 144, 230
Spenlow, Lavinia 137
Sphynx', 'Sophronia; *see* 'The Marchioness' 87
Spiker, Henry 138
Spottletoe, Mr 115
Spottletoe, Mrs, née Slyme 115
Squeers, Fanny 67, 68, *75*
Squeers, Mrs 68, *68*, 71
Squeers, Wackford (33), 63, *68*, 69, 70, *71*, *73*, 74, 75, 78, 117, 140–141
Squeers, Wackford 'Junior' 69
Squod, Phil 152
Stables, Hon Bob 152, 159
Stagg 92, *95*, 96
Stareleigh, Mr Justice 44
Startop 185, 188
Steerforth, James 134, 136, 137, 138, 139, 143, 226
Steerforth, Mrs 134, 138
Stiggins 44, *44*, 231
Strong, Annie 135, 138, 144
Strong, Dr 135, 138, 144
Stryver 177, 179
Summerson (eventually Woodcourt), Esther (30), (31), 147, 148, 149, 150, 151, 152, 153, 154, 157, 158, 159
Sweedlepipe, Poll (Paul) 115, *115*
Swiveller, Dick 69, 79, 80, 81, 82, 84, *84*, 86, 87

Tacker 115
Tangle 152
Tapley, Mark 111, 112, 113, 115, *115*, 119
Tappertit, Sim 89, 91, 92, 95, 96, 97
Tappleton, Lt 44
Tartar *196*, 198
Tattycoram (32), (33), 171, 224
Tigg, Montague 113, *113*, 115
Tim, Tiny *98*, 101, *101*, 106, 109
Tippins, Lady 193
Tisher, Mrs 199
Tix 69
Todgers, M, Mrs (28), 111, 112, 113, 115, 117, 119
Tom 179
Tomkins, Miss 44
Toodle, Mr 127
Toodle, Mrs (Polly) 127
Toodle, Rob(in) ('Biler') 126, 131
Toots *13*, 122, 125, 127, 127
  sartorial preoccupations of 127
Tope 199
Tope, Mrs 199
Toppit, Miss 115
Towlinson, Tom 127
Tox, Miss Lucretia 126, 127
Tozer 127
Traddles, Tommy 131, 133, 134, 135, 138, *138*
Trent, Fred (32), 78, 79, 82
Trent, Nell(y); *see* Nell(y), Little
Trimmers 69
Trotter, Job 40, 44, 48
Trotwood, Betsey (30), (31), 131, 134, 143, 226
Trundle 44
Tuckle 44
Tulkinghorn (28), 147, 148, 149, 153, 158, *158*, 159
Tungay 139
Tupman, Tracy (30), (31), 41, 44, 45, 47
Turveydrop, Mr 22, *152*, 153
Turveydrop, Prince 153
Twemlow, Melvin 193, 194
Twinkleton, Miss 199
Twist, Oliver 14, (30), (31), 46, *50*, 52, 53, 54, *54*, 55, 56, 57, 58, *58*, 59, 81, 85

Varden, Dolly 92, *93*, 97
Varden, Gabriel (28), 91, 92, 96, 97
Varden, Martha 91, 92
Veck, Meg 203, *203*
Veck, Toby ('Trotty') 203, *203*
Veneering, Anastatia 192, 193
Veneering, Hamilton 192, 193, 194
Vengeance, The 179
Venus (28), 192, 193, 194, 195
Verisopht, Lord (Frederick) (28), 63, 64, 69, 70, 96, 167
Vholes 153, 157
Vuffin 79

Wackles, Jane 79
Wackles, Melissa 79
Wackles, Mrs 79
Wackles, Sophy 79
Wade, Miss (32), (33), 171, 224
Waldengarver 185
Wardle (later Snodgrass), Emily 39, 44, 49
Wardle (later Trundle), Isabella 44, 45
Wardle, Mr 40, 41, 42, 44, 45, 47
Wardle, Rachael (30), (31), 41, 44, 45, 47
Waterbrook 138, 139
Watty 45
'Weevle' 150
Wegg, Silas 193, *193*, 194, 195
Weller, Sam 12, 13, 15, *16*, (30), (31), 39, 40, 42, 44, 45, 45, 47, *47*, 48, 80, 86, 215
  boosts *Pickwick Papers'* readership 47
  with Pickwick prefigures Jeeves–Wooster relationship 45
Weller, Tony 39, 45, *45*, 47
Wemmick, John 183, 185
West, Dame 79, 84
Westlock, John 113, 115
Westwood 69
Whiffers 45
Wickam, Mrs 127
Wickfield, Agnes (30), (31), 139, 144
Wickfield, Mr (30), (31), 134, 139
Wicks 45
Wilfer (later Harmon), Bella 191, 193, 194, 195
Wilfer (later Sampson), Lavinia 193
Wilfer, Mrs 193, 194
Wilfer, Reginald (aka 'Rumty'/'The Cherub') 193
Willet, John 92, 96
Willet, Joseph/Joe 92, 96
William, Sweet 79
Winkle, Nathaniel (30), (31), 41, 43, 45, 48, 49, 78, 224
Winkle Sr 45, 49
Witherden 79, 86
Witherfield 45
Withers 127
Wititterley, Henry 69
Wititterley, Julia 66
Wolf 115
Woodcourt, Allan 149, 153, 154, 159
Woodcourt, Mrs 153
Wopsle 183, 185
Wopsle, Miss 185
Wrayburn, Eugene (30), (31), 191, 192, 193
Wren, Jenny *190*, 191, 193, *193*, 195
Wugsby, Mrs Colonel 45

Zephyr, The 45

A complete set of the works of Charles Dickens, published in London by Chapman and Hall in 1874. The 32 volumes are bound in half blue morocco, with gilt titles and spine decoration and marbled endpapers. Even when they were published these books were expensive, priced at two guineas (£2 2s [£2.10]) a volume; today such a fine Victorian set can fetch upwards of £7,000/$11,000, roughly commensurate with inflation (equivalent to £8,400/$13,200).

This edition published in 2011 by Worth Press Ltd

Designed, arranged and produced by Bookcraft Ltd www.bookcraft.co.uk

ISBN 978-1-84931-025-3

Printed in China

Dickens characters illustrated by the Victorian artist Kyd (Joseph Clayton Clarke), clockwise from top left: The Artful Dodger (Oliver Twist), *Bill Sikes* (Oliver Twist), *Mr Pickwick* (Pickwick Papers), *Captain Cuttle* (Dombey and Son), *Wackford Squeers* (Nicholas Nickleby) *and Mrs Gamp* (Martin Chuzzlewit).